LAW OF CONTRACT

LAW OF CONTRACT

Sixth Edition

Richard D. Taylor, MA, LLM, Barrister
Forbes Professor of English Law and
Head of Department of Legal Studies at the
University of Central Lancashire

Series Editor: C.J. Carr, MA, BCL

BLACKSTONE
PRESS LIMITED

This edition published in Great Britain 1998 by Blackstone Press Limited, Aldine Place, London W12 8AA. Telephone: 0181-740 2277

© Richard D. Taylor, 1985
Second edition, 1987
Third edition, 1989
Fourth edition, 1992
Reprinted, 1993
Fifth edition, 1995
Sixth edition, 1998

The right of Richard D. Taylor to be identified as author of this work has been asserted in accordance with ss. 77 and 78 of the Copyright Designs and Patents Act 1988.

ISBN: 1 85431 779 2

British Library Cataloguing in Publication Data
A CIP cataloguing record for this book is available from the British Library

Typeset by Montage Studios Limited, Horsmonden, Kent
Printed by Bell & Bain Limited, Glasgow

CONTENTS

Preface to the first edition   vii

Prefaces to the second, third, fourth, fifth and sixth editions   ix

Table of cases   xi

1   *Efficient and creative study*   1

Lectures — Textbooks — Reading cases — Statutes — Journals
and articles — Seminars and tutorials — Essays and presentations
— How to use this book — Conclusion

2   *Examinations and how to take advantage of them*   21

Revision — Organisational matters — Sitting the examination —
Conclusion

3   *Agreement*   42

Underlying themes — Key issues — The examination —
Conclusion

4   *Consideration*   58

Definition of consideration — Past consideration — Existing
duties — Part payment of a debt — The examination

5   *Terms of the contract*   80

The distinction between terms and representations — Conditions, warranties and innominate terms — Implied terms — The
examination

6   *Exemption clauses*   100

Historical development — Incorporation of exclusion clauses —
Interpretation of exclusion clauses — Unfair Contract Terms Act
1977 — The examination — Conclusion

7   *Misrepresentation*   127

Basic requirements — Remedies for misrepresentation — The
examination — Conclusion

8   *Mistake and frustration*   150

Mistake — Frustration — The examination

9   *Privity and remedies*   180

Remedies — Privity — The examination — Conclusion

10   *Illegality and inequality*   210

Illegality — Inequality of bargaining power — The examination

Bibliography   233

Index   235

PREFACE TO THE FIRST EDITION

Have you ever thought, 'If only I had known then what I know now, I would have got much more out of that period of my life'? I think that even most of the people who have succeeded in examinations would admit that this is to some extent true of their experiences as a student. This book attempts to tell you *now* the sorts of things that otherwise you might later wish you had known *then*. It is designed to put a slightly older and wiser head on younger or less experienced shoulders. It will not of course remove the need for you to work — the series title stands for Success Without Tears, not Success Without Trying — but it will help to ensure that the work you do is productive and not wasted.

Although it does cover the central areas common to most contract syllabuses and offers ways of looking at the substantive law which you should find helpful, it is not a textbook in the conventional sense and thus does not attempt to cover every nook and cranny of the subject. Rather, it is designed to be used alongside conventional textbooks (and other sources) and to help you to get the most out of them. It is aimed primarily at law students studying for first degrees in England and Wales, but it may well be that students taking other courses involving contract law will find within it a useful outline of the major topics and how to study them.

It is a pleasure to record my thanks to the publishers and the series editor not only for their encouragement and patience but also for introducing me to the delights of Chinese restaurants and multi-storey car-parks! My thanks are also due to Lesley Mellodey and Madeleine Bousfield for their cheerful assistance with the typing. I should also like to thank all those who have taught me in the past and hope that they are not too embarrassed at anything they might read herein. Finally, I could not fail to record my appreciation and gratitude for the support and patience of my wife, Karen, and two young children, Deborah and Damian. I have taken account of the comments and suggestions of the latter two individuals in particular, wherever appropriate. Errors and omissions which remain are of course their responsibility!

Richard Taylor
Oswaldtwistle
October 1985

PREFACE TO THE SECOND EDITION

It is a measure of the success of the book and of the series that it has been necessary to produce a second edition less than two years after the first. I have taken the opportunity to add a new section on essays and presentations and to reflect new developments in the case law, particularly in the areas of frustration and remedies. One of the most pleasing aspects of the reaction to the first edition has been the variety of readers who have written in to express their satisfaction, from the gentleman who was helped towards his first at Oxford to those who found the book useful on 'A'-level courses. I thank them all for their kind and constructive comments and hope that the second edition continues to please. Having placed responsibility for errors and omissions in the first edition on my children, I suppose that I should now give them the credit for any plaudits but I hesitate to do so as they quickly grow older and shrewder and will no doubt soon be demanding a share of the royalties!

May 1987

PREFACE TO THE THIRD EDITION

The book has been thoroughly updated to take account of developments since the second edition in the hope that it will continue to be of maximum utility to students. My worst fears expressed in the preface to the second edition have been fulfilled in that not only do my children now demand a share of the royalties but they spend them in advance!   *September 1989*

PREFACE TO THE FOURTH EDITION

The text has been updated again to take account of developments over the past two years, particularly in the area of consideration and performance of existing duties. The escalating cost of bringing up my children makes me thankful that students do continue to find the book useful enough to purchase it in increasing numbers, and that I have not accumulated offspring with quite the same frequency or regularity as new editions have continued to be produced.   *January 1992*

PREFACE TO THE FIFTH EDITION

There have again been a number of new developments to take account of over the past three years especially in respect of implied terms, unfair contract terms, undue influence and damages for fraud and misrepresentation. My sentiments in respect of my children continue much as before save for the additional point that as they go through their teens, preparation of this edition has had to fit in with my extensive commitments as their unpaid taxi driver.   *April 1995*

PREFACE TO THE SIXTH EDITION

Prefaces become shorter as my children become larger and indeed at only 15 my youngest has outstripped me as my eldest continues to divert my finances, now as a first year university student. She is now old enough to disclaim (quite unreasonably) any responsibility which I had previously sought to ascribe to her for errors or omissions in this work but as a non-law student she is also exempt from the subtle pleasures of having to read it.

Two other important things have happened since the previous edition, both of which I expect to recur before the next. There have been a number of important appellate decisions and Blackburn Rovers became Premier League Champions in May 1995. Readers will find both of these phenomena reflected in this sixth edition.   *Richard Taylor*
                                                                   Oswaldtwistle
                                                                   May 1998

TABLE OF CASES

Adams v Lindsell (1818) 1 B & Ald 681   46
Addis v Gramophone Co. Ltd [1909] AC 488   185
Ailsa Craig Fishing Co. Ltd v Malvern Fishing Co. Ltd
    [1983] 1 WLR 964   103, 112, 113, 123
Alder v Moore [1961] 2 QB 57   189
Alec Lobb (Garages) Ltd v Total Oil GB Ltd [1985]
    1 All ER 303   217, 218, 219, 222, 225, 228, 232
Allcard v Skinner (1887) 36 ChD 145   224
Amalgamated Investment & Property Co. Ltd v John Walker & Sons Ltd
    [1976] 3 All ER 509   155, 175
Amoco Australia Pty Ltd v Rocco Brothers Motor Engineering Pty Ltd
    [1975] 1 All ER 968   219
Anangel Atlas Compania Noviera S.A. v Ishikawajima-Harima Heavy Industries Co. Ltd
    (No. 2) [1990] 2 Lloyd's Rep 526   66
Andrews Brothers Ltd v Singer & Co. Ltd [1934] 1 KB 17   102
Angel v Jay [1911] 1 KB 666   158
Anglia Television Ltd v Reed [1972] 1 QB 60   182
Appleby v Myers (1867) LR 2 CP 651   171, 172
Archbolds (Freightage) Ltd v S. Spanglett Ltd [1961] 1 QB 374   211, 212
Archer v Brown [1984] 2 All ER 267   138
Archer v Cutler [1980] 1 NZLR 386   227
Ashmore, Benson, Pease & Co. Ltd v A. V. Dawson Ltd [1973] 2 All ER 856   211
Associated Japanese Bank International Ltd v Crédit du Nord SA
    [1988] 3 All ER 902   156, 173
Astley v Reynolds (1731) 2 Barn KB 40   222
Atkinson v Denby (1862) 7 H & N 934   214
Atlas Express Ltd v Kafco Ltd [1989] 1 All ER 641   70, 223
Attica Sea Carriers Corporation v Ferrostaal Poseidon Bulk Reederei GmbH
    [1976] 1 Lloyd's Rep 250   192
Attwood v Lamont [1920] 3 KB 571   220
Attwood v Small (1838) 6 Cl & F 232   131
Avery v Bowden (1856) 6 E & B 953   173

B & S Contracts & Design Ltd v Victor Green Publications Ltd [1984] ICR 419   223
Bailey v Bullock [1950] 2 All ER 1167   185
Baldry v Marshall [1925] 1 KB 260   101

Balfour v Balfour [1919] 2 KB 571   74
Baltic Shipping Co. v Dillon (1993) 176 CLR 344   186
Banco Exterior Internacional v Thomas [1997] 1 All ER 46   224
Bank Line Ltd v A. Capel & Co. [1919] AC 435   167, 177
Bank of Credit & Commerce International v Aboody [1989] 2 WLR 759   224
Bannerman v White (1861) 10 CBNS 844   81
Barclays Bank v Fairclough Building [1995] 1 All ER 289   188
Barclays Bank v O'Brien [1993] 4 All ER 417   224
Barton v Armstrong [1976] AC 104; [1975] 2 All ER 465   132, 133, 222
Bell v Lever Brothers Ltd [1932] AC 161   156, 157, 173, 175
Beswick v Beswick [1968] AC 58   193, 203, 205, 208, 209
Bettini v Gye (1876) 1 QBD 183   86
Bigos v Bousted [1951] 1 All ER 92   212, 214, 231
Bisset v Wilkinson [1927] AC 177   129
Black Clawson International Ltd v Papierwerke Waldhof-Aschaffenburg AG
   [1981] 2 Lloyd's Rep 446   177
Blackpool & Fylde Aero Club v Blackpool Borough Council [1900] 3 All ER 25   49
Bliss v S. E. Thames Regional Health Authority [1985] IRLR 308   185, 186
Bolton v Mahadeva [1972] 1 WLR 1009   191
Boomer v Muir (1933) 24 P2d 570   198
Boulton v Jones (1857) 2 H & N 564   152, 153
Boustany v Pigott (1993) 109 LQR 530   225
Bovis v Whatlings Construction, The Times, 19 October 1995   113
Bowerman v ABTA, The Times, 24 November 1995   55
Bowmakers Ltd v Barnet Instruments Ltd [1945] KB 65   215
BP Exploration (Libya) Ltd v Hunt (No. 2) [1979] 1 WLR 783   171, 172
Branchett v Beaney [1992] 3 All ER 910   186
Bridge v Campbell Discount Co. Ltd [1962] AC 600   190
Bridge v Deacons [1984] AC 705   217
Brikom Investments Ltd v Carr [1979] QB 467   72, 74, 131
Brinkibon Ltd v Stahag Stahl und Stahlwarenhandelsgesellschaft mbH
   [1983] 2 AC 34   45
British Crane Hire Corporation Ltd v Ipswich Plant Hire Ltd [1975] QB 303   107, 122
British Movietonews Ltd v London & District Cinemas Ltd [1952] AC 166   162
British Westinghouse Electric & Manufacturing Co. Ltd v Underground Electric
   Railways Co. of London Ltd [1912] AC 673   187
Bunge Corporation v Tradax Export SA [1981] 2 All ER 513   86, 97
Butler Machine Tool Co. Ltd v Ex-Cell-O Corporation (England) Ltd
   [1979] 1 WLR 401   44, 51, 52
Butterworth v Kingsway Motors Ltd [1954] 1 WLR 1286   197
Byrne & Co. v Leon Van Tienhoven & Co. (1880) 5 CPD 344   3, 4, 6, 7

C & P Haulage v Middleton [1983] 3 All ER 94   182, 187, 207
Canada Steamship Lines Ltd v The King [1952] AC 192   109
Car & Universal Finance Co. Ltd v Caldwell [1965] 1 QB 525   135
Carlill v Carbolic Smoke Ball Co. [1893] 1 QB 256   47, 49, 55
Casey's Patents, Re [1892] 1 Ch 104   76
CCC Films (London) Ltd v Impact Quadrant Films Ltd [1985] QB 16   182, 183, 207
Cellulose Acetate Silk Co. v Widnes Foundry (1925) Ltd [1933] AC 20   189
Central London Property Trust Ltd v High Trees House Ltd [1947] 1 KB 130   73, 79
Chandler v Webster [1904] 1 KB 493   162, 163, 167, 168
Chapelton v Barry Urban District Council [1940] 1 KB 532   106
Chaplin v Hicks [1911] 2 KB 786   185
Charnock v Liverpool Corporation [1968] 1 WLR 1498   200
Chichester v Cobb (1866) 14 LT 433   66
CIBC Mortgages v Pitt [1993] 4 All ER 433   224, 225
Clark v Earl of Dunraven [1897] AC 59   44

Clea Shipping Corporation v Bulk Oil International Ltd [1984] 1 All ER 129   192
Cleveland Petroleum Ltd v Dartstone Ltd [1969] 1 WLR 116   217
Co-operative Insurance Society v Argyll Stores [1997] 2 WLR 898   194
Collins v Godefroy (1831) 1 B & Ad 950   67, 68, 71
Combe v Combe [1951] 2 KB 215   60, 62, 76, 78
Cooper v Phibbs (1867) LR 2 HL 149   157
Cox v Philips Industries Ltd [1976] 3 All ER 161   185, 186
Crabb v Arun District Council [1976] Ch 179   74
Cresswell v Potter [1978] 1 WLR 255 n   225
Cricklewood Property & Investment Trust Ltd v Leighton's Investment Trust Ltd
    [1945] AC 221   164
CTN Cash and Carry Ltd v Gallaher Ltd [1994] 4 All ER 714   223
Cundy v Lindsay (1878) 3 App Cas 459   152
Currie v Misa (1875) LR 10 Ex 153   58, 59, 60
Curtis v Chemical Cleaning & Dyeing Co. [1951] 1 KB 805   105
Cutter v Powell (1795) 6 TR 320   191

D & C Builders Ltd v Rees [1966] 2 QB 617   73, 79
Daulia Ltd v Four Millbank Nominees Ltd [1978] Ch 231   48
Davies v London & Provincial Marine Insurance Co. (1878) 8 ChD 469   128
Davis & Co. (Wines) Ltd v Afa-Minerva (EMI) Ltd [1974] 2 Lloyd's Rep 27   146
Davis Contractors Ltd v Fareham Urban District Council [1956] AC 696   160, 162
Dawnay Day & Co. v D'Alphen, The Times, 24 June 1997   217
De la Bere v Pearson Ltd [1908] 1 KB 280   75
De Lassalle v Guildford [1901] 2 KB 215   82
De Rivafinoli v Corsetti (1833) 4 Paige Ch 264   194
Dean v Ainley [1987] 3 All ER 749   207
Denny, Mott & Dickson Ltd v James B. Fraser & Co. Ltd [1944] AC 265   161
Derry v Peek (1889) 14 App Cas 337   27, 138
Dick Bentley Productions Ltd v Harold Smith (Motors) Ltd [1965] 2 All ER 65   81, 82
Dickinson v Dodds (1876) 2 ChD 463   33, 50
Dimmock v Hallet (1866) LR 2 Ch App 21   129
Doyle v Olby (Ironmongers) Ltd [1969] 2 QB 158   138, 141
Dunlop Pneumatic Tyre Co. Ltd v New Garage & Motor Co. Ltd [1915] AC 79   189
Dunlop Pneumatic Tyre Co. Ltd v Selfridge & Co. Ltd [1915] AC 847   60, 201, 206

Earl of Aylesford v Morris (1873) LR 8 Ch App 484   225
East v Maurer [1991] 2 All ER 733   130, 141, 146
Eastham v Newcastle United Football Club Ltd [1964] Ch 413   216, 219, 221
Edgington v Fitzmaurice (1885) 29 ChD 459   130, 132
EE Caledonia Ltd v Orbit Value Co. Europe [1994] 1 WLR 1515   109
Eliason v Henshaw (1819) 17 US (4 Wheat) 225   51
Errington v Errington [1952] 1 KB 290   48, 56
Ertel Bieber & Co. v Rio Tinto Co. Ltd [1918] AC 260   161
Esso Petroleum Co. Ltd v Harper's Garage (Stourport) Ltd [1968] AC 269   217, 218
Esso Petroleum Co. Ltd v Mardon [1976] QB 801   83, 130, 138, 139, 148
Esso Petroleum Ltd v Commissioners of Customs & Excise [1976] 1 All ER 117   13
Evening Standard Company Ltd v Henderson [1987] IRLR 64   193
Export Credits Guarantee Department v Universal Oil Products Co.
    [1983] 2 All ER 205   190

Felthouse v Bindley (1862) 11 CBNS 869   33, 43, 53
Ferguson v Davies [1997] 1 All ER 315   78
Fibrosa SA v Fairbairn Lawson Combe Barbour Ltd [1943] AC 32   161, 168, 170
Fisher v Bell [1960] 3 All ER 731   11, 12
Foakes v Beer (1884) 9 App Cas 605   71, 72, 73, 78
Foley v Classique Coaches Ltd [1934] 2 KB 1   52

Forsikrings Vesta v Butcher [1988] 2 All ER 43   188

Galbraith v Mitchenall Estates Ltd [1965] 2 QB 473   190
Gamerco SA v ICM/Fair Warning (Agency) Ltd [1995] 1 WLR 1226   169
Geier v Kujawa [1970] 1 Lloyd's Rep 364   107
George Mitchell (Chesterhall) Ltd v Finney Lock Seeds Ltd
   [1983] 2 AC 803   16, 101, 104, 112, 113, 117, 123, 125
Gibson v Manchester City Council [1979] 1 WLR 294   44, 55
Gilbert Steel Ltd v University Construction Ltd (1976) 12 OR (2d) 19   66
Glasbrook Brothers Ltd v Glamorgan County Council [1925] AC 270   67, 68
Goldsoll v Goldman [1915] 1 Ch 292   220
Goldsworthy v Brickell [1987] 1 All ER 853   224
Gran Gelato Ltd v Richcliff (Group) Ltd [1992] 1 All ER 865   131
Green v Portsmouth Stadium Ltd [1953] 2 QB 190   213
Green (R. W.) Ltd v Cade Brothers Farms [1978] 1 Lloyd's Rep 602   118
Greig v Insole [1978] 3 All ER 449   216
Grist v Bailey [1967] Ch 532   158, 173, 175, 176
Grogan v Meredith Plat Hire, The Times, 20 February 1996   105

Hadley v Baxendale (1854) 9 Exch 341   183
Hansa Nord, The [1976] QB 44   88, 97
Harbutt's 'Plasticine' Ltd v Wayne Tank & Pump Co. Ltd [1970] 1 QB 477   17, 102, 103
Harris v Watson (1791) Peake 102   69
Harse v Pearl Life Assurance Co. [1904] 1 KB 558   213, 214
Hart v O'Connor [1985] 3 WLR 214   227
Hartley v Ponsonby (1857) 7 E & B 872   65, 68, 76
Hartog v Colin and Shields [1939] 3 All ER 566   151
Harvela Investments v Royal Trust Co. of Canada [1985] 2 All ER 966   48, 49
Hayes v Dodd [1990] 2 All ER 815   186
Hedley Byrne & Co. Ltd v Heller & Partners Ltd
   [1964] AC 465   39, 75, 105, 128, 129, 138, 139, 140, 143, 145, 147
Heilbut, Symons & Co. v Buckleton [1913] AC 30   82
Hennessy v Craigmyle [1986] IRLR 304   222
Henthorn v Fraser [1892] 2 Ch 27   33
Herne Bay Steam Boat Co. v Hutton [1903] 2 KB 683   164
Heron II, The [1969] 1 AC 350   184
Heywood v Wellers [1976] 1 All ER 300   186
Hill v C. A. Parsons & Co. Ltd [1972] Ch 305   193, 206
Hillas & Co. Ltd v Arcos Ltd (1932) 147 LT 503   155
Hoenig v Isaacs [1952] 2 All ER 176   191
Hoffberger v Ascot International Bloodstock Bureau Ltd (1976) 120 SJ 130   187
Hollier v Rambler Motors (AMC) Ltd [1972] 2 QB 71   107, 108, 109, 110, 112, 122, 123
Holwell Securities Ltd v Hughes [1974] 1 All ER 161   33, 46
Hongkong Fir Shipping Co. Ltd v Kawasaki KK Ltd [1962] 2 QB 26   85, 86, 89, 93, 97, 164
Hopkins v Tanqueray (1854) 15 CB 130   97
Houghton v Trafalgar Insurance Co. Ltd [1954] 1 QB 247   108
Hounslow London Borough Council v Twickenham Garden Developments Ltd
   [1971] Ch 233   192
Howard Marine & Dredging Co. Ltd v A. Ogden & Sons (Excavations) Ltd
   [1978] QB 574   39, 139
Hughes v Liverpool Victoria Legal Friendly Society [1916] 2 KB 482   214
Hummingbird Motors v Hobbs [1986] RTR 276   129
Hyde v Wrench (1840) 3 Beav 334   51

In re Selectmove Ltd [1995] 1 WLR 474 (see also (1994) 110 LQR 353   53, 72, 73, 78
Ingram v Little [1961] 1 QB 31   152
Interfoto Picture Library Ltd v Stiletto Visual Programmes Ltd
   [1988] 1 All ER 348   107

Jackson v Horizon Holidays Ltd [1975] 1 WLR 1468;
    [1975] 3 All ER 92   10, 200, 201, 203, 205, 206
Jackson v Union Marine Insurance Co. Ltd (1874) LR 10 CP 125   178
Jarvis v Swans Tours Ltd [1973] QB 233   185
JEB Fasteners Ltd v Marks, Bloom & Co. [1983] 1 All ER 583   132, 133, 144
Johnstone v Bloomsbury Health Authority [1991] 2 WLR 1362   90
Joseph Constantine Steamship Line Ltd v Imperial Smelting Corporation Ltd
    [1942] AC 154   166

Karsales (Harrow) Ltd v Wallis [1956] 1 WLR 936   102
Kearley v Thomson (1890) 24 QBD 742   214
Kehoe v Borough of Rutherford (1893) 27 A 912   198
Kiriri Cotton Co. Ltd v Dewani [1960] AC 192   213, 214, 230
Krell v Henry [1903] 2 KB 740   162, 163, 164, 167, 176

L'Estrange v F. Graucob Ltd [1934] 2 KB 394   101, 102, 105, 118
Lampleigh v Brathwait (1615) Hob 105   64
Levison v Patent Steam Carpet Cleaning Co. Ltd [1977] 3 All ER 498   103
Lewis v Averay [1972] 1 QB 198   152
Liverpool City Council v Irwin [1977] AC 239   90, 91, 95
Lloyds Bank Ltd v Bundy [1975] QB 326   223, 226, 232
Lockett v A. & M. Charles Ltd [1938] 4 All ER 170   200
Long v Lloyd [1958] 1 WLR 753   135
Luxor (Eastbourne) Ltd v Cooper [1941] AC 108   48

M & S Drapers v Reynolds [1956] 3 All ER 814   220
Magee v Pennine Insurance Co. Ltd [1969] 2 QB 507   156, 173
Mahmoud and Ispahani, Re [1921] 2 KB 716   212, 229
Manchester Diocesan Council for Education v Commercial & General
    Investments Ltd [1970] 1 WLR 241   51
Maritime National Fish Ltd v Ocean Trawlers Ltd [1935] AC 524   165
McArdle, Re [1951] Ch 669   63, 64
McCutcheon v David MacBrayne Ltd [1964] 1 All ER 430   107, 122
McLeish v Amoo-Gottfried & Co., The Times, 13 October 1993   186
McRae v Commonwealth Disposals Commission (1950) 84 CLR 377   155, 156, 182
Mendelssohn v Normand Ltd [1970] 1 QB 177   107
Mihalis Angelos, The [1971] 1 QB 164   86, 95, 97
Miller's agreement, Re [1947] Ch 615   202
Mountford v Scott [1975] Ch 258   48

National Carriers Ltd v Panalpina (Northern) Ltd [1981] AC 675   160, 164, 166, 176
National Westminster Bank plc v Morgan [1985] 1 All ER 821   223, 224, 226, 227, 232
Naughton v O'Callaghan [1990] 3 All ER 191   141
New Zealand Shipping Co. Ltd v A. M. Satterthwaite & Co. Ltd
    [1975] AC 154   45, 67, 68, 119, 122
Nordman v Rayner & Sturgess (1916) 33 TLR 87   164
North Ocean Shipping Co. Ltd v Hyundai Construction Co. Ltd
    [1979] QB 705   65, 66, 68, 69, 70, 222, 228, 229
Notcutt v Universal Equipment Co. Ltd [1986] 1 WLR 641   162, 176

Odenfeld, The [1978] 2 Lloyd's Rep 357   192
O'Sullivan v Management Agency & Music Ltd [1985] QB 428   216
Olley v Marlborough Court Ltd [1949] 1 KB 532   105
Oscar Chess Ltd v Williams [1957] 1 WLR 370; [1957] 1 All ER 325   81, 96, 158

Page One Records Ltd v Britton [1967] 3 All ER 822   193
Paget v Marshall (1884) 28 ChD 255   154

Pao On v Lau Yiu Long (1980) AC 614   64, 67, 222
Parker v South Eastern Railway Co. (1877) 2 CPD 416   101, 106
Parsons Brothers Ltd v Shea (1966) 53 DLR 2d 36   172
Partridge v Crittenden [1968] 1 WLR 1204; [1968] 2 All ER 421 DC   11, 12, 46, 55
Pearce v Brooks (1866) LR 1 Ex 213   211
Phang [1993] JBL 242   91
Pharmaceutical Society of Great Britain v Boots Cash Chemists (Southern) Ltd
    [1953] 1 QB 401   53
Philips Hong Kong v A-G of Hong Kong (1993) 61 BLR 41   189
Phillips Products Ltd v Hyland [1987] 2 All ER 620   104, 125
Phillips v Brooks Ltd [1919] 2 KB 243   152
Photo Production Ltd v Securicor Transport Ltd [1980] AC 827   103, 112, 120
Pinnel's Case (1602) 5 Co Rep 117a   71, 72, 73, 78
Pitt v PHH Asset Management [1993] 4 All ER 961   74
Planché v Colburn (1831) 8 Bing 14   198, 199, 205, 207, 208
Posner v Scott-Lewis [1986] 3 WLR 531   194
Poussard v Spiers (1876) 1 QBD 351   86
Price v Strange [1977] 3 All ER 371   195, 208
Provident Financial Group v Hayward [1989] IRLR 84   193

Quinn v Burch Brothers (Builders) Ltd [1966] 2 QB 370   187

Radford v De Froberville [1978] 1 All ER 33   205, 207, 208
Raffles v Wichelhaus (1864) 2 H & C 906   150, 154
Raggow v Scougall & Co. (1915) 31 TLR 564   70, 76
Raphael, The [1982] 2 Lloyd's Rep 42   109
Reardon Smith Line Ltd v Hansen Tangen [1976] 3 All ER 570   84, 85
Redgrave v Hurd (1881) 20 ChD 1   131, 132
Richardson, Spence & Co. v Rowntree [1894] AC 217   101, 107
Riverlate Properties Ltd v Paul [1975] Ch 133   153, 154
Roscorla v Thomas (1842) 3 QB 234   63
Routledge v McKay [1954] 1 All ER 855   81
Rowland v Divall [1923] 2 KB 500   197
Royscot Trust Ltd v Rogerson [1991] 3 All ER 294   138, 141
Rust v Abbey Life Assurance Co. Ltd [1979] 2 Lloyd's Rep 334   53
Ruxley Electronics v Forsyth [1996] AC 344   186, 207
Ryan v Mutual Tontine Westminster Chambers Association [1893] 1 Ch 116   194

Scally v Southern Health and Social Services Board [1991] 3 WLR 778   91
Scammell (G.) & Nephew Ltd v Ouston (H. C. & J. G.) [1941] AC 251   52
Scandinavian Trading Tanker Co. AB v Flota Petrolera Ecuatoriana [1983] 2 AC 694;
    [1983] QB 529   73, 190
Schawel v Reade [1913] 2 IR 64   97
Schebsman, Re [1944] Ch 83   202
Schroeder (A.) Music Publishing Co. Ltd v Macaulay [1974] 1 WLR 1308   216, 217, 218, 219
Schuler (L.) AG v Wickman Machine Tool Sales Ltd [1974] AC 235   98
Scotson v Pegg (1861) 6 H & N 295   66, 67, 68, 78
Scriven Brothers & Co. v Hindley & Co. [1913] 3 KB 564   154
Shadwell v Shadwell (1860) 9 CBNS 159   62, 66, 68, 69, 76
Shepherd (F. C.) Ltd v Jerrom [1986] 3 WLR 801   165
Shanklin Pier Ltd v Detel Products Ltd [1951] 2 KB 854   82, 128
Shell UK Ltd v Lostock Garage Ltd [1977] 1 All ER 481   91, 117, 196
Shelley v Paddock [1979] QB 120   138, 212
Shuey v United States (1875) 92 US 73   5, 6, 7, 49, 56
Singer v Tees & Hartlepool Port Authority [1988] 2 Lloyd's Rep 164   119
Smith New Court v Scrimgeour Vickers [1996] 4 All ER 769   141, 142
Smith v Bush [1989] 2 WLR 790   117, 124

Smith v Hughes (1871) LR 6 QB 597   44, 150, 152
Smith v Land & House Property Corporation (1884) 28 ChD 7   130
Smith v South Wales Switchgear Ltd [1978] 1 All ER 18   108, 123
Solle v Butcher [1950] 1 KB 671   150, 157, 158, 173, 175
Spurling (J.) Ltd v Bradshaw [1956] 1 WLR 461   106, 107
St Albans City and District Council v International Computers Ltd, The Times,
    11 November, 1994   116
St John Shipping Corporation v Joseph Rank Ltd [1957] 1 QB 267   211, 212, 231
Stevenson, Jaques & Co. v McLean (1880) 5 QBD 346   51
Stewart Gill Ltd v Horatio Myer & Co. Ltd [1992] 2 All ER 257   115, 117, 124
Stilk v Myrick (1809) 2 Camp 317   59, 62, 65, 71, 76
Stockloser v Johnson [1954] 1 QB 476   190
Strongman (1945) Ltd v Sincock [1955] 2 QB 525   82, 212, 229, 230
Suisse Atlantique Société d'Armement Maritime SA v NV Rotterdamsche
    Kolen Centrale [1967] 1 AC 361   102, 112
Sumpter v Hedges [1898] 1 QB 673   199
Super Servant Two, The [1989] 1 Lloyd's Rep 148   165, 166

Tai Hing Cotton Mill v Liu Chong Hing Bank [1985] 2 All ER 947   91
Tamplin (F. A.) Steamship Co. Ltd v Anglo-Mexican Petroleum Products Co. Ltd
    [1916] 2 AC 397   177
Taylor v Bowers (1876) 1 QBD 291   214, 230
Taylor v Caldwell (1863) 3 B & S 826   161, 166
Taylor v Chester (1869) LR 4 QB 309   215
Telephone Rentals v Burgess Salmon, The Independent, (1987) 22 April   192
Texaco Ltd v Mulberry Filling Station Ltd [1972] 1 WLR 814   217
Thake v Maurice [1984] 2 All ER 513   83, 95, 148, 154
Thomas v Thomas (1842) 2 QB 851   64
Thomas Witter v TBP Industries [1996] 2 All ER 573   136
Thompson v London, Midland & Scottish Railway Co. [1930] 1 KB 41   101, 106
Thornton v Shoe Lane Parking Ltd [1971] 2 QB 163   105, 106
Tinn v Hoffmann & Co. (1873) 29 LT 271   51
Tito v Waddell (No. 2) [1977] Ch 106   194, 196
Tsakiroglou & Co. Ltd v Noblee Thorl GmbH [1962] AC 93   162
Tweddle v Atkinson (1861) 1 B & S 393   62, 75, 206

United Dominions Trust (Commercial) Ltd v Eagle Aircraft Services Ltd
    [1968] 1 WLR 74   120
Universe Tankships Inc. of Monrovia v International Transport Workers Federation
    [1983] 1 AC 366   228, 229
Upton-on-Severn Rural District Council v Powell [1942] 1 All ER 220   33, 43

Vandepitte v Preferred Accident Insurance Corporation of New York [1933] AC 70   201
Verrall v Great Yarmouth Borough Council [1981] QB 202   195
Victoria Laundry (Windsor) Ltd v Newman Industries Ltd [1949] 2 KB 528   183, 184, 185
Vitol SA v Norelf Ltd [1996] 3 All ER 193   53

W. J. Tatem Ltd v Gamboa [1939] 1 KB 132   164
Waldron-Kelly v British Railways Board [1981] CLY 303   118
Walford v Miles [1992] 1 All ER 453   75
Ward v Byham [1956] 3 All ER 318   67, 68
Warlow v Harrison (1859) 1 E & E 309   76
Warner Brothers Pictures Inc. v Nelson [1937] 1 KB 209   193
Watkin v Watson-Smith, The Times, 3 July 1986   225
Watkins & Son Inc. v Carrig (1941) 21 A 2d 591   70
Watson v Prager [1991] 1 WLR 726   219
Watts v Morrow [1991] 4 All ER 937   186

Watts v Spence [1976] Ch 165   141
Wayne Tank & Pump Co. Ltd v Employers Liability Assurance Corporation Ltd
   [1974] QB 57   102
West London Commercial Bank Ltd v Kitson (1884) 13 QBD 360   130
White & Carter (Councils) Ltd v McGregor [1962] AC 413   173, 191, 192
White v Bluett (1853) 23 LJ Ex 36   75
White v John Warwick & Co. Ltd [1953] 2 All ER 1021   109
White v Jones [1995] 1 All ER 691   202
Whittington v Seale-Hayne (1900) 82 LT 49   134
Wight v British Railways Board [1983] CLY 424   118
Wilkinson v Clements (1872) LR 8 Ch App 96   195
William Sindall v Cambridgeshire County Council [1994] 1 WLR 1016   136
Williams v Bayley (1866) LR 1 HL 200   223, 230
Williams v Roffey Bros [1991] 1 QB 1   65, 66, 68, 72, 76, 78
Williams v Williams [1957] 1 All ER 305   71
Wilson v Best Travel [1993] 1 All ER 353   90
With v O'Flanagan [1936] Ch 575   128, 146
Wong Mee Wan v Kwa Kin Travel [1995] 4 All ER 745   90
Woodar Investment Development Ltd v Wimpey Construction UK Ltd
   [1980] 1 All ER 571   202, 203, 205, 206
Wroth v Tyler [1974] Ch 30   185, 196
Wyatt v Kreglinger & Fernau [1933] 1 KB 793   218, 219

Yates Building Co. Ltd v R. J. Pulleyn & Sons (York) Ltd (1975) 119 SJ 370;   33, 51, 56

1 EFFICIENT AND CREATIVE STUDY

Advising someone on how to study is rather like trying to identify the secrets of a happy marriage — what works well for one person or couple may well be a recipe for disaster for others — the only difference is that in marriage there is always somebody else to blame if things go wrong whereas in studying for examinations you stand or fall by your own efforts. This difference is in fact worth emphasising, particularly for degree-level students, since one of the things that distinguishes a degree course from most other courses that you might have previously taken is the extent to which you are expected to work on your own, organise your own time and create your own way of looking at the subject. The secret of success is realising this at an early stage and devising an efficient and creative pattern of study which suits your own character and with which you can feel comfortable. This applies not only to when you study but also to how you study. Whether you choose to work a lot in the evenings in order to leave time free for, e.g., daytime activities or whether you prefer to work 'office hours' or some combination of the two approaches, it is important to plan some sort of routine. It can be a different sort of routine for different days of the week, as long as you are clear which routine applies to which day and as long as you keep to it. How long you need to allocate varies from one individual to another, but you are asking for trouble if you think you can work less than a 40-hour week. You must review your programme as your course progresses and if you find that you have allocated insufficient time for study then obviously your programme has to change. It is better to start off with a timetable which you think you have a reasonable chance of adhering to rather than an over-generous programme which you know you have no chance of maintaining since the latter may well encourage you to develop inefficient techniques and habits which it is difficult to get out of later on.

Of course, recognising that what is effective is to some extent a personal thing does not mean that there are *no* ground rules to be followed at all and just as there are some basic do's and don'ts for a happy marriage, like *do* speak to each other and *don't* beat your spouse, so too there are similar imperatives and injunctions for successful study such as, *do* listen to your lectures and *don't* write your exam scripts in Gaelic.

Happily, the advice that can be given goes further than such obvious statements since the course on which you are embarking, or something very similar to it, has been taken by thousands of students before you and you can benefit from their experiences and learn from their errors without actually suffering from the associated pain. That is not to say that successful study is totally painless and that you will not make errors yourself in trying to devise your own personal style. Nothing can be achieved without a certain amount of hard work but your effectiveness and efficiency will increase as you learn what works best for you. Knowing that you are going to improve, however, doesn't mean that you have to start from scratch. The aim of this chapter will therefore be to set you on the right track from the outset and to give you an idea of where the track is supposed to lead because it has been said with some justification that the commonest form of stupidity is forgetting what it is you are trying to do.

LECTURES

The point just made, about remembering what you are trying to do, is particularly true of lectures. The purpose of attending lectures is not to compile a verbatim account of every single word that the lecturer utters but to gain an understanding of how the materials which comprise the subject-matter of a particular area of your course fit together and what sorts of issues, problems and possible future developments can arise from those materials. There is no point trying to obtain a word-perfect account of everything the lecturer says:

   (a)   Because you would be unlikely to be able to reproduce it all again in an examination room.
   (b)   Even if you could so reproduce it, the examiner would not thank you for it because you would not be answering the particular question set.
   (c)   And this is related to (b), you will be so busy trying to write down every word that you will not have the time to think about what is being said and understand it.

Without an *understanding* of the material you will have no chance of answering problem questions which any contract examination will require of you and an examinee who reproduces a lot of material learned parrot fashion in answer to an essay question leaves the impression that he has a parrot-like intellect with no understanding of the material which he recites. Since the purpose of attending lectures is to gain an undersstanding of the subject, the first think you should do is *listen* to what the lecturer has to say and *think* about its meaning and then make your own note or paraphrase of what you *understand* him to have said. As a general rule it is better to translate the lecturer's form of words into your own form of words, even at the risk of the loss of some degree of accuracy, since the creative effort of translating into your own words necessarily involves making at least some attempt to understand what the lecturer has said, and material understood, even if only imperfectly, the first time round is much more easily revised on second and subsequent occasions. Also, understanding an issue at this stage rather than compiling a quantity of notes about it, will assist you in your own reading and seminar preparation involving that issue. Of course, it may well be that despite making the effort to understand what the lecturer is saying, there are parts of what he says that don't seem to make much sense. Assuming that your lecturer is not just incompetent, all you can do here is to make a brief accurate note of what is being said, perhaps indicating in your margin that you were puzzled and if possible why, so that you can go back to the issue later on when you have yourself done more work and have a better chance of understanding. Even here you should not be writing down every single word but merely sufficient to enable you to identify later on the issue that the lecturer has raised and which requires further thought from you. Remember, any notes that you make are for your use later on and the notes should be no more than you require to enable you to recall the material at that later stage. Let us take an example of what a lecturer might actually say and how you might listen to it and take notes.

> LECTURER. When one turns to revocations, however, one finds that the postal rule is inapplicable and that in general the revocation has to be actually received before it can take effect. Thus in *Byrne* v *Van Tienhoven* the defendants dispatched their offer on the first of the month from Cardiff and the plaintiffs received it on the eleventh and immediately accepted it. In the meantime the defendant had posted a revocation on the eighth which, however, was held to be ineffective because it was not received until the twentieth, well after the acceptance had taken place.
>
> In fact one can see from looking at the case that to apply a postal rule to revocations would go a long way towards undermining the postal rule established for acceptances. The advantage to the acceptor of knowing that he has a binding contract once he has posted his letter for acceptance and the ability to act safely in reliance on that knowledge would be largely destroyed by the mere possibility of a revocation having already been dispatched but not yet received. Whilst it is not logically

impossible to apply the postal rule to both acceptances and revocations, it makes much better practical sense to confine the rule to acceptances only and *Byrne* v *Van Tienhoven* is consistent with the prevailing objective approach.

Suggested note

> Revocations: Disting. from
> Acceptances.
>> No postal rule.
>> Must normally be received.
> *Byrne* v *Van T.* Offer 1st, acc. 11th,
> revoc. posted 8th. Received 20th —
> too late.
> Any other rule wld sit uneasily
> with P. rule for acc. Peace of mind
> given to acceptor by P. rule would
> be illusory if unreceived posted
> revoc. could be effective.
> P. rule for both situations not
> logically imp. but *Byrne* v *Van T.*
> rule makes more sense and is
> consistent with objective approach.   **?**

Note that in the first paragraph of the lecture, the process of note-taking has not involved much translating, merely cutting down, since in that paragraph the lecturer is concerned merely with stating the basic rule and outlining the facts of the leading case. Some abbreviations have been used — how much you use abbreviations is a matter of personal choice, always remembering that the purpose of taking notes and using abbreviations is not to produce something elegant but something that will be meaningful to you when looked at later.

In the second paragraph, the lecturer is commenting on the legal rule, and here the process of translating the commentary into your own words is more evident and important because it is a way of automatically checking that you are understanding what the lecturer is saying and that what you are writing down will later be meaningful to you. The note supposes that the last sentence of the extract from the lecturer is not immediately understood by the student so the note reverts to using the lecturer's words in an abbreviated form and a question mark in the margin reminds the student that this is something he didn't fully understand and needs to think about again.

If your margin starts to disappear under the weight of numerous question marks, this suggests two possible explanations:

(a)   That your lecturer is incapable of making any point clearly and intelligibly. This is not impossible but before conveniently absolving yourself by jumping to this conclusion, you should check with a cross-section of other students whether they are experiencing the same difficulty.

(b)   It is more likely that you are not doing the necessary preparatory work or reading that the lecturer is expecting of you, in which case the remedy lies in your own hands.

It has to be said that lecturers do vary in their expectations in this matter, and indeed the same lecturer may adopt a different attitude at different stages in a course. It may be that early on in a course, particularly a course like contract which is often taught in the first year, the lecturer assumes little in the way of existing understanding in his audience. Even here, though, it will not do you any harm to have read the relevant section of your textbook before attending the lecture — you are going to have to read it several times anyway so you might as well make a start. Later on in a course, the lecturer certainly will expect and assume a certain level of understanding at least of material that has gone before in the course which perhaps he is going to draw on in dealing with new issues. If you can see from the lecture hand-out that the next lecture on, say, damages for breach is going to draw comparisons with damages for misrepresentation covered earlier in the course, then it makes sense, before the lecture, to refresh your memory of that topic by reading through your notes. Even if this doesn't actually pay tremendous dividends in understanding the lecture, it will not be wasted as it will make your eventual revision of that topic that much easier.

You will have noticed that the sample note above leaves plenty of space around the notes made. Despite the rising costs of paper and the no-doubt straitened financial circumstances under which you are operating it would be a false economy to try to save money by cramming your notes into a smaller quantity of paper because you will later on want to add to and amplify your notes as, hopefully, your understanding of the subject deepens. At a later stage still, you will need to cut them down again before the examination but it is much easier to 'distil' one complete set of notes in this way than to have to combine at a later stage a number of different sets of notes made at different times. If you leave sufficient spaces in your lecture notes they can eventually serve quite well as your 'master' set rather than having to create a totally new 'master' incorporating all the different sources of notes you have made during the year. Indeed, the spaces that you leave in a lecture may be just as important as the notes that you make.

So, going back to the earlier sample notes, let us suppose that for your seminar reading you are referred to the case of *Shuey* v *United States* (1875) 92 US 73 but the case is not specifically dealt with in the lecture. When you have read the case you will realise that it represents a modification to the proposition that revocations have to be actually received and that in the case of an offer made to a large number of unidentifiable persons, the revoking offeror may succeed if reasonable steps are taken to bring the revocation to the attention of potential acceptors. Thus you might want to amend your note of *Byrne & Co.* v *Leon Van Tienhoven & Co.* (1880) 5 CPD 344 in the following manner:

Revocations: Disting. from Acceptances.

No postal rule.

Must <u>normally</u> be received.

Compare *Shuey* v *US*.
Offer of reward in newspaper withdrawn by similar means even though revoc. did not come to attention of offeree. No conflict with p. rule for acc. since p. rule not applicable even to acceptor in *Shuey*.

Byrne v *Van T.* Offer 1st, acc. 11th, revoc. posted 9th. Received 20th — too late.

Any other rule wld sit uneasily with P. rule for acc. Peace of mind given to acceptor by P. rule would be illusory if unreceived posted revoc. could be effective.

P. rule for both situations not logically imp. but *Byrne* v *Van T.* rule makes more sense and is consistent with objective approach. **?**

The more you add to and modify your original set of lecture notes, the more you will be creating your own distinctive view of the subject which will help make your eventual examination script seem fresh and original to the examiner. Furthermore, the more your notes are your own individual creation, the more easily will you be able to recall them in the pressures of the examination.

One final point about lectures: it should already be clear that they are not a one-way process. You should be participating by thinking about, interpreting and translating what the lecturer is saying, but it can be more overtly reciprocal in that the lecture may provide an opportunity to ask questions. Again, individual lecturers' attitudes vary. Some prefer not to have their delivery interrupted by questions and will take questions at the end of the lecture. Personally, whilst I think that may be appropriate for a one-off lecture or a relatively short series where interruptions may otherwise prevent the lecturer getting through all he plans to say, I don't think it is really suitable for a series of lectures that is to continue for a whole academic session since to leave five or ten minutes for questions may be far too long on some occasions and not long enough on others. So most lecturers are happy to take questions during the course of their lecture and unless they have made it clear that this is not so you should not be afraid of asking such questions. The lecturer will be only too pleased to know that at least someone is taking a sufficiently close interest in what he is saying (as opposed to the words he is speaking — so don't ask him if he actually said revocation or withdrawal) to want to ask a question about it. As already indicated, though, there are questions and questions and no one is going to be pleased if you ask a question that everyone knows is going to be asked in a subsequent seminar or tutorial or which it is obvious from the lecture hand-outs is going to be answered later in the lecture. The sorts of questions which are legitimate and which will be welcomed are those that arise from material which the lecturer has already covered. Thus if the lecturer did deal with both *Byrne* v *Van Tienhoven* and *Shuey* v *United States* without pointing out or explaining the obvious difference in approach between them, it would be legitimate to ask him to explain the apparent inconsistency between them. It might just be that he or she has forgotten to say something that was intended to be said (lecturers are, believe it or not, ordinary humans — or at least most of them are) or perhaps the lecturer has deliberately omitted to point out the inconsistency in order to see if the class is awake! If your question receives a reply that still leaves you in the dark it is best not to pursue the point unless the lecturer invites you to do so, but to seek clarification after the lecture has finished, or perhaps from your seminar tutor after you have done some further reading if that might help. What you should not do is to ignore your confusion and hope it goes away — it is likely to reappear in the exam room where no help is at hand. Most lecturers and tutors are only too happy to discuss issues with students who are prepared to take the trouble to think about them — but it is very difficult to help the student who doesn't tell you what it is that troubles (or interests) him.

TEXTBOOKS

The law of contract has a substantial history as an academic subject, indeed some would argue that in some sense the academic subject was created first and then the law hijacked to fit the academic myth. At any rate, the textbooks have a lengthy pedigree, none more so than *Anson's Law of Contract* first published in 1879 and now in its 26th edition. It was generally regarded as the most conventional of the available textbooks and has been primarily responsible, at least on this side of the Atlantic, for the preservation of the classical theory of contract in a purer form than the realities of the situation would otherwise have allowed (see Atiyah in *The Rise and Fall of Freedom of Contract*, pp. 681-7). Nonetheless it offered a straightforward account of the subject and was therefore quite suitable for students taking contract as a first-year subject provided that they were aware of its rather orthodox tradition, but the 1984 edition has now become hopelessly out of date.

Cheshire, Fifoot & Furmston's Law of Contract (first published in 1945) is not dissimilar in outlook but at the time of writing is in its 13th edition which was published in 1996 so it is therefore much more up-to-date than the 1984 edition of Anson a new edition of which is expected shrotly.

The third and most recent in origin (1962) of the three major textbooks is Treitel, *The Law of Contract*, now in its 9th edition, 1995. Whilst it is not, and would not claim to be, a revolutionary or radical text, Trietel is the most contemporary in outlook and explores the difficult issues in most depth. It spends less time detailing the facts of cases and more time on analysis and comment and is therefore most suitable for the student of contract at second or third-year level, or for the slightly more ambitious first-year. For those seeking a more concise but nonetheless intelligent account of the law, Downes' *Textbook on Contract* (5th ed., 1997) and McKendrick's *Contract Law* (3rd ed., 1997) provide readable alternatives.

It should be emphasised that the above are only personal views about the essential characteristics of the major texts and that you should obviously pay most attention to the advice of the person responsible for your own particular course. However, it does seem to me to be rather a waste of resources for all, say, 80 students on a particular course to buy the same textbook when the different books all have something slightly different to offer. Given that groups of students often live and work together, share a house, or perhaps have some even cosier arrangement, it would seem to be sensible to share their resources and provide themselves with access to a range of textbooks rather than each individual purchasing his own copy of the same book like some magic talisman for success.

Having decided which textbook you are going to buy, the next question is what are you going to do with it? Now the answer to that question might seem obvious — read it — but that is the last thing that some students seem to want to do. Some paint it pretty colours whilst others underline long sections of it, some so much that the only sections that stand out are those which aren't coloured or underlined. Some copy it out in great detail like medieval scribes whilst others appear to learn whole paragraphs off by heart which then appear unattributed in the middle of their termly essays. Of course emphasising, underlining, note-taking, even wholesale quoting *if acknowledged*, can all have some utility sometimes but, like most things in life, only in moderation, and the first thing you must do with your textbook is *read it*. Don't try to make any notes of a chapter (or a smaller section if you have been specifically set one to read) until you have read it through at least once and seen the structure of the discussion and what seem to be the major features and what are merely incidental illustrations. Some would say that noting textbooks is a waste of time anyway and that your time would be better spent reading the book again. The best course in my view is a compromise which doesn't involve making a separate set of notes but does involve, once you have read the book once or twice and have had your lectures in the area, going through the textbook carefully again and every time you come across something significant or important, locating where in your lecture notes something is said on that issue or a related issue and amplifying your lecture notes accordingly in the light of the textbook discussion. Obviously, if you do not have any existing notes on a particular topic, you must create a separate set of notes from your textbook but do make sure that your notes are in outline form and do not merely reproduce large sections of the textbook.

If you feel that underlining etc. the book will help you in a subsequent reading then by all means do so but do it in a way that emphasises the important material rather than submerges it. It may give you a curious sort of satisfaction to underline neatly every line in a ten-line paragraph but a much more economical, effective and less unsightly way of achieving the same result is to put a single vertical line in the margin as here. It goes without saying that the only books you mark are those which belong to you.

READING CASES

Cases are still the most important source of the law of contract and so much of your directed reading will comprise lists of decided cases. It is therefore important to understand how to go about reading them and what you are supposed to get out of the process. I have often been asked a question along the following lines by students at the start of their studies: 'Why should I go to the trouble of reading long and complex cases when the textbook writers and my lecturers have already done it and extracted the relevant information for me?' The inquisitor will often attempt to reinforce his question by pointing out that the text writers (and, it is sometimes somewhat grudgingly conceded, his lecturers) are far more learned and able to interpret the cases properly. The answer to this question lies in recognising that the real purpose of reading cases is not merely to learn the rule or principle which the case is authority for but to gain an insight into *how* the courts arrive at those principles and rules and how the judges interpret facts and apply legal principles to those facts. Even the law of contract is not a fixed and immutable body of rules and it is quite useless merely to acquire a static picture of the rules at any particular moment if you cannot interpret new cases which may be decided or have no real insight into how the principles can be applied to factual situations (with which you will undoubtedly be confronted in the form of problem questions in the examination). It is only by reading decided cases and familiarising yourself with the way that judges manipulate other cases (and indeed statutes) and apply the law to the facts that you will be able to develop your own technique for doing so. In one sense, it doesn't really matter which cases you read — they could be cases about the law of sewers and drains or other such exciting subjects — as long as you read plenty of them but it might as well be contract cases as reading those cases will also incidentally help to familiarise you with the actual rules and principles of contract law.

In any event, it is a mistake to think that each case represents one or more specific rules or principles which can 'correctly' be deduced from it. Even if you ignore the phenomenon of different judgments agreeing on the result but disagreeing on the reasons why (see, e.g., *Jackson v Horizon Holidays Ltd* [1975] 3 All ER 92 where the Court of Appeal upheld the trial judge's award of damages but Lord Denning MR and James LJ had significantly different reasons) even a single closely reasoned judgment contains a great number of potential 'rules' which can be deduced from it (see Twining and Miers, *How to Do Things with Rules*, 3rd ed.). Which rules the case eventually substantiates depends on the attitude taken by later cases so it is the relationship between groups of cases that is important and you can only properly understand these relationships by observing the way judges handle groups of cases. The great American jurist Karl Llewellyn (in *The Bramble Bush*, a series of lectures first published in 1930 and, rather like this book, aimed directly at law *students*) for this reason advised students not to start making notes of the first case on a reading list until at least the second one had been read. (Even allowing for the difference between American legal education in the 1930s and modern English legal education, *The Bramble Bush* is well worth reading and chapters 3 and 4 in particular in the present context.) Every case in fact presents a number of choices of legal rules which later courts can make and it is only by careful study of the way in which judges make their choices that you can learn how to predict how the court will react to new choices and thus learn how to advise on how the law will be applied to problems or how the law might develop in the future.

Having convinced you, hopefully, of *why* you should read cases, I should offer some advice as to *how* you should do it. Understanding why is of course the key to understanding how. You should not be aiming merely for a note of the facts and of which side won and the main reason why. You can usually get that from the headnote. You should also be noting such things as what arguments were rejected by the court and why, for that will tell you whether similar arguments are likely to succeed on another slightly different set of facts, whether the court came to its decision reluctantly or not, for that will tell you whether the case is likely to be interpreted broadly or narrowly in the future, and, last but not least, whether there are any flaws in the court's reasoning or arguments that you think should have been considered but were not. This last point is important because it is what makes the case memorable and distinctive from your point of view and it is also what makes the study of law interesting. Obviously, in a good number of cases you will be happy to agree with the case and will not wish to criticise the reasoning or the failure to consider some other line of argument but even here it is useful to note *why* you agree with it. The process of working out why you agree (or disagree) with the case will help imprint the case on your memory and it is much easier to remember matters that you have views about than material about which you are indifferent or complacent. Taking a creative attitude to the reading of cases will help bring the subject alive and not only make you more efficient but make your studies more interesting and enjoyable. Most people fare best at tasks that they enjoy and work is no burden if it can be turned into a pleasure. Of course, there will be times when you would rather be doing something else but these times can be kept to a minimum if you can make your studies a source of at least some satisfaction.

At the risk of stating the obvious I should perhaps add that you should not let your own views completely displace the hard facts of the case or the reality of what the court actually said. You should be able to tell the examiner what the orthodox view of the case is before explaining what you yourself think of it. The point is that forming and having a view *about* something automatically entails knowing and recalling the 'something' itself.

In case you have found the above rather abstract and theoretical, let me take an example of how you might note a particular case taking as an example *Partridge* v *Crittenden* which will appear at a fairly early stage in most contract reading lists, bearing in mind that the precise method you adopt for yourself must at the end of the day be a matter of personal choice depending on what is likely to be most meaningful to you.

Partridge v *Crittenden* [1968] 2 All ER 421 DC
Classified adv. page in bird periodical — 'Bramblefinch cocks, . . . hens, 25s. each', words 'offer for sale' not mentioned. Appellant (Partridge!) supplied bird — convicted by mags of 'offering for sale' a live wild bird contrary to Protection of Birds Act 1954.

  Div. Court quashed conviction because advert constituted an invitation to treat, not an offer. (NB. Injustice here only apparent; offence of selling also available and should be used in these circs.)
Fisher v *Bell* (shop-window display not an offer) followed.
Ashworth J: Words 'offer for sale' not used — use of these words would not necessarily make any difference, but their absence strengthens appellant's case. *Fisher* v *Bell* (Parker CJ) is directly in point — 'equally plain' in that case and this that not an offer, only invitation to treat.
Parker CJ. 'I agree and with *less reluctance* than in *Fisher* v *Bell*' because business sense in treating adverts and circulars as invitations to treat unless they come from manufacturers — otherwise advertiser might be inundated with binding acceptances which given limited stocks he could not supply — as pointed out by Lord Herschell in *Grainger & Son* v *Gough*.
Per Me. Parker's point about limited supplies seems a telling one but has no application to *Fisher* v *Bell* situation which he seems less confident

about despite being a party to the decision. Despite headnote mentioning absence of words 'offer for sale', that doesn't seem terribly
significant.

Notice that this note makes as much use of Parker CJ's judgment as of
Ashworth J's even though the latter is four or five times as long because a lot
of Ashworth J's judgment is taken up with the question of whether the
particular bird sold was a wild one 'other than a close-ringed specimen'
within s. 6(1) of the Act, a question which is totally irrelevant to your contract
course. It is worth mentioning that the copy of the report I used to compile
this note from had actually been marked in pencil at various points by some
moron, if you will pardon the expression, who had read it before me. You can
tell he was a moron not only because he had marked a book that others have
to read, but also because the parts that he had underlined were the parts
relating to whether the bird was close-ringed. That is a rather obvious
illustration of why you shouldn't rely on any markings put on law reports by
previous students as they are just as likely to be misleading as helpful.
Someone else had underlined the fact, mentioned in Ashworth J's judgment,
that the words 'offer for sale' nowhere appear, which merely served to
distract attention from the next sentence in his judgment which was as
follows: 'I ought to say I am not for my part deciding that that would have
the result of making this judgment any different, but at least it strengthens
the case for the appellant'. Anyone unaware of that sentence would not be
able to discuss with appropriate subtlety, e.g., an exam problem which had
an advert expressly using the words 'offer for sale'. The same is true of anyone
who just relied on the headnote which specifically mentions the absence of
these words and which might mislead you into attaching too much
significance to this fact.
    Notice also that by reading the judgments you get a feeling of the
relationship between the case and the earlier case of *Fisher* v *Bell* [1960] 3 All
ER 731 and that whilst Ashworth J thought both were 'equally plain' Parker
CJ was less happy about *Fisher* v *Bell* even though it was his own decision.
That could be important to you if you wanted to argue in an essay or a
problem that the rule about displays of goods in a shop window is less
defensible than the *Partridge* v *Crittenden* rule, or ought not to be followed or
ought to be distinguished in a particular case etc.
    Of course the major point, and the one you have highlighted as your reason
for agreeing with the case is Parker CJ's point about limited stock. This will
be important if confronted with a question involving an advertisement where
the problem of limited supplies does not exist.
    Partridge v *Crittenden* is a relatively short case and some cases you will be
asked to read are much longer but the same principles apply to them all, and
indeed these principles are much more important for longer cases since the

potential for wasted effort is correspondingly greater. Firstly, read the case through. You don't know what is significant until you have seen the whole picture. Secondly, *summarise* the facts which you consider significant and the actual result of the case. Thirdly, extract from each judgment the factors which each judge found significant and also which factors or arguments he rejected or found insignificant. Of course, in cases of multiple judgments you need only note the second and subsequent judgments where they differ in some way from the previous ones. Finally, ask yourself how *you* would have decided the case and summarise your own views. (The expression 'per me' is one way of indicating these and at the same time clothing them with a sort of spurious authority but any other way will do as long as you clearly distinguish your own views from those of the court.) One other useful device which you might find will help you to remember the case later on is to make a note of anything in the case that strikes you as amusing (like the name of the appellant, Partridge, in this case) or ironic (like the fact that if the prosecution had framed the charge slightly differently, the issue would never have arisen).

Having done all that, you are ready to move on to the next case on your list. A purely practical point can be made here. Suppose that the next case is say, *Esso Petroleum Ltd* v *Commissioners of Customs & Excise* [1976] 1 All ER 117 and, warming now to the exciting task of reading cases, you go along to the shelf and eagerly look for volume 1 of the 1976 *All England Law Reports* where your reading list tells you the case is reported and you find that all copies of that volume have been taken and you can't trace it in the time you have available. Do not despair, or what is more common, use it as an excuse for not reading the case. Look the case up in the *Current Law Case Citator* or in the index of cases in *Chitty on Contracts* where you will find that the case is also reported at [1976] 1 WLR 1. The chances are that that volume is still on the shelves and you can read the case equally well in that volume. Do take care though that you are not reading the same case reported in a lower court when you are supposed to be reading the report of a successful appeal! All the above, of course, will be rarely necessary if, like most law students, you hunt in a pack and occupy an area of the library together where law reports etc. can be passed around and shared (like good jokes and illicit pleasures).

One final point about reading cases relates to casebooks. There are now a number of casebooks on the market, including Smith annd Thomas's *A Casebook on Contract*, the less conventional, *Contract Cases and Materials*, by Beale, Bishop and Furmston and the more concise *Casebook on Contract* by Poole. Smith and Thomas originally was regarded as quite a novel work in the English context and was primarily designed for a type of teaching imported from America, the so-called case method. Nonetheless, even for those students (the majority) where this method is not *de rigueur*, casebooks constitute a convenient and up-to-date collection of sources for those (such as part-time students) whose access to a good law library is limited. There is usually nothing lost if a case substantially extracted in the casebook is read there rather than in the reports (although one must be careful where only a small snippet is extracted to illustrate a particular point) and the questions and comments etc. can be useful stimuli for further thought on, or criticism of, the case. Of course, you would lose quite a lot if you *never* read a case in the reports (not least the important skill of how to use a law library properly but that is unlikely given that there are always cases on your reading list which the casebook does not contain, including most obviously those decided after the publication of the casebook). Unless your own tutors insist on it, a casebook is certainly not necessary but can be a useful purchase especially for those who like to work and find they can work efficiently at times when the library is normally closed. Certainly one advantage of reading casebooks is that there are no headnotes on which you can rely which forces you into the sound practice of working out yourself from the judgments what the principal issues are. Some casebooks have the additional merit of including materials from other jurisdictions (or disciplines) which may not be readily available in your own library. Whilst this is only occasionally true of Smith and Thomas or Poole, Beal, Bishop and Furmston are rather more adventurous on that score. Wheeler and Shaw is a more recent and substantial addition to the available casebooks and tries to locate the cases in a broad and challenging range of theoretical perspectives. It is probably best suited to those studying contract at 2nd or 3rd rather than 1st year level.

STATUTES

Although contract is still an essentially case-law-based subject, statutory material is becoming an increasingly important part of the syllabus, most obviously in areas such as exclusion clauses, misrepresentation and frustration. More will be said about particular statutes in the appropriate chapters later in the book but a few general remarks would not be out of place at this stage because the way students handle statutes is often a cause of disappointment to examiners. Statutes are not something to be frightened of, quite the reverse, because at least in a statute you have a definitive formal statement of a legal rule and do not have the problem that arises from case law of distilling a legal rule or principle from a number of lengthy judgments. The problem is rather one of interpretation of the rule itself and the language of statutory provisions tends to be somewhat convoluted and obscure at first sight because the statutory words have to stand or fall on their own and do not have the background of the facts of a case as an aid to their meaning.

   Again the key is to *read* the words of the sections which you are required to understand, work out what they mean to you and then translate that meaning into your own summary of the particular provision. If there are any decided cases on the application of the section then compare your own interpretation with that of the cases and then modify your own interpretation accordingly or, if you disagree with the court's interpretation, make a note of the difference and why you think the court's approach is open to criticism. If there are no decided cases as yet, then you can only compare your understanding of the provision with the comments of the textbooks or other commentators. A useful source of such commentaries is the *Current Law Statutes* series. These are a useful place to start from if on a first reading you cannot make head or tail of the statute but if you can manage it, the statute will be more deeply impressed on you if you can first of all grapple with it on your own.

Once you have worked out what the intention and effect of a provision is you have achieved the most important part of your task. That is much more important than learning to recite unthinkingly the precise words of a section but there is a place for learning by heart key sentences or phrases of a section which may be worth quoting in an examination. The point is that you will only know which sections, sentences or phrases are worth learning *after* you have understood the meaning of the whole. More detailed advice on this matter will be provided at appropriate points later in the book.

JOURNALS AND ARTICLES

Much of what has already been said about reading cases and statutes is equally applicable to articles — especially that you must read the whole piece through first before trying to make a note from it. It is best to leave the reading of an article until you have completed your own reading of the cases and statutes which are likely to be discussed in it so that you have had a chance to formulate your own view of the cases and how they fit together (or not, as the case may be) and thus have something against which to test the views of the writer of the article. Just as in reading cases, you should make a separate note of the extent to which you agree or disagree with the writer, or whether you think he is saying anything useful etc. It is not usually necessary to make detailed notes of the whole chain of reasoning of the author (although obviously you must try to follow and understand the reasoning as you read) for the writer will be anxious to defend his ultimate conclusions against the most erudite professor who might wish to challenge him by anticipating in advance every counter-argument and awkward if obscure precedent he can think of. You will not normally be expected to be able to recall how the author disposes of some half-reported 18th-century case but what is important is the way he deals with cases that *are* on your own reading list and the arguments of policy and principle which he deploys or rejects. On the other hand, merely noting down his conclusions will not be enough since without examining the reasoning which supports them and noting the major strands of that reasoning you will find that the conclusions mean little to you when later you wish to utilise them in an examination.

Case notes and shorter articles on recent developments have to be looked at slightly differently. There is likely to be less surplusage in the form of rebutting possible objections to the author's theory but even so you must remember that you are unlikely to be able to refer in detail to all the arguments in an examination. There is no point noting again the facts of the case if it is one which you have already noted although you may find that the author has discovered some background material not mentioned in the law report — if so it is worth adding this to your existing note of the case. Again your priority must be to understand the comments that the writer makes and to consider whether you agree with him and make a note of why. When it comes to the examination you will then be able to display not only your knowledge of contemporary opinion but also your willingness to evaluate issues for yourself.

Take for example a case note of *George Mitchell (Chesterhall) Ltd* v *Finney Lock Seeds Ltd* [1983] 2 AC 803, an important House of Lords case on exclusion clauses, at (1983) 46 MLR 771. The note is three and a half pages long but most of the first two sides is taken up with setting the scene by summarising the facts, the decisions of the lower courts and the context of the previous case law on the subject. You need not note this unless in reading it you find there is anything which you can usefully add to your existing notes of the case. (This is no criticism of the author as such case notes have to be intelligible to people other than law students who have only just read the relevant material.)

However, towards the bottom of the second page the author does begin to give his views when he criticises the distinction, reaffirmed by the House of Lords, between the interpretation of exclusion clauses on the one hand and mere limitation clauses on the other. This is worth noting, but not without the author's reasons, i.e., that the Unfair Contract Terms Act 1977 operates equally on both types of clause. Do you agree with the writer? Do you find his reasoning adequate? Can you think of additional reasons that might support his view, e.g., the fact that the limitation on damages on the facts was so low (in effect one-third of 1% of the actual damage) as to make it very close in practical effect to an exclusion clause.

The writer then goes on to point out that the case was actually interpreting the provisions of the Supply of Goods (Implied Terms) Act 1973 which have now been replaced by the Unfair Contract Terms Act 1977. This is a useful point which perhaps you had omitted to notice in your own reading of the case. If so, note it now.

The author then lists three points which emerge from the House's decision. Compare these with your own notes — do you agree that these three points emerge, or had you missed any of them? On a personal note, I think that point two is misleading and ignores the distinction which the writer has already pointed out, between the Supply of Goods (Implied Terms) Act 1973 provisions and the terms of s. 11 of the Unfair Contract Terms Act 1977. If that sort of point occurs to you, then again note it down as a point which you can later use as evidence of your independence of mind (suitably tinged with an awareness of your own fallibility).

Finally, the note ends with a question — what would the result of the earlier case of *Harbutt's 'Plasticine' Ltd* v *Wayne Tank & Pump Co. Ltd* [1970] 1 QB 477 be if it were to be decided today, given the change in attitudes and applicable rules in the meantime. The author can afford to leave the question unanswered but it would be a useful exercise for you to try to answer it and if the examiner has been reading the note and decides to set a question which effectively asks the same question, it is an exercise that could produce spectacular rewards.

SEMINARS AND TUTORIALS

To a large extent, preparing for seminars and tutorials is a question of following the above advice in relation to following your lectures and reading law reports and journals. However, you will not obtain maximum benefit if you merely complete the reading and allow no time for conscious preparation for the seminar or tutorial. Firstly, and most obviously, you need to have prepared outline answers to any questions or problems specifically set for discussion, otherwise you are likely to find that the discussion rushes by at a pace which you are unable to follow or contribute to. Some may think it is a clever economy of effort to merely listen to others discussing a problem and to make copious notes of their answers but if they have rarely gone through the process for themselves they will find it difficult to do in the isolation of the examination room.

Secondly, and equally importantly, you ought to use the seminars to ask questions that are *not* specifically set for discussion but which have occurred to you or have troubled you whilst preparing for the seminar. You need have no fear of upsetting your tutor who will be delighted to discuss something, in addition to the questions with which he is all too familiar, with someone who is interested enough to raise his own questions. The whole point of a seminar is to give you the opportunity to clear up points about which you are doubtful or to explore further issues in which you are interested. Of course, you must consider the interests of other students in your group and cannot expect to completely hijack the seminar. Most tutors are willing to continue discussions outside the seminar if there is not time to accommodate you within it. Perhaps I should add that there is no rule forbidding students to discuss issues between themselves *before* a seminar and refine their queries in advance. You can then together bombard your tutor with your combined thoughts and whilst most tutors would usually enjoy the exercise you can sometimes watch one squirm as he or she attempts to repel the combined broadside.

Again, there is no point in trying to take notes of everything that everybody says in a seminar but if something is said which you feel is significant or helps to shed new light on a particular case or problem, then by all means make a brief note providing that in doing so you do not lose track of what is going on.

ESSAYS AND PRESENTATIONS

An important part of the process of studying (and increasingly of assessment) involves the art of writing essays and, in some cases, the skill of presenting a paper to a seminar or tutorial group. More will be said in the later chapters about detailed techniques for dealing with essays and problems and about their specific content but some more general remarks can be made here. Essay-writing should be viewed as an exercise in communication. No matter how good the content, if it is not presented in an attractive and helpful manner, it will not receive the credit that its substance might otherwise deserve. Thus it is important to plan one's essay carefully so that it has a logical structure which makes it easy for the reader to follow the argument. Subheadings, provided that there are not too many of them, can be helpful in this respect as can a *brief* introduction explaining the approach which the rest of the essay is going to take. It should also be remembered that length is no virtue in itself and that all tutors prefer a concise and punchy piece of work to one that rambles on and takes twice as long to say the same thing. Quotations should be kept to a minimum and only used where absolutely necessary, e.g., where part of your essay is making a point about the quotation and the quotation is necessary in order to make your own point intelligible. Your tutor will be primarily interested in your own views rather than your ability to quote from others. You should, of course, never reproduce a passage from elsewhere without acknowledging that it is a quotation as the crime of plagiarism is even worse than the fault of excessive use of quotations.

Students on many courses are now increasingly asked to present their essays, or a summary of them, to a seminar group. Unless you are specifically asked to do so, simply reading out your essay is not usually what is required for the simple reason (amongst others) that it can be extremely boring unless the essay happens to be a literary gem. Again, planning your presentation is the secret of success. The preparation of charts and diagrams, illustrating the key points you are going to make and the issues which you are going to discuss, can make an otherwise dry topic come to life. If you have access to an overhead projector, you can meticulously prepare colourful slides in advance making the presentation appear much more professional than having to make a somewhat rushed use of a blackboard, during the actual seminar. Provided that your written essay or paper is actually going to be handed in and read by your tutor, you should also take the opportunity to digress from your written paper where appropriate and to expand on points made in your essay particularly with respect to issues which are difficult to explain adequately on paper but which lend themselves to oral discussion backed up with a visual display.

HOW TO USE THIS BOOK

It would be rather remiss of me if, having advised you on how to listen to lectures, read cases and journals and prepare for seminars, I said nothing about how you should use this book. Being reasonably substantial, it will of course serve as a suitable base on which to place hot sustaining drinks at times when such are required for continued study and it will also serve as a suitable missile for hurling (the hot drink preferably having been removed) at unwelcome intruders who seek to interrupt your efforts. It is, however, despite the absurdly low price at which it is sold, a rather expensive item if confined to such uses and there are in fact more appropriate ways of realising its utility. I *would* suggest that you read this chapter at an early stage but for the fact that you have obviously already read it so I shall confine my advice to subsequent chapters. Chapter 2 is no doubt the obvious one to read after chapter 1 but its contents are most directly in point once the material in your course has been covered for the first time. Nevertheless, I think that you can benefit from reading it at an early stage if only to give you an insight into what you will be doing later on with the notes which you are assiduously compiling. As for the remaining chapters, dealing with substantive topics, you will find these most helpful if you read them *after* you have read the appropriate chapter in your textbook and possibly attended a few lectures on the area but it is best at this stage not to bother with the latter parts of each chapter dealing with sample questions. When you have completed your own first reading of cases and articles on a topic you could then go back to the chapter in this book and see how much more sense the first part of each chapter now makes and make any amendments and adjustments to your notes that seem appropriate. You can then look at the sample questions but before reading what I have to say about answering them, it is best as always to work out how *you* would go about answering them and then compare what I have to say about the matter. You may well find that you have thought of useful approaches that I have not but it is even more likely that there are also suggestions of mine that you will find helpful. Certainly our combined approaches are likely to be better than either in isolation and should result in you developing your own individual and yet experienced style which you can then apply to questions and problems which you are given as course work or in examinations. When you have successfully negotiated the end-of-course examination you should then be lavish in extolling this book's virtues to the following year's students but be careful not to depress the market by selling it second-hand to no doubt eager customers! If kept in good condition, unstained by tea or coffee, it will appreciate in value and become a rare collector's item, a valuable artefact to be passed on to your doubtless numerous progeny!

CONCLUSION

You may feel that the advice in this chapter constitutes a counsel of perfection that you could not realistically hope to follow but it is better to set your sights high in order to leave a little margin for error. It is surprising what you can achieve when you know what you are trying to do and with just a little self-discipline and planning you will not only do well in your studies but perhaps even enjoy them. If you give priority to your studies, you will also find that you will be able to enjoy the leisure time that remains in a much more relaxed and carefree way. The essential message of this chapter is that the only studying which is worth doing involves *thinking* about what you are reading or listening to and *creating* your own ideas about it. This will inevitably familiarise you with the subject itself and the standard theories within it. The unthinking and mechanistic compiling of notes that the untutored mistake for study is not only boring and unproductive but, thankfully, unnecessary.

2 EXAMINATIONS AND HOW TO TAKE ADVANTAGE OF THEM

Most students regard examinations as something to be feared, something to be 'got through' with as little damage as possible and without being caught out on too many points. Now I don't want to pretend that examinations are an ideal method of assessment, or that students do not feel under pressure at exam times or that sitting in an examination hall for three hours in the middle of summer is the pleasantest occupation imaginable. However, you have to deal with the situation as it is and you will deal with it with much more success and less worry if you adopt a positive rather than a negative attitude from the start.

The first thing to remember is that examiners are not trying to catch people out or trip them up with unfair questions. They want to see people pass and pass well and exmainations are designed to provide students with an opportunity to display what they have learned rather than to winkle out bits they might have missed. Generally speaking, you are given marks for the knowledge, ability and understanding that you display rather than having marks knocked off for the points that you omit or get wrong (although there are some issues that are so central and obvious that ignorance of them is only consistent with having done no work at all and which will be penalised accordingly). If questions contain subtleties they are not designed to catch people out but to give the better students the opportunity of distinguishing themselves. If you have been accepted on to a course, then you should have no doubts that you are capable of at least passing it. The only reasons you can possibly fail are either:

(a)   you are idle and do insufficient work, in which case you will have only yourself to blame, or

(b)   you do not understand what is expected of you or how to go about achieving it.

You are removing this latter possibility by reading this book and the former possibility will automatically disappear if you put into practice what you have read. Indeed the main cause of idleness is boredom and lack of motivation and the main thrust of the previous chapter was that efficient and creative study carries its own rewards and satisfactions. Once you have dispelled the fear of failure you can look forward to the examination as the culmination of your efforts and as a chance to show just what you can do.

A second point to remember about examinations is that they normally only last for three hours (or less) and thus you have a strictly limited time to show the examiner the breadth and depth of your understanding. The limited time available is one of the reasons that assessment by examinations is criticised but, once again, you have to deal with the system as it is and recognising the fact of the limited amount of time is the first step to devising strategies to cope with the problem and perhaps even turn it to your advantage.

One of the reasons that I have stressed the need to think creatively and critically throughout your course is the very fact that you will have very little time to think in the examination. You cannot hope to formulate a convincing answer to whether, e.g., the doctrine of consideration serves a useful purpose if you have not thought about the issue before you go into the examination room but merely learned the facts and results of the leading cases. Your views and opinions on the key issues in the law of contract should be bubbling over ready to spill out in the examination should a question give them the opportunity to do so. But how do you know what these key issues are that you should have thought about? I have tried to identify some of them in the later chapters of this book but different courses emphasise different areas and a much more direct guide to your own course is available in the form of past papers. A study of these, before you start your revision, is invaluable and provides the nearest thing to seeing the paper in advance. Of course no examiner is going to set precisely the same question twice in exactly the same words but by analysing the papers over a three or four-year period you will see a pattern emerging whereby certain topics re-emerge, albeit in different form, almost every year. By putting together what you know from the past papers with your knowledge of what matters have been looked at in detail on your particular course, you should be able to make an educated guess as to the likely topics that will arise in your examination paper. Try putting yourself in the examiner's shoes and ask yourself what sort of questions you would set to test whether the students had followed your course and learned something from it. You will then see that, given the limitations of a three-hour examination, the examiner's room for manoeuvre is strictly limited. It would be unwise though to use this sort of analysis to exclude topics from consideration — its value lies more in identifying issues to which one should pay especial attention and on which one should have already formulated views.

Talk of past papers leads on to another point related to the constraints of a time limited examination. The number of questions you will be expected to answer will be such that you will have between approximately 35 and 45 minutes at most to answer each question and can be expected only to write between about 1,000 and 1,500 words per question. This means that it is far more relevant to write course-work essays of that sort of length, which requires discipline and selection and conciseness of expression, rather than write long, rambling essays which all too often lack direction and say very little in two or three times that number of words. Of course your own course may actually *require* you to do any essay of a specified length in which case, obviously, you must do it and such an essay can provide a useful opportunity to study a particular area in greater than usual depth. It must also be added that in doing course-work, your work will be expected to be rather more polished and authoritative than would be expected in an examination so that a limit of what you could write in an exmaination should not be adhered to too strictly. However, in addition to course-work that you are required to do, for which obviously you should adhere to the guidelines laid down by your tutors, there is nothing to stop you from writing examination-type answers to questions from past papers. Most tutors, given reasonable notice, are quite happy to go through these with you to assess whether you are approaching them in the right way and even if this is not possible the very fact of going through the exercise and addressing your mind to the sorts of issues that may confront you in the examination room will prove an enormous benefit.

There are two caveats that perhaps I should add in respect of the above uses of past papers.

(a)   There is little point in starting the exercise too early for you will lack the material to deal properly with most of the questions, particularly any questions which straddle two or more areas of the syllabus. It could be highly misleading for you to think that you had answered a question on exemption clauses if you had not yet covered the topic of privity or of remedies that such a question might also raise. The safest course is to leave your study of past papers until your first run through the course is complete — you will have plenty to occupy your time until then in any case and past papers can seem misleadingly daunting before that stage.

(b)   You should bear in mind that the past papers are *past* papers and that the more in the past they are the less reliable guide they constitute to the likely shape of the current year's paper. Not only do syllabuses and examiners change but issues that are topical in one year may not be so in another. Some issues are fairly timeless but a question prompted by a particular decision in one year is less likely to recur, particularly if the decision has been reversed or supplanted by subsequent cases.

Remember also that examination papers are usually set several months in advance so that cases decided in the intervening period offer no clues to the likely content of a paper (unless the imminence of the decision was well-known) which is not to say that the actual decision will not constitute very useful material in a question that has already been set.

REVISION

Having said that examinations are not to be feared, it must at once be added that they must be carefully prepared for — a process generally described as revision. Admittedly, in one sense you are preparing for an examination right from the start of your course but you would have a somewhat distorted view of things if you let that dominate your thoughts right from the beginning. Your purpose from the outset should be to gain as complete an understanding of the syllabus as possible in a manner which is consistent with being able to display that understanding in an examination at the end of the course. If you think only of the examination from the outset you will not acquire the understanding of the subject which is necessary to do yourself justice in the examination.

However, once you have completed the syllabus for the first time and acquired some sort of overall understanding, your thoughts will obviously, and quite properly, turn more directly to the issue of the examination. On many courses, this is the period from about Easter onwards, the main revision period. (This does not necessarily imply that an earlier formal period of revision is not beneficial — revision, e.g., during the Christmas vacation of the material covered up to that point will make later revision much easier and it may be essential if you are to benefit fully from any mid-course examinations.) For courses which run for a semester rather than a full year, the revision period will of course tend to be shorter.

The word 'revision', I am afraid, is a word which is much abused. It is often assumed to mean nothing more than looking at material again (and again and again) in order to 'learn' it and be able to reproduce it in the examination. Of course, certain things do have to be committed to memory, not least names of cases, but to describe that process alone as revision is not only incorrect as a matter of definition but also likely to result in underachievement in the examination. If you look up the verb 'revise' in a dictionary you will find that it means 'to examine and amend faults in' and that definition is much closer to what you should actually be doing in this period. You have to remember that many of the notes which you currently have were made at a time when your understanding of the subject was partial and incomplete. Not only that, they are far too voluminous to be useful on their own in preparing for an examination. It is not so much a question of amending the faults in what you already have, although doubtless you will find some of these, but of remedying areas that are weak, drawing together and amplifying issues, and distilling and reducing your notes to a manageable form. Let us take these three processes in turn and examine in detail what should be involved.

Remedying Weak Areas

No matter how efficiently you have organised your time during the course, there are likely to be some topics that you did not cover properly due to illness or other unavoidable causes. You may, for example, have some lecture notes on misrepresentation but if for some reason you were only able to read a few of the cases yourself, these notes may not mean all that much to you. Obviously you need to remedy this (you should ensure that there are no more than one or two such areas by the time the revision period comes around) and in a sense this remedial work is pre-revision in nature. It is tempting to decide that an area that is initially weak is one that can be left out of the examination but the danger is that by failing to understand the area properly in the first place you miss its important connections with topics that you do expect to deal with, e.g., as far as misrepresentation is concerned, its relationship with the terms of a contract and the remedies for their breach. You cannot hope to be able to decide which areas to give priority to until you have a reasonably good understanding of the whole subject. It is also worth bearing in mind that a topic in which you are initially weak, but which receives special attention at the start of the revision period when your study techniques have improved and you are better able to see its relationship with other areas, can quite often turn out to be a star performer in the examination.

Drawing Together and Amplifying

Once you have remedied any obvious gaps in your notes and in your overall knowledge of the subject you can start amplifying your understanding of that subject by bringing out more openly the relationships between the topics that so far you have largely reviewed in isolation. How can you identify these inter-relationships? One way is to take the opportunity of reading some of the literature that perhaps you were not specifically directed to read at any particular point of the course but to which references may have been made. Books like, for example, Gilmore's *The Death of Contract* or Fried's *Contract as Promise* or Atiyah's *An Introduction to the Law of Contract* (the word 'introduction' in the title is misleading, it is best read once an overall grasp of the subject has been obtained) have particular themes running through them which they try to illustrate by reference to various areas of contract law.

Earlier on in your course you would probably find these books in places confusing if not unintelligible but now you should be in a position to understand and evaluate them. (This is particularly true of Collins' *The Law of Contract* as to which it is worth comparing the reviews in 1986 CLJ 503, 102 LQR 628 and 1987 NILQ 408.) The way in which they bring together different areas of contract to support their own general thesis will set off your own thoughts about the way the whole subject fits together. You will probably get the opportunity in some question in the examination to show your awareness of their views of the subject but even if you do not, your exposure to this type of theory will enable you to discuss any question in a more mature and reflective style. Furthermore, seeing how others classify groups of cases and view particular issues will enable you to see more clearly the essentials of the outlook which your lecturer or the standard textbooks have presented to you. It is rather like looking at a painting of a particular scene by one artist and being asked to identify the major characteristics of his style. It is much easier to do if another picture of the same scene painted by a different artist is placed by its side. For this reason, it can be interesting to look at textbooks from other jurisdictions — particularly the Commonwealth where the law of contract is still fundamentally similar to our own. Waddams's *The Law of Contracts* is an excellent example and it is also worth dipping into overseas casebooks like Swan and Reiter which you may find in your library, to see how far the issues that have arisen in the English cases also arise overseas and whether any different solutions are offered in the Commonwealth than at home.

The time you can spend on this sort of exercise of course limited and you must not attempt it until you have properly covered the reading to which you are specifically directed but you may well find by broadening your reading in this way that the subject begins to really come alive and that you are prepared to willingly devote more time to your studies than you ever thought possible. Obviously you cannot read all these books and it is not always necessary to read the whole of a book in order to get something useful out of it. A few minutes spent studying the contents page and an intelligent use of the index can enable you to focus on the areas of a book which are of most relevance to your course or which deal with a topic in which you have developed a particular interest. So if one takes, as an extreme example, Atiyah's *The Rise and Fall of Freedom of Contract*, it would be a daunting task, and indeed rather foolish, to try to digest well over 700 pages in the context of preparing for an examination for the law of contract. However, by studying the contents one can quickly identify the sections which will best repay reading. An introduction, particularly if as in Atiyah's case it is relatively short and to the point, is usually worth reading as it will summarise the questions which the author is interested in and the themes which he is later going to explore. You are not going to be directly concerned with the next six chapters of this particular book which are subtitled 'The Story to 1770' although when you look in the index you may find there are one or two sections that you wish to read. You may be more interested in the next nine chapters (part 2) entitled 'The Age of Freedom of Contract: 1770–1870' and in particular chapters 14 and 15 dealing with freedom of contract in the courts, but even these total just over 100 pages and a quick dip into them would probably reveal them as too detailed and historical in nature for your purposes. Part 3, 'The Decline and Fall of Freedom of Contract 1870–1970', is clearly most in point but you may well feel that you cannot afford to read the whole thing and that you must give the chapters on the condition of England and the intellectual background a miss in order to concentrate on the chapters entitled 'The Legal Background, 1870–1970' and 'The Decline of Freedom of Contract, 1870–1970' which seem of most direct interest. You would probably also want to read the last chapter, 'The Wheel Come Full Circle', as it is likely to draw together and summarise much of what has gone before. That still means 120 pages to be read but remember, this is not a set book that you have to know inside out, but an exercise in exposing yourself to ideas and you need only make notes of points that strike you as particularly illuminating or interesting, such as perhaps the comments made upon *Derry* v *Peek* (1889) 14 App Cas 337, or the discussion of freedom of contract and freedom of trade, and weave these comments into your own existing notes of those areas.

Another possible way of developing the relationship between different parts of the syllabus is to note the extent to which your past examination papers require you to do this. This may not be very great if the subject is studied at first-year level but it is likely to be more evident in other courses where questions are more likely to ask you to identify themes that recur in different sections of your course, obvious ones being 'how does the law of contract deal with inequality of bargaining power?' or 'how far is the law of contract based on promise as opposed to reasonable reliance?' Even if you are not asked wide-ranging questions of this nature, it will still be useful in, say, a question specifically on misrepresentation, to show that you are aware of its role in protecting reliance rather than in protecting the expectations engendered by a promise. Evidence of wide reading and of an appreciation of the wider issues underpinning any question will usually receive credit from the examiner which is disproportionately high to the extra work involved, for in reading more widely you are inevitably refamiliarising yourself with the cases and problems which are central to your course in a manner which is less burdensome because it is more interesting. I should emphasise again that broadening your horizons in this way should not take up too large a portion of your revision timetable, but to omit it completely is to neglect an opportunity not only to improve your eventual performance but to receive full benefit from the course which you are following.

A more obviously economical way of increasing your understanding of the subject and of keeping your revision interesting and thus efficient is to search the current year's issues of the leading periodicals for notes of any important cases decided in the last 12 months or so. Your reading list may well have referred you to the law reports of the case but perhaps the list was compiled before any comments on the case had been published. By the time the revision period comes along it is more than likely, if the case is an important one, that it will have been noted in one of the periodicals. It should not take you long to check what has been published in most of the leading journals such as the *Modern Law Review, Law Quarterly Review* and *Cambridge Law Journal,* to name but three, and the material that you find should enable you to impress the examiner with your awareness of the latest trends in the case law. As always, it is not a question of merely being able to reproduce what someone else has said about the latest cases but showing your initiative in being aware of what has been said and in having a view of your own. The cases that are attracting attention in the periodical literature are also likely to be amongst those that are influencing the examiner when he is devising questions for the examination.

Cases only decided since your reading list was compiled are also well worth reading since even if they don't add much to the previous position, there will often be a discussion of the previus case law within them and the mere fact of following a judgment discussing the cases already on your reading list will help to reinforce your knowledge and understanding of them. On top of that, the examiner will once again give you credit for initiative and for being willing to interpret the case for yourself. It is not difficult to track down any recent cases there might be, the contract section of the monthly issues of *Current Law* being one good place to look and the cumulative index to the *All England Law Reports* being another. Remember though, the point made before, that very recent decisions are of little value in assessing the likely content of the examination as the paper has in all probability already been set. The point again is really that by diversifying the sources of your notes, you keep your revision interesting and avoid the danger of boredom (which can be just as much of a problem as lack of time, the former often leading to the latter) whilst simultaneously making yourself more familiar with the subject-matter of the course.

Clearly, you can only hope to engage in this sort of revision if you start your revision process at a suitably early stage. Nevertheless, there obviously does come a time when you have to stop going to new sources or returning to old ones and have to consolidate the material that you have. This is the part of the revision process which many mistake for the whole when really it is merely the third and final, though no doubt most essential, phase.

The Process of Distillation and Reduction

No matter how efficient and well organised you have been in your acquisition of notes up to now, they will not be arranged in the best possible form for learning from. They have been compiled in the order in which you have read the material and even if you have managed to organise them so that all your notes on a particular topic are collected together and interwoven, it will inevitably be a rather messy and disorganised patchwork. In addition, you should have rather a lot of material, certainly too much to recall in the form of a mental picture, even if you limit yourself to one area of the syllabus, like consideration. What you need to do now is to reduce all your notes to a series of schemes, pictures, tables or diagrams which in outline form can represent your understanding of the subject and which are simple enough for you to memorise in detail. This does not mean that you can then forget the rest of your notes, you obviously cannot, but the reduced versions which you can literally memorise will serve as indexes or triggers which will release when necessary the more detailed knowledge that is there in the background. Rather like a certain brand of lager, the only schemes, tables etc. which will do this are those which you have devised for yourself for it is the process of devising the schemes etc. that creates the association between the detail and the plan which will enable you to remember the detail when it is required. The principal features of your plans could be borrowed from the way your lecture hand-outs are organised or from textbook headings or from a combination of these and other sources but the ultimate shape of *your* scheme will probably be unique even though it shares many common features with other people's pictures of the subject.

You cannot expect, of course, to go straight from the level of great detail to the level of the most easily remembered scheme. It has to be done in stages and each stage must be capable of triggering off the next more detailed stage. Figures 2.1 and 2.2 are examples of the sort of thing you might produce in an area like exclusion clauses, first at a fairly detailed level looking just at one issue within that area, the question of incorporation, and then, reduced still further, to form part of a more general picture of the larger area.

Figure 2.1 — Incorporation

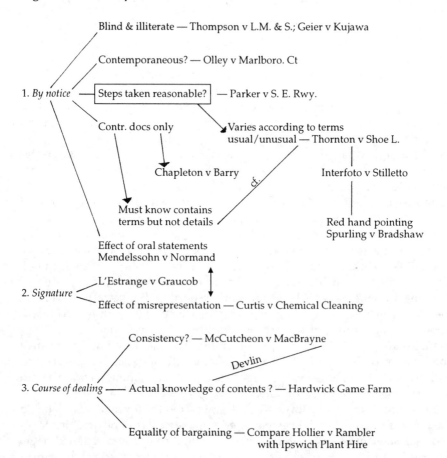

Figure 2.2

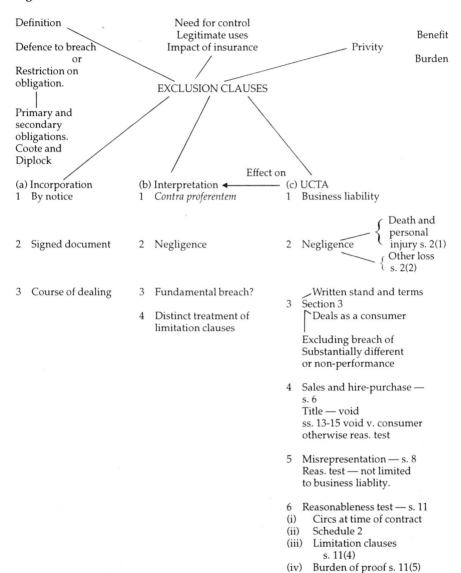

Before arriving at Figure 2.2, you will have had to create a number of other schemes similar to Figure 2.1 dealing in more detail with areas like interpretation and statutory controls which can then be simplified before being incorporated in Figure 2.2. You will then have perhaps five or six sides of notes or plans which encapsulate your understanding of exclusion clauses and which can serve as reference points when you need to recall any particular area in detail. Again, it should be stressed that the plans or schemes themselves do not mean that much — it is the process of producing them and the associations which that process creates that are important. My plans may not mean all that much to you, even after you have studied exclusion clauses, but they do signify a lot to me because I am the person who has produced them. Similarly, any plans that you produce may not be terribly significant to others, but that does not matter as long as they have meaning for you.

You will have noted that the names of cases appear quite frequently and one of the commonest worries of law students, especially in their first year, is whether they will be able to recall the cases and their names. An important point to remember is that it is not really that crucial to be able to reproduce the actual names of cases in the examination, provided that you can refer to them in such a way as to indicate that you have read them and appreciate their significance for the particular point you are discussing. Your answer will be that much more polished if you can refer to the case name accurately, but 'X v Y' or 'the case where the option had to be exercised by notice in writing' are much better than failing to discuss the relevant case at all.

Having said that, case names are worth learning, not only to make your answers more fluent and convincing, but as convenient pegs on which to hang legal principles and by which to remember them. You will already have lists of cases on seminar sheets or lecture hand-outs which are not just arranged in some haphazard fashion but which are grouped according to the issues to which they relate and which are often ordered in a way that mirrors the logical or historical development of a particular rule. You can take advantage of these ready-made lists as another index which you can commit to memory which can again trigger off the more detailed knowledge that you have about the cases. If you write in the margins at the side of each case on your reading list some key feature about the case which will help you to link the name of the case with the greater detail which you possess about the case, and make yourself thoroughly familiar with your annotated list, then you should find in the examination that you can mentally picture that list in order to remember the name of the case which you want. Again, the information which is actually on your case list is pitifully inadequate but it is the process of identifying the key feature which you associate with the case that is important and which enables you to use the mental picture of the case as a key to unlock in the examination your full knowledge and understanding of the case. The fact that this will help you to remember the actual names of the cases is an additional bonus.

As an illustration, take half a dozen cases from an offer and acceptance reading list:

	Holwell Securities Ltd v Hughes [1974] 1 All ER 161 *'Notice in writing to'. Postal rule excluded.*
Acc. Birkenhead Liverpool	Henthorn v Fraser [1892] 2 Ch 27 *Postal rule applicable — but only where reas. to use post.*
	Yates Building Co. Ltd v R. J. Pulleyn & Sons (York) Ltd (1975) 119 SJ 370 *Acc. by regd post — Mandatory/directory — prejudice to offeror?*
Objective test	Felthouse v Bindley (1862) 11 CBNS 869 *No Acc. by silence — nephew/uncle horse.*
	Upton-on-Severn Rural District Council v Powell [1942] 1 All ER 220 *Wrong fire brigade — objective test.*
Subjective approach	Dickinson v Dodds (1876) 2 ChD 463 *Revoc. by 3rd party Reas. to rely on?*

This method may not look terribly elegant and perhaps will not work for everyone but I found it helpful and if you think it might work for you, try it.

ORGANISATIONAL MATTERS

Revision Timetable

Having discussed the processes that can be involved in revision and having seen the variety of things that it can encompass, it is obvious that you need to plan your revision programme carefully. The amount of time you have to organise will vary from between about eight weeks down to about two or three weeks depending on your course (to be shared usually with other subjects besides contract). If the period that you have available is closer to the two-week end of the spectrum then it is to be hoped that you have little in the way of remedial work to be done and you will need to spend most of your time undertaking the third process, reduction and distillation. The nearer you are to the other end of the spectrum, the more you should feel able to undertake more of the broader reading necessary to amplify your understanding of the subject. However you decide to balance the various types of revision, you need to devise a programme which you can then follow fairly closely without having to waste time each day working out what you are going to do next. Let us suppose that you are on a year long course and that you have six weeks to go before your first examination, and that you have four examinations in one week, none of which you feel is weaker or stronger than any other. You need to draw up a chart showing the dates of the exams and the time available to you. You then need to decide how to programme your revision into it. Are you going to split your revision within the days, so that, e.g., you revise one subject in the morning and a different one in the afternoon or are you going to dedicate whole days or groups of days to one subject? Some people prefer the former approach but personally I think that it is much better to work in blocks of days since that gives you the opportunity to immerse yourself in a subject and make yourself feel really at home with it. Working with small blocks of time may prevent you from ever getting totally bored with one subject but this shouldn't really be a problem if you approach your revision in the right frame of mind and view it as a period in which to deepen your understanding rather than merely as a process of committing material to memory. In addition, repeatedly switching from subject to subject may mean that you spend a significant proportion of each revision period working out where you last left off and where you want to go to next. So, if I was planning my revision, I would probably devise a timetable something like this:

Week	S	M	T	W	Th	F	S
1		4	4	4	2	2	
2		1	1	1	3	3	
3		3	3	4	4	4	
4		2	2	2	1	1	
5		1	1	3	3	3	
6		4	4	2	2	1	1
7		Exam 1	Exam 2	3	Exam 3	Exam 4	

Notice that I have left Saturdays and Sundays free since it is important that you provide yourself with breaks and periods of relaxation to ensure that you are fresh and alert for the periods when you do work. (The break days don't have to be weekends — it depends on what suits your own leisure and social pattern.) This applies also to the days themselves. You will not maintain a programme that involves working 12 or 13 hours a day for very long unless you are a complete workaholic. The weather is usually irritatingly fine when you need to work the hardest so take advantage of it and enjoy some fresh air for an hour or two in the afternoon. It is usually best to do a full morning's work so that you can do something relaxing with a clear conscience, at least for part of the afternoon. If you feel you must work during the whole afternoon, make sure you do something different in the evening. Of course, there may be days when you feel you can work all day and most of the evening too. There is nothing wrong with that as long as you don't allow every day to become like that because if you do you are likely to become stale by the time of the examination itself when you wish to be at your sharpest.

Returning to the revision timetable, it might be worth explaining how I decided to order the subjects in the particular way that I did. Essentially I worked back from the day of the examinations. Since subject 1 is the first exam, it seemed sensible to have the final revision period for that subject last although notice that the day before the first exam is left notionally free. That doesn't mean that I would do *no* work that day but I would keep it as light as possible, to ensure that I was as fresh as possible for the start of the examination week. E2 follows fairly quickly on E1 so I need to have that subject fully sewn up before sitting E1. Therefore the last two days of revising E2 are the next on the timetable. Then comes the last two days of E4, rather than E3 since at least I will have the Wednesday after the first two examinations to refamiliarise myself with E3 so it seems sensible to have the revision of E4 nearer to the examinations themselves. After that (or rather before, since I am working backwards) it is just a case of allocating blocks of two and three days to each subject in a reasonably equal sort of way. That way, each subject ends up with seven or eight days' revision allocated to it. Within that seven or eight days I would expect the first day or so to be taken up with any remedial work necessary, perhaps the next couple of days in amplifying my understanding, e.g., undertaking any broader reading that I felt I ought to do and the next two or three days trying my hand at some past questions and beginning to distil and reduce the notes that I already have. The final two days allocated to each subject will be spent further reducing these distilled notes and plans, making sure I actually know them and also just reading through the full set of notes that I have to refresh in my mind details that my reduced notes represent.

You yourself will probably wish to have a different sort of emphasis on the different types of revision, depending on the sort of work that you have done on your subject earlier in the year, and a different allocation of the days to different subjects. The important thing is to devise a programme which suits you, to know why you have devised it in a particular way and (this should follow automatically from the previous point) not to allow yourself to be diverted from it without some very good reason. If you do this, you will arrive at your first examination in a relaxed and confident frame of mind, knowing that you have prepared in a business-like and efficient manner and that you will be able to perform to the best of your ability on the day that matters.

SITTING THE EXAMINATION

The Day Before

Rather than trying to cram in as much last-minute revision as possible, you should be making sure that you are properly organised to take the examination at the proper location. Have you checked the place and starting time of the examination and have you got the proper equipment, i.e., at least two good pens and any materials which are permitted (e.g., statutes although this is unlikely in a contract paper) in the examination room? These may seem obvious points, and indeed they are, but every year someone misses an examination because they mistakenly think it is an afternoon rather than a morning examination and many more impair their performances because they arrive slightly late and extremely flustered, having gone in error to building B at the other side of town rather than to building A where the examiantion is to be held. Whilst I have never known anyone fail an examination because their writing implements have let them down, there are many papers whose legibility clearly deteriorates as the felt-tip pen begins to dry up and fade and legibility can certainly affect marks obtained (to say nothing of the retarding effect of having to use an inefficient pen).

Attending to such mundane matters is not of itself time-consuming and can save you invaluable time later and still leaves time for last-minute revision if you feel that will help you. What you should not do is work until very late at night since a good night's sleep and an alert mind in the morning will be much more important than a few extra cases crammed in when you really need to be asleep (cases which you probably won't remember anyway if you are short of sleep the next day). I am not saying that you should not look at your notes at all the night before the examination but that what you do should be done in a relaxed manner, in the spirit that what you are doing isn't actually necessary, merely helpful, so that you can stop and do something else or go to bed when it starts to get on your nerves. You should only be looking at material with which you are already familiar (like your reduced notes and plans) in order merely to reinforce it in your mind. Personally, I did find it helpful to look at my case lists (suitably annotated) the night before in order to ensure that I was completely familiar with the case names and their relationships with one another — I find that material looked at just before bedtime (as long as I go to bed at a reasonable time) and then attempted to be recalled first thing in the morning, sticks remarkably well for the rest of the day. To ignore completely the urge to indulge in last-minute revision is to ignore the fact that examinations only actually test what you can remember on one particular day and there is nothing wrong with last-minute revision as long as you recognise its limitations and don't allow it to become an obsession.

The Day of the Examination

You will inevitably feel a certain amount of tension on the actual day of the examination and as long as this does not get out of hand, this is not a bad thing as it is probably related to a build-up in adrenalin which will help you to perform to the peak of your ability. To avoid the tension being heightened to such an extent that it becomes counter-productive you should try to keep your mind off the examination for at least some of the time immediately prior to actually turning up at the examination hall. If your examination is in the morning, try to eat a decent breakfast as you will not perform well on an empty stomach and read the newspaper over breakfast or talk to someone about something interesting, anything other than law. (This is not meant to imply that law is not interesting, but talking about law or about what you have or haven't revised etc. at this stage is more likely to induce unwarranted anxiety than a calm and collected approach to the examination.) If your examination is in the afternoon, there is no harm in reading through your notes again in the morning in a relaxed fashion but don't work so hard that you are feeling jaded by the time the examination comes round in the afternoon. Ensure that you arrive at the examination hall in good time but not so early that you have to wait outside for half an hour listening to X describing the amount of revision *he* or *she* has done or Y recounting the legendary status that this particular examination has achieved as the one that students fail. Once at your desk, do make sure you have no prohibited materials (such as this book!) with you — allegations of cheating are so much more distressing if you are in fact innocent and even if you can eventually rebut the allegation, the fact of having been accused will no doubt affect your performance.

Once the papers are distributed, read the instructions carefully even though you think you know how many questions etc. are required to be answered in how long — there may have been a change which you don't know about — and do check that the paper is the one that you are supposed to be taking — it is just possible that there is an examination on the law of contract being taken by some students on another course in the same hall. It is quite common for examinations to allow 10 minutes' reading time — if this applies to you, you must obviously take full advantage of it and first read each question carefully and then start to plan which questions you can best answer and how. Even if you are not given reading time, it is not a bad idea to act as though you are in the sense that you spend the first 10 minutes *just* reading the paper and planning which questions to answer, without actually beginning to write anything down in your answer book. This will prevent you from diving into a question which looks quite attractive at first sight but which turns out to involve issues on which you are not well prepared when it is too late to change your mind. If you have to answer, say, five questions, and you have identified four definites but cannot decide on the fifth then don't waste any more time, get on with the first four — you will feel better able to cope with the fifth when you have your first four answers under your belt. What you must be careful of in this situation though is subconsciously trying to score enough marks on the first four questions so as to make the fifth largely irrelevant. The way in which papers are marked makes this almost impossible and you must stop each answer once you have used up the proportion of time properly allocated to it. If you feel you can write more, then leave a space so that if you do have time left over at the end, you can go back and add to your earlier answer. It is not a bad idea to leave a couple of sub-headings as pointers to remind yourself what issues you still wanted to discuss. This will help you if you do go back at the end when time is bound to be severely limited and even if you don't get the chance to go back, it will indicate to the examiner the points that you still want to discuss — of course you will get far more marks if you do actually go on to discuss these points. It is absolutely crucial that you do make a reasonable stab at the fifth question (or fourth if you are only required to do four) even if it is a little shorter than the other questions. Failure to do so is more likely to be regarded as being due to inadequate revision or lack of work during the year than due to shortage of time and this is justified since if you are thoroughly prepared you will be able to answer the questions properly in the allotted time. Furthermore, most students pick up a good deal more than half their marks in the first half of each answer so it is more efficient to ensure that you produce at the very *least* a half-length answer to your last question than produce an answer any less than that in order to spend extra time on an earlier question.

This is not the place to give detailed advice on answering individual questions as this is dealt with in each of the remaining chapters of this book but it is worth making some fairly general points at this stage.

(a)   Read the question properly and answer the question set. All too many students just fasten on to a particular word or phrase in an essay question, e.g., the word 'consideration', and regurgitate all they know about consideration instead of reading the question and identifying what particular angle the examiner wishes them to investigate. If the question says 'critically evaluate' or invites you to consider any reforms that are necessary it is clearly not sufficient merely to describe the law as it stands.

(b)   Plan your answer in outline before you start to write it. This need not be shown on the question paper but it certainly does not harm to do this. No doubt your ideas will develop in more detail as you are actually writing your answer, but you are not absolutely tied to a plan once you have formulated one and you can depart from it where it seems sensible to do so. The point about a plan is that it is likely to give your answer more shape, it will help you to direct your arguments to some sort of logical conclusion and it enables you to concentrate on the issue on which you are actually writing rather than having to be thinking at the same time about what issue you are going to discuss next. Also, having a plan prevents you from embarking on a question and then finding a quarter way through it that you have really got very little to say on the area covered by that question.

(c) *Citing cases*. A common defect, particularly of examinees taking law papers for the first time, is that they discuss questions, particularly problem questions, quite sensibly and logically but fail to back up their arguments with any relevant case law. This can be disastrous as the examiner will at best conclude that you don't understand how to use cases properly and at worst that you haven't ever read any. If an answer refers to and discusses relevant cases, even if the arguments based on those cases are found to be misconceived, you can at least be given credit for knowing the relevant cases. An answer without cases on the other hand is rather like an answer to a mathematical problem which gives the right answer but doesn't show any working — the answer could be an intelligent guess and so no credit is given for it. It doesn't matter too much if you cannot remember the full case name or indeed any of the case names — it is always better to say 'in the case where ...' rather than not to refer to the case at all. On the other hand, don't go to the extreme of making your answers just a series of accounts of cases with no discussion of their significance or application to the question which you are answering. The aim should be to extract from the case only what is material to the isue which you are discussing and in doing this you demonstrate that you not only know the case thoroughly but understand its significance. So, for example, if you were discussing Section 2(1) of the Misrepresentation Act 1967 and the burden which that section places on the representor to show reasonable grounds for his statement, you would need to discuss the case of *Howard Marine & Dredging Co. Ltd* v *A. Ogden & Sons (Excavations) Ltd* [1978] QB 574. It would be wasteful and unnecessary to cite the whole of the facts and the various opinions of the three judges in the Court of Appeal. Instead you could say something like this:

> The burden placed upon the representor is not an easy one to discharge as is illustrated by *Howard Marine* where a majority of the Court of Appeal held that the representor did not have *reasonable* grounds for making the statement about the capacity of the barges even though he had based his statement on Lloyd's Register (the shipping world's Bible) since he had access to the true figures given in the original shipping documents.

Of course there are other issues discussed in that case such as the effect of s. 3 of the Act on exclusion clauses and the applicability of the *Hedley Byrne* principle but those aren't the aspects of the case relevant to the particular issue you are discussing. A straight factual account of the case that included them would be largely irrelevant. The discussion of the case I have suggested on the other hand shows your ability to *select* relevant material from the case, and yet *in passing* shows a sufficient knowledge of the detailed facts of the case and the fact that the decision was not unanimous. What is more it does it fairly swiftly and economically so that you can quickly get on to the next issue or relevant case and score some more marks. Further examples of how to use cases are provided in subsequent chapters of this book.

As it is near the end of this chapter, I should say something about the end of the examination. The standard advice here is to leave five or ten minutes to read over your paper and check for obvious errors etc. The advice I would give is perhaps rather controversial here, but I don't really think there is a great deal of use in doing this. If you have missed an odd word out which changes the sense of what you intended to say, the examiner will probably read it in the intended sense if it is clear from the rest of what you are saying that you know what you are talking about. I have hardly ever had the sort of time available at the end of an examination to enable me to read the whole paper through and you will usually score more marks in any time that you do have available by completing any answer that you have had to curtail. Of course, if you find you have the time, do read through your paper as this might remind you of additional points that you could usefully make. But the notion of checking for errors at the end of a three-hour examination period is not to my mind terribly realistic and is unlikely to produce any substantial improvement on your mark.

Finally, there is one very simple way in which you can improve your chances of obtaining a good mark, and that is to cultivate an easily readable style of handwriting which you can execute at speed. Your arguments will seem much more fluent if the examiner can read them without having to stop to try and decipher every other word and if your script can be read quickly the examiner is much more likely to look at it in a benevolent light. It is just amazing the number of students who seem deliberately to invite the examiner's wrath by writing in styles that defy sensible reading. You may think that your handwriting is fine because you can read it easily yourself but this does not automatically follow and the only way to be sure is to ask someone else to read it. It is too late to try to improve your handwriting two days before the examination. You ought to start trying to modify your style as soon as possible if you think it is likely to be a problem (if your handwriting is poor in normal circumstances, it will probably be significantly worse in the pressure of the examination room). If you are not sure how to improve it, try experimenting with different types of pens — this won't effect a complete cure but could mitigate some of the worse symptoms. It would be silly if you lost marks in the examination due to something like your handwriting which you can do something about in advance.

CONCLUSION

Examinations are a fact of life. As a result, some would think that they ought not to be talked about or discussed openly in public, but if you prepare properly for them and are clear on what you are expected to do there is nothing to fear. Examinations can even be turned to your advantage — if examiners really wanted to fail students (and the reverse is true in actual fact) they would want more than two or three hours in which to ask you questions, not all of which you have to answer. The scales are hardly weighted in the examiner's favour and by following the advice in this chapter you can tip them even more firmly in your own direction.

3   AGREEMENT

This topic should be your 'starter for 10' — or even more. It is not conceptually difficult and yet has sufficient intricacies and potential depth to provide the opportunity to score high marks. Students do not, however, always perform as well as they ought to in this area simply because it is a topic which is dealt with at an early stage in a subject that for many students represents their first exposure to case law. Thus it is particularly important to re-examine this topic at a later stage in your course when you have improved your powers of analysis of case law and the contents of this chapter should prove to be of especial value to you both the first and second time you consider this area. In considering any particular issue in this branch of the law it is important to be aware of certain themes which underlie the whole area.

UNDERLYING THEMES

The Objective Test of Agreement

Many contractual rules are supposedly based on the actual intentions of the parties and are thus given a power and legitimacy which they might otherwise lack. This appeal to the will of the parties is often merely an ideal and in reality other external factors play a key role. Nowhere is this more true than in the formation of contract where the dominant approach is an objective one, i.e., one which attaches significance to outward appearances rather than to internal, subjective mental states. Of course, in many instances the parties will be subjectively in agreement with each other, there will be the *consensus ad idem*, the meeting of minds, to satisfy the purist *and* there will be the outward, objective indications of that agreement. Such cases, however common, are unlikely to lead to litigation or if they do the issue litigated is hardly likely to be whether there was agreement. It would be obvious that there was agreement so the matter in dispute is more likely to be some other issue such as what is the appropriate remedy for breach of the agreement. The cases which result in disputes about agreement and which are therefore your concern are those where the external signs of agreement are lacking or deficient or ambiguous in some respect. It is in these critical cases that the law of contract adopts its objective approach.

You may well observe that this is inevitable since, as Brian CJ once put it, little knowing how often he was to be quoted, 'the devil himself knows not the intent of a man', i.e., it is impossible to know what actually went on in the parties' minds (they will later say whatever suits their case best) and thus you have to judge them on what they have said and done. Whilst your observation would be true up to a point, it underestimates the strength of the objective approach to agreement since the objective approach may still prevail where it is quite clear to the court that the actual intentions of one, or both, of the parties would dictate a different result. Thus in *Felthouse* v *Bindley* (1862) 11 CBNS 869 Willes J noted that: 'the auctioneer was told that [the horse] was already sold. It is clear, therefore, that the nephew in his own mind intended his uncle to have the horse at the price his uncle had named, £30 15s.' Willes J might have added that it was also clear that the uncle, having said that he would consider the horse his if he heard no more and having heard nothing for six weeks, also believed, correctly, that he and his nephew were in agreement. And yet, because nothing was done to evidence this agreement, at least before the horse was sold to the third party, the court refused to give it legal effect. Conversely, in *Upton-on-Severn Rural District Council* v *Powell* [1942] 1 All ER 220, the court did find that there was a contract to pay for fire services even though it was clear that the defendant thought he was arranging to receive them free of charge and the plaintiffs initially intended not to charge.

These two cases represent perhaps the extremities of the objective approach and there is more to be said about *Felthouse* v *Bindley* later in this chapter but they do illustrate the point that the objective approach is not merely a device for avoiding the difficulties of proving mental states. The real reason for the objective approach is not that the *courts* might have difficulty in determining the parties' true intentions after the event (they have to do that often enough anyhow) but that the *parties themselves* at the time of the alleged contract cannot know one another's intentions. They can only act on what it *appears* the other party intended and so the law of contract enforces agreements which it appears that a person has made since to do otherwise would mean no one could safely rely on any agreement, it always being possible that the other party meant something different from what he said. Most of the specific 'rules' on offer and acceptance only make sense in this light and, indeed, understanding this reason for the objective approach helps to make sense of those exceptions which go to prove the rule. For example, where one party *knows* that the other's contractual intention differs from what is suggested by the objective test, the reason for the objective test disappears, as does the test itself. See *Smith* v *Hughes* (1871) LR 6 QB 597, where it was held that there would be no contract for the sale of oats if the plaintiff knew that the defendant mistakenly thought it was a term of the contract that the oats were 'old', i.e., superior, even if objectively it looked (to a reasonable bystander) like an agreement for 'new', i.e., inferior, oats. Thus the objective test is primarily concerned with how things look to the other party, not to the reasonable bystander. See the note in (1986) 102 LQR 363 by Atiyah for some further thoughts on the significance and rationale of the objective approach.

The Reduction to Offer and Acceptance

Given that the law generally adopts an objective test and looks for external evidence of agreement, what does the law count as such evidence? It could adopt a very free and liberal approach whereby anything at all potentially counts as evidence, i.e., you just look at all the circumstances and see if the parties appear to have reached agreement. The trouble with this approach is that you can easily end up looking at what each party actually intends and ignoring the standpoint of the parties themselves — what did it appear to each party that the other party intended? More importantly, it can openly reveal the extent to which the law is unpredictable. Instead, therefore, lawyers prefer to break down human conduct into smaller more manageable units which they can classify as offers or invitations to treat, as acceptances, counter-offers or requests for information, as revocations or rejections. This at least has the advantage for you as a student that you can break down a problem into manageable chunks and it also has the advantage for lawyers that it at least appears to make the law more certain (but note Atiyah's comments about conceptual reasoning in *An Introduction to the Law of Contract* at pp. 58–60).

The first, more liberal, approach was indeed suggested by Lord Denning MR in *Butler Machine Tool Co. Ltd* v *Ex-Cell-O Corporation (England) Ltd* [1979] 1 WLR 401 and again in *Gibson* v *Manchester City Council* [1979] 1 WLR 294 but in the first case the majority of the Court of Appeal based their decision on the more traditional offer and acceptance analysis (and indeed this formed an alternative ground for Lord Denning). In the *Gibson* case, the House of Lords actually reversed the Court of Appeal's decision that looking at the evidence as a whole there was a concluded agreement and instead held that there had been no matching offer and acceptance. Lord Diplock recognised that there may be certain types of exceptional contracts which do not fit neatly into the normal analysis of offer and acceptance but that the exchange of correspondence was not one of them. *Clark* v *Earl of Dunraven* [1897] AC 59 is a good example of the sort of exceptional case that Lord Diplock probably had in mind, where all the entrants to a race where unambiguously agreeing to be bound to one another by the rules but the large number of competitors and the different times at which they entered made it artificial and virtually impossible to identify individual offers and acceptances.

It is worth contrasting Lord Diplock's view that it is only exceptional cases 'which do not fit easily into the normal analysis of offer and acceptance' with Lord Wilberforce's view in *New Zealand Shipping Co. Ltd v A. M. Satterthwaite & Co. Ltd* [1975] AC 154 that the traditional approach is 'often at the cost of forcing the facts to fit uneasily into the marked slots of offer, acceptance and consideration'.

What you as a law student must reveal is an awareness of this occasional unease with the analytical tools, felt to differing degrees by different judges at different times, and yet at the same time demonstrate the ability to manipulate the concepts of offer and acceptance with the best of them. To do this effectively, you must be aware of the following, third underlying theme.

The Prima Facie Nature of the Rules

Most students at the start of their contract course are on the look-out for rules — after all that is what law consists of, or so they think. (The precise extent to which this is true is a question you should be glad I am not going to try to answer here.) If you are one of those students, you will not be disappointed initially in studying agreement in contract. You will hear, if you have not already done so, of the postal rule, the rule that a revocation must actually have been received, that silence is no acceptance and so on and so forth. What you may not have appreciated is that any legal rule, especially as formulated in textbooks and law reports, is likely to have a number of unstated exceptions to it, some obvious, some less obvious. Take for example the rule that a person who intentionally strikes another is guilty of an assault — this clearly doesn't apply if the person doing the striking is acting in self-defence. One can of course restate the rule to include the exception, e.g., a person who intentionally strikes another except in self-defence is guilty of an assault and you can argue endlessly about whether this is really one rule or two but it would quickly become an unmanageable rule if you tried to state within it all its possible exceptions. One of the skills of a lawyer is to know what sort of exceptions there might be to any given rule and where they might be found, and an important skill of an examinee is to be able to recognise an exception when you are presented with one.

What is true of rules in general is even more true of the so-called rules of offer and acceptance. The House of Lords itself in effect recently recognised this in *Brinkibon Ltd v Stahag Stahl und Stahlwarenhandelsgesellschaft mbH* [1983] 2 AC 34 where in dealing with acceptancce by telex, Lord Wilberforce, for example, pointed out that 'no universal rule can cover all such cases: they must be resolved by reference to the intentions of the parties, by sound business practice and in some cases by a judgment where the risks should lie'.

Thus the 'postal rule', that an acceptance takes effect when posted, would be more accurately stated as follows: an acceptance normally takes effect when posted if that would be consistent with the parties' apparent intentions. The most important part of this restated rule is the second part because (a) it is the part which is common to most of the so-called rules in this area and (b) it is the part of the rule in which the examiner is most likely to be interested. He will assume that you have heard of the shorter version of the postal rule and will give you some, but not too much, credit for revealing this to be so but he is more likely to be impressed by a demonstration that you are aware of its limitations. Thus the important case in this area is not so much *Adams* v *Lindsell* (1818) 1 B & Ald 681, which is generally regarded as the case where the postal rule originated, but a case like *Holwell Securities Ltd* v *Hughes* [1974] 1 WLR 155 where the postal rule was held *not* to apply to a posted acceptance because the terms of the offer made it clear that the offeror only intended to be bound on receipt of the acceptance.

Similarly, students are almost always aware of the fact that in *Partridge* v *Crittenden* [1968] 1 WLR 1204 the Court of Appeal held that an advertisement in a newspaper only constituted an invitation to treat and too readily assume that all such advertisements will only be invitations to treat and not offers. The examiner is much more concerned to know *why* the advertisement was only an invitation to treat, e.g., because the advertiser, assuming him to be a reasonable and sensible person, can't have intended to be bound by replies to his advert since his stocks were limited and he had no way of knowing how many replies he would receive. Therefore the examiner is quite likely to set a problem where the advertisement lacks one of these factors, e.g., where the advertiser's stocks are unlimited or where, as in the problem discussed later in this chapter, the number of replies are limited. As will be seen in investigating particular issues in the following pages, offer and acceptance is an area which abounds with opportunities for distinguishing leading cases in this way. There are a great number of thorny little problems which an examiner can pick on but it is not the purpose of this book to offer a comprehensive survey. Instead I shall concentrate on a number of issues which are central in themselves and which also illustrate techniques which can be applied to other issues with which you may be asked to deal.

KEY ISSUES

Unilateral Contracts

This is a phrase which is freely bandied about by writers and students alike but not often explained or understood. It should be contrasted with bilateral contracts, which means two-sided so that a unilateral contract must therefore only be one-sided! Of course, this is wrong because, just like the tango and many other pleasures, a contract takes two. What is one-sided, however, in a unilateral contract, is the obligation. Only one party assumes an obligation, i.e., promises to do anything, whereas in a bilateral contract both parties assume obligations and make promises. The well-known *Carlill* v *Carbolic Smoke Ball Co.* case [1893] 1 QB 256 illustrates the point well. The Smoke Ball Co. promised £100 to anyone who bought and used their product and who nonetheless caught flu, so clearly they made a promise and the court enforced their obligation to pay Mrs Carlill. She, however, didn't make any promises, she merely bought and used the smoke ball and caught flu. She was never under any obligation to do any of this, she could have stopped using the product at any time without incurring any *liability* to anyone, although of course she had to comply with all the company's conditions before she became *entitled* to anything. Thus the contract was unilateral — only one side, the company, was under any obligation. By way of contrast, the typical contract for the sale of land is a classic example of a bilateral contract. Both parties commit themselves in advance, the seller promises to deliver a good title and the purchaser promises to pay the price. Both parties assume obligations for the breach of which, if they fail to perform, they may be sued.

Offers leading to unilateral contracts are usually readily recognisable, being in the firm, 'If you fulfil the following conditions,' (e.g., find my lost dog, purchase my product etc.) 'I promise to do X in return' (usually pay you a sum of money). The essential point though is that 'you', the promisee, must not be yourself promising to perform the condition, e.g., promising to find the lost dog, because if you are, the contract will be bilateral. It will be pretty clear in most cases that no promise is being made in return — it would be pretty rash for anyone actually to promise to find a lost item and the objective approach will normally assume that no such promise is being given or is to be implied.

You may well be admiring the logic of this distinction between unilateral and bilateral contracts and yet wondering why, apart from for semantic reasons, the distinction needs to be made. The answer is that the normal rules for offer and acceptance are often not applicable, or only applicable with modification, to unilateral contracts. This is true of the *Carlill* case where, remember, an advertisement was treated as an offer even though advertisements are often construed only as invitations to treat. It would have been absurd to have decided otherwise since that would involve that a person fulfilling the conditions in this type of advert would merely be making an offer in response to the advert. The advertiser could then reject this 'offer' with impunity, having already had the benefit of seeing the conditions fulfilled (in the sense of increased sales or in the reward cases of having had his property found). Similarly, the requirement of communication of acceptance, except in the sense of communication of the fact that the condition has been fulfilled, is not normally required in unilateral contracts. (Indeed if a person did communicate in advance that he was accepting this type of offer, e.g., of a reward for finding lost property, he would be in danger of converting it into a bilateral contract whereby he agrees or promises to find the property or at least to spend a reasonable amount of time and effort searching for it whereas the essence of a unilateral contract is that the acceptor makes no promises to do anything.)

Furthermore, the rules for revocation are arguably different for unilateral contracts (or more accurately, for offers which have the potential to be converted into unilateral contracts by acceptance. Lord Diplock appears to have overlooked this point in *Harvela Investments* v *Royal Trust Co. of Canada* [1985] 2 All ER 966 at p. 969 where he seems to envisage the creation of a unilateral contract before the offeree has done anything at all that could constitute acceptance). The normal rule is of course that revocation is possible at any time before acceptance but this can appear to operate harshly where a person has started to perform the conditions requried to complete a unilateral contract but has not yet completed them. The usual, faintly absurd, example is of A promising B £50 if he walks from London to York, or, if it is an American discussion, if he walks across the Brooklyn Bridge (which might be more realistic, the £50 perhaps being regarded as danger money!). It would certainly look unfair, when B has walked nine tenths of the way to York (or nine tenths of the way across the bridge) if A could suddenly appear and say 'I revoke my offer'. Thus there are suggestions in the textbooks and cases that a unilateral offer cannot be withdrawn once the other party has started to perform. This was certainly Denning LJ's approach in *Errington* v *Errington* [1952] 1 KB 290 and also that of the Court of Appeal (*obiter*) in *Daulia Ltd* v *Four Millbank Nominees Ltd* [1978] Ch 231. The main point to note about this special rule is that there is disagreement both about its theoretical basis (a popular one being that the offeror makes a separate implied promise not to revoke once the offeree starts to perform) and also, consequently, about the extent to which the rule is universal in unilateral contracts. (The implied promise not to revoke theory would not be applicable, for example, to cases where the reward is great compared to the actual effort needed to earn it and where the offeree can be assumed to take the risk of the offer being withdrawn, see *Luxor (Eastbourne) Ltd* v *Cooper* [1941] AC 108.)

If one wishes to be creative in this area (if not, you can skip this paragraph) one might also point out that there is a difference between saying that there is a rule of law that an offer cannot be withdrawn after a certain stage (this appears to be the effect of Treitel's view) and saying on the other hand that withdrawing it will be a breach of a secondary promise not to withdraw (apparently Cheshire and Fifoot's view). Under the latter approach the offer will indeed be withdrawn (but see *Mountford* v *Scott* [1975] Ch 258) and the action will be for breach of the secondary promise and it is not necessarily the case that the damages for breach of that promise will be as high (given the duty to mitigate, see chapter 9) as would be the case under the former, rule of law, approach. Being more creative still, one might argue that this suggests that the implied promise theory is preferable in that it might provide some sort of compromise between the interests of the offeror and the offeree. Ironically Treitel seems to favour a compromise solution but his theory is perhaps less likely to achieve it.

Finally one might note that loss caused by withdrawal is not only a phenomenon in unilateral contracts, an offeree in a bilateral contract can easily incur substantial expenses before discovering that the offer has been withdrawn but the difference is that these expenses have not been requested by the offeror in the same way as they have been in the unilateral contract situation. Similarly, someone invited to tender or make an offer can suffer loss in reliance on the invitation if the offer or tender they submit is not accepted. This loss is normally, quite properly, not recoverable but it may be different if the offer or tender is not treated in the manner anticipated or stipulated in the invitation. In this connection the courts increasingly appear to be prepared to discover a preliminary unilateral contract which effectively binds A, who has requested B to act in a particular way, to enter into a subsequent bilateral contract with B. *Harvela Investments* v *Royal Trust Co. of Canada* [1985] 2 All ER 966 is one example of this (unilateral contract to accept the highest bid i.e., to enter a bilateral contract with the highest bidder to buy/sell shares) and the interesting and more recent case of *Moran* v *University College Salford (No. 2), The Times*, 23 November 1993 is arguably another (unilateral contract to enter into a bilateral contract to provide tuition/pay fees etc. i.e., to accept a student's offer to join a course if he refrained from going to another institution and sought to enrol at Salford at the start of the term). In each case, the completed unilateral contract leads to a subsequent bilateral contract and B's requested reliance is protected by restricting A's freedom to avoid the creation of the subsequent bilateral contract. *Blackpool & Fylde Aero Club* v *Blackpool Borough Council* [1900] 3 All ER 25 is a similar sort of case where, however, the unilateral contract did not go so far as involving an obligation to *accept* B's tender or offer but merely to *consider* it (as that is all A had promised in the invitation to tender).

One further point that ought to be mentioned here is the question of communication of revocation of offers made to the whole world (or to a large number of unidentified persons) — e.g., how would you revoke an offer like that in *Carlill*? You can't comply with the normal rule requiring actual communication, i.e., notification, since you don't know who the potential acceptors are. It is generally accepted that the test laid down in the American case of *Shuey* v *United States* (1875) 92 US 73 is a sensible one, i.e., that the offeror must merely take reasonable steps (e.g., by issuing a similarly prominent advert) to revoke his offer, even if it does not actually come to the attention of the offeree. The point to be noted is that this rule is *not* dependent on the contract being a unilateral one. Its rationale is the impossibility of contacting all the offferees directly and that they should know that the offer is likely to be withdrawn and this can be true of an offer leading to a bilateral contract as well as to one leading to unilateral contract. However, the rule will often coincide with a unilateral contract situation because unilateral contracts are often created by offers to the whole world but note that an offer to a specific individual can give rise to a unilateral contract — see the earlier discussion of B walking to York — in which case any revocation would have to be communicated.

Revocation of Offers

From the foregoing, one can see that the issue of revocation is particularly likely to arise in relation to unilateral contracts but it is clearly an issue that can crop up in other contexts as well. The prima facie rule, that revocation must be communicated, has already been adverted to above and it should be stressed that there is no 'postal rule' exception to this, as many examination candidates unfortunately seem to think. Those who are aware that there is no postal rule applicable to revocations are also usually to be found pointing out that as a result of *Dickinson v Dodds* (1876) 2 ChD 463 a revocation may be communicated by a third party and need not be communicated by the offeror. This is true if one takes the case at face value but one should note carefully the reservations that have been expressed about this rule, since the examiner will give more marks for appreciating the reservations than for merely observing the rule itself. Thus both Treitel and Anson note that the rule may put an unfair burden on the offeree to decide whether the third party can be relied on or not. It should be noted that the so-called third party in the case itself subsequently became the agent of the offeree so that this was not really a problem on the actual facts. If one is presented with a situation which looks ripe for the application of *Dickinson v Dodds* in an exam it would be advantageous to show that you are aware of this and to query whether the third party is one on whom the offeree can be expected to rely, instead of just mechanically reciting the propositon that an offer can be revoked by a third party.

Acceptance of Offers

The postal rule and the importance of the qualifications to it have already been noted. A related issue, also popular with examiners, is that which arises where the offer states one method for acceptance and the offeree uses another. The cases normally discussed in this connection are an old

American case, *Eliason* v *Henshaw* (1819) 17 US (4 Wheat) 225 a decision of Buckley J in the Chancery Division in 1969, *Manchester Diocesan Council for Education* v *Commercial & General Investments Ltd* [1970] 1 WLR 241 and some dicta of Honeyman J in *Tinn* v *Hoffmann & Co.* (1873) 29 LT 271. All these cases are however, succinctly discussed in a later Court of Appeal decision, *Yates Building Co. Ltd* v *R. J. Pulleyn & Sons (York) Ltd* (1975), the facts of which are readily intelligible and which neatly illustrates the relevant principles. Why the decision is not discussed in all the textbooks (or even cited in some) is a little difficult to understand but perhaps it has something to do with the fact that the case is only fully reported in the *Estates Gazette* (237 EG 183) with a rather brief report also available in the *Solicitors' Journal* (119 SJ 370). Essentially, the case involved an option (i.e., an offer) which stipulated that acceptance should be by recorded or registered post and he acceptance was actually made by ordinary post. The offerors therefore returned the acceptance, which it was not disputed had arrived within the stipulated time-limit, saying they were not bound by it since it did not accord with the prescribed mode, and by the time it was too late for the offerees to accept by the correct means. Lord Denning MR pointed out that one has to look at the purpose for stipulating registered or recorded post and noted that it was for the benefit of the offeree and that since the letter had actually arrived no one, certainly not the offerors, had been prejudiced. His Lordship also drew a useful distinction between mandatory stipulations, where the offeror is in effect saying, accept by this method and no other, and those which are merely directory where a different mode of acceptance will suffice provided it is equally efficacious from the offeror's point of view. The decision is given further weight by the fact that Scarman LJ also gave a concurring judgment in which, although he queried Lord Denning's use of the terms 'mandatory' and 'directory', he adopted a similar distinction between obligatory and permissive modes of acceptance. You may feel that Scarman LJ's terminology expresses more clearly the nature of the distinction which will be further illustrated in the specimen problem at the end of this chapter.

Counter-offers

It should first be noted that a counter-offer not only terminates an offer, as in *Hyde* v *Wrench* (1840) 3 Beav 334, but can also itself be converted into a contract by acceptance (this did not occur in *Hyde* v *Wrench* but may be a possibility in an examination problem — see also the *Butler* case below). Secondly, a key distinction to be aware of is that between a counter-offer and a mere request for information which leaves the offer untouched and of which the case of *Stevenson, Jaques & Co.* v *McLean* (1880) 5 QBD 346 affords a good example. This is really a gem of a case since it also illustrates several other points, namely, that a *revocation* (telegraphed at 1.25 p.m.) does not take effect until received (at 1.46 p.m.) and that an *acceptance* (telegraphed at 1.34 p.m.) does take effect when *sent* even though the revocation has already been transmitted though not received. It is also a good example of the objective approach to agreement since a contract was found to have been created at 1.34 p.m. even though the offerors had sent their revocation and no longer wished to be bound. The essence of a request for information is that, unlike a counter-offer, the offeree does not by his conduct show that the original offer is unacceptable to him but instead is merely postponing his decision until he can obtain clarification of certain points. A more recent case illustrating a counter-offer (which was this time accepted and resulted in a contract) is *Butler Machine Tool Co. Ltd* v *Ex-Cell-O Corporation (England) Ltd* [1979] 1 WLR 401 which again is an examinee's dream which can be utilised in a variety of contexts. I have already discussed it in the context of alternatives to the offer and acceptance approach and it is also an example of the problem of the battle of forms. In many cases companies negotiate with each other on their own respective forms, the terms of which continually conflict with one another. The classical rules of offer and acceptance may well mean that no agreement is ever actually reached even though in some cases hundreds of thousands of pounds' worth of business is done under these non-existent 'contracts'. The *Butler* case itself was rather exceptional in that the tear-off acknowledgement made it relatively easy to prefer one set of terms to the other but that will not normally be the case. A useful way of looking at this problem is suggested by Professor Atiyah, i.e., to distinguish between executed and executory contracts. Where the contract is executed, i.e., already carried out or performed, it would be ridiculous to say there never was a contract and so the courts will find some way, as in *Butler*, of preferring one set of terms to the other. Where, however, the contract is still executory, i.e., to be performed in the future and not yet acted on, the court may well feel free to conclude that no agreement has been reached and therefore refuse to enforce it. Indeed, the extent to which an alleged contract has been acted on by the other party may be a potent though unexpressed factor in the approach taken to a wide variety of issues by the courts. See, e.g., the problem of certainty and compare the cases of *G. Scammell & Nephew Ltd* v *H. C. & J. G Ouston* [1941] AC 251 (executory and not sufficiently certain) and *Foley* v *Classique Coaches Ltd* [1934] 2 KB 1 (partially executed and therefore upheld). It is therefore a distinction which you too can usefully point out to an examiner.

Silence as Acceptance

Virtually all students can recite the prima facie rule that silence does not constitute acceptance but closer examination reveals that this rule, like most others, is not universally applicable. Such examination also reveals the importance of asking for what reason it is being asserted that a contract exists.

In *Felthouse* v *Bindley* (1862) 11 CBNS 869, the contract was being set up to show that the horse now belonged to the uncle so that the uncle could sue a third party (the auctioneer) for the conversion of the horse. The court may well have been inclined to reach a different result if no third party or questions of title had been involved and it had merely been a question of the uncle suing the nephew, who in this case would still have had possession of the horse, for breach of contract. The same sort of point could be made about, e.g., *Pharmaceutical Society of Great Britain* v *Boots Cash Chemists (Southern) Ltd* [1953] 1 QB 401 where the question of whether a display of goods amounted to an offer or an invitation to treat was being asked in order to decide whether Boots were guilty of what perhaps seemed at most to be a technical breach of the criminal law. It is by no means certain that a court would adopt the same approach in a case brought by a shopper against a supermarket which refused, e.g., to sell to him goods displayed on its shelves, particularly if the goods had been specially promoted or advertised.

To return to *Felthouse* v *Bindley*, it is important to appreciate that the rationale for the rule is that the offeror should not be able to impose on the offeree the burden of rejecting an offer (and see also the Unsolicited Goods and Services Act 1971 giving further protection to offerees in this connection). Thus there is no reason at all why the rule should apply if it is the *offeree* who is trying to enforce the contract, having relied on the offeror's statement that silence will constitute acceptance — if for example the nephew in *Felthouse* v *Bindley*, relying on the uncle's statement that he would treat silence as an acceptance, had turned down other offers for the horse in the meantime and was now suing the uncle for failure to take delivery of the horse. Similarly if the offeree is the person responsible for introducing silence as a mode of acceptance (cf. *In re Selectmove Ltd* [1995] 1 WLR 474), there is no real objection to making the offeree liable and note that where a court feels that the 'contract' ought to be enforced it can treat prolonged silence as acceptance by conduct as in *Rust* v *Abbey Life Assurance Co. Ltd* [1979] 2 Lloyd's Rep 334 (see also the observations of Lord Steyn in *Vitol SA* v *Norelf Ltd* [1996] 3 All ER 193 at p. 201).

THE EXAMINATION

A number of central themes and issues have now been investigated and enough has been said to enable you to deal intelligently with any particular issue with which you are confronted. The remaining part of the chapter will be devoted to the analysis of an examination question in order to reveal how examiners provide you with the opportunity to demonstrate your understanding of the law. Offer and acceptance lends itself quite readily to problem questions and does not overtax the examiner's reserves of imagination so more often than not the question will be a problem rather than an essay in this area. (If an essay were to be set it would probably focus on one of the three underlying themes identified earlier.) Therefore the following problem will be taken as an example:

Bob places the following advertisement in the *Oldburn Weekly Gazette* published on 1 May:

> Scoop purchase — a dozen brand-new 16 inch colour TVs, £100 each. Will be sold to the first 12 replies received enclosing a cheque for £100. Write to PO Box 12.

On the 7th, Fred posts a letter saying he wishes to buy one of the sets and enclosing £100 cash. In the meantime, Bob's supplier has let him down and so Bob places an advertisement in the *Weekly Gazette* published on the 8th, announcing that the sets are no longer available. Fred's letter arrives on the 9th and is among the first 12 received.
Discuss.

A short introduction is never out of place provided that you do not delay dealing with the issues raised by the facts for too long, so you could preface your answer to this problem with some remarks about the search for an offer and a corresponding acceptance as the normal approach to discovering agreement. This is a useful opening gambit for many types of problems but do remember to slant your answer accordingly if the question reveals a situation where the traditional offer and acceptance analysis is in some way inappropriate.

Next you should take the facts stage by stage and examine the possible legal implications of each stage in the sequence of events. Thus the first issue will be the status of the advertisement — is it an offer or an invitation to treat? The answer depends of course on the offeror's intention but you can point out that this has to be objectively assessed. Does Bob *appear* to readers of the advertisement to be willing to be bound by a simple acceptance? In many problems, the answer to this question will be deliberately ambiguous and your answer will at this point have to divide into two, one part examining the effect on the rest of facts if the advert is assumed to be an invitation to treat, the other part examining the implications if the advert is regarded as an offer. Don't be afraid of hedging your bets in this way. It will soon become apparent if one of the alternatives is a non-runner. In this problem, for example, if you are tempted to assume that the advert is only an invitation to treat you will then find that Fred's letter is at most an offer to buy which Bob never accepts — end of question — so there must be more substantial arguments suggesting that the advert is an offer which will then lead on to other issues.

There are in fact at least three aspects of this advertisement which you could identify as supporting it being an offer:

(a)   The words 'will be sold' imply a definite commitment on Bob's part and evidence that willingness to be bound which is the essential feature of an offer. Contrast the council's letter in *Gibson* v *Manchester City Council* [1979] 1 WLR 294 which said 'The corporation *may* be prepared to sell' (emphasis added) and which was only regarded as an invitation to treat.

(b)   The advertisement limits the number of possible acceptances to 12 — the first 12 — so the danger, which influenced the court in *Partridge* v *Crittenden* [1968] 1 WLR 1204 of the advertiser being swamped with a large number of acceptances which he could not supply is not present.

(c)   The advertisement seems to envisage a unilateral contract. If the reader satisfies the conditions laid down and is among the first 12 replies received he becomes entitled to the promised TV set but he never makes any promises himself. Such advertisements, as in *Carlill* v *Carbolic Smoke Ball Co.* [1893] 1 QB 256, normally only make sense as offers and are thus treated as such under the objective approach (see *Bowerman* v *ABTA, The Times*, 24 November 1995 for a modern illustration of the objective approach in *Carlill*).

Having established that the advert is almost certainly an offer (and being reassured in this on seeing that the question would die a quick death if it were only an invitation to treat) the next issue is whether Fred validly accepts by sending his letter on the 7th. All too many students are so pleased to see a posted acceptance that in their excitement they only remember the shortened version of the postal rule (see above) and conclude that Fred's letter takes effect when posted, overlooking the fact that the offer requires the replies to be *received*, thus effectively excluding the normal rule. Some students are still unconvinced even when this is pointed out to them, arguing that the offer actually authorises the post by saying 'write to PO Box 12'. The fact remains, however, that whilst Bob authorises the use of the post, he is clearly not willing to be bound until the letter is actually received. In any case, a few moments reflection shows that the letter can't take immediate effect on posting since one doesn't know until it is received whether it fulfils the condition of being amongst the first 12. So as usual, the examiner has set a problem where the postal rule is excluded and can't apply.

However the letter does arrive on the 9th and is amongst the first 12 received. Ignoring for the moment the question of Bob's attempted revocation, would there be a valid acceptance on the 9th? The question does not have Bob asking for a cheque, and Fred sending cash instead, for nothing. One might simply argue that Fred has not fulfilled the stipulated conditions and cannot therefore claim to have accepted the offer but the examiner would also expect you to discuss wehether sending cash as opposed to a cheque can be regarded as merely a different mode of acceptance. The issues then would be (a) whether the requirement of a cheque is mandatory or directory in Lord Denning's sense in *Yates Building Co. Ltd* v *R. J. Pulleyn & Sons (York) Ltd* (1975) 237 EG 183 (or obligatory or permissive in Scarman LJ's terminology) and (b), if it is only directory, i.e., permissive, whether cash is equally efficacious from Bob's point of view. As to (a), there is nothing in the advertisement to suggest that it is mandatory (such as 'Cheques only' or 'No cash') so you must at least investigate the positon under (b) if it is only directory. As to this, most people regard cash as being better rather than worse than a cheque but on the other hand Bob may well not want the security problems associated with dealing with cash, and remember that if the offer receives a heavy response he will have to make a lot of refunds which he can do most easily by simply returning cheques. Much depends on the reason why Bob stipulated a cheque — or rather his apparent reason — was it for his own protection or for that of prospective purchasers? Again, don't be afraid to give alternative answers to this issue. The question says 'Discuss', not reach a definitive conclusion. Indeed the examiner will be positively impressed by your ability to see both sides of the argument.

Having recognised that there may be a valid acceptance by the 9th, the remaining issue is whether the offer is still open on that date. Bob tries to withdraw on the 8th but there is no suggestion that this withdrawal has been communicated to Fred, as is normally required. However, the examiner has again selected a situation where the normal rule may not be applicable. Instead the exceptional rule suggested by the American case of *Shuey* v *United States* (1875) 92 US 73 might be applicable (because Bob cannot know to whom he should communicate his revocation until he receives an acceptance by which time it is too late) and a revocation in the next issue of the *Weekly Gazette* seems to be reasonable in the circumstances.

Nonetheless, you can always expect an examiner to give you some opportunity to distinguish a leading case and it should be remembered that if there is a contract here, it is unilateral in nature. Hence it may be possible to argue that Bob cannot revoke once Fred has started to perform — i.e., posted his letter. See the earlier discussion of revocation in unilateral contracts although this is not such a strong case perhaps as, e.g., *Errington* v *Errington* [1952] 1 KB 290 where the offerees had paid out a substantial amount of money in part performance. In our problem, Fred has not changed his position to any great extent (apart from the cost of postage!) although he has effectively committed himself (if Bob chooses to treat his letter as an acceptance he will be bound) so that it is arguable on the grounds of equality that Bob should not have the freedom to withdraw. Note also that in *Shuey* the Supreme Court spoke of the offer being revocable 'before anything had been done in reliance on it'. Again the essential point is to discuss the question of revocation and to show that you are aware of the different possible solutions to this issue. The better your understanding of the possible solutions and of their rationales the better will be your discussion of the problem.

Finally, what you must not do with this problem is to try to answer it by saying that Fred will never be able to prove that his letter was amongst the first 12 received or that Fred shouldn't be so foolish as to send such a large amount of money through the post or that it is not Bob's fault that his supplier has let him down etc. On the last point, Bob may well have a contract with his supplier on which he can sue (if he hasn't then perhaps he should not have placed the advertisement) and on the first two points, you should accept the facts of problems as given although it would not be out of order to comment briefly that as a matter of practicality Fred may have difficulty in proving that his letter was amongst the first 12, as long as you don't use that as an excuse for failing to discuss whether it constitutes an acceptance.

CONCLUSION

This is a topic which most students find reasonably interesting first time round and with which, even at that stage, they do not find unduly difficult. Despite that, it is still a topic worth a detailed second look during the revision period since by that time you will be able to discern subtleties and points of significance which were not obvious to you at the very early stage of the course when the subject was first studied. If you do this and take notice of the themes and issues discussed in this chapter, you can be confident of making a solid start to your contract examination.

4 CONSIDERATION

Having grappled with the rules of offer and acceptance and perhaps having found them not to be too bad after all, the student will normally be confronted with the doctrine of consideration where the going is often thought to become considerably tougher. There is some justification for this in that there is no real agreement about the true basis of the requirement of consideration, the cases often seem to turn on somewhat arbitrary distinctions and the student can at times feel lost in an area where rules abound but appear to be conveniently ignored wherever it suits the courts to do so. However, by being aware of the conflicting themes underlying the doctrine and by appreciating the reasons for the distinctions which the law has developed you can nevertheless cope with the sorts of questions which an examiner is likely to throw at you. Indeed you can expect to pick up bonus points in an area where examiners will express their delight at those answers which show any real understanding.

DEFINITION OF CONSIDERATION

We will start with a definition since this is where most student essays begin, in particular with the statement of Lush J in *Currie* v *Misa* (1875) LR 10 Ex 153 at p. 162, that 'a valuable consideration in the sense of the law, may consist either in some right, interest, profit or benefit accruing to the one party or some forbearance, detriment, loss or responsibility, given suffered or undertaken by the other'. Unfortunately, many essays do not analyse this statement any further and merely go on to recite the leading cases without asking how far they accord with this definition or what particular interpretation of it they support. Further analysis of this definition *is* necessary because as stated the definition tells us very little other than that consideration can be looked at from two angles — that of the promisee, the person providing the consideration, and that of the promisor, the person for whose promise it is being given. This in itself is important enough, but it fails to tell us what *sort* of benefits and detriments the law will regard as sufficient reason for enforcing a promise. In particular, a distinction needs to be drawn between *legal* benefit and detriment on the one hand and mere *factual* benefit and detriment on the other. Generally speaking, it is not enough that a factual benefit is being received or that a detriment in fact is being incurred if the promisee is neither doing more than he is already legally obliged to do nor the promisor receiving more than he is already legally entitled to insist on. Thus the general rule is that if, as in *Stilk* v *Myrick* (1809) 2 Camp 317, A promises B extra money to do what B is already contractually obliged to A to do, there is no consideration, no legal benefit or detriment, even though in fact A may benefit more from B's performance than he would if B refused to perform and paid damages for breach of contract instead. Whether this is a sensible approach for the law to take is another matter and will be discussed later in this chapter but the point is that it generally has, at least formally, taken this approach and therefore it is a point that you should be aware of in discussing the definition in *Currie* v *Misa*.

Another aspect of the *Currie* v *Misa* definition is that, whilst in one sense it looks at both sides of the consideration, it does not look at both sides of the contract. As noted in chapter 3, it takes two to contract and in the classic bilateral contract each side will be making promises. For example, on the 1st of the month, A, a schoolteacher taking a party of schoolchildren abroad on the 15th, promises B, a coach operator, £50 in return for B's promise to collect A and his party from the airport on their return at the end of the month. Initially the agreement is totally executory. A's promise to pay is executory consideration for B's promise to collect. It is both a detriment to A (in the words of Lush J in *Currie* v *Misa*, he undertakes the responsibility of paying £50) and also a benefit to B (although it would be sufficient if it were either of these). Thus if B on the 7th (having been offered a more lucrative job for the end of the month) tries to get out of the agreement, it can be enforced against him (in the sense that he will be liable to pay damages for its breach — see chapter 9). However, this is only to look at half of the agreement. The other half is B's promise to collect as executory consideration for A's promise to pay. Again, the promise to collect is both a detriment (responsibility) to B and a benefit to A. If A tries to escape from the agreement on the 7th (perhaps because X has offered to collect the party for only £40) then A's promise would be enforceable and A would be liable to pay damages for its breach.

Thus the definition of consideration is *potentially* applicable twice to this contract since the definition focuses on just one promise whilst the contract consists of two. But the issue of consideration usually only actually arises in relation to one party's promise when that party has refused to perform it properly or at all. That is why the definition concentrates on whether the plaintiff has provided consideration for the defendant's promise and is not directly concerned with whether the defendant's promise would have constituted consideration for the plaintiff's. On which side of the contract one is looking for consideration depends of course on who it is who is failing or refusing to perform; if it is A who is declining to pay, then one is concerned with whether B's promise to collect is consideration and if it is B who is declining to collect, the question will be whether A's promise to pay is consideration.

Another point to emerge from my example and to be noted about the *Currie v Misa* definition is that the question of whether consideration is a benefit or detriment has to be looked at in isolation from the value of what is being given in return. Thus it is still a detriment to A to promise to pay £50 even though he is getting in return a service from B which is presumably worth an equivalent amount to him. The service in return (or rather the promise of it) has to be ignored in deciding whether A's promise constitutes a benefit or detriment — being obliged to pay £50 is a detriment if looked at in isolation from the service which is promised in return and which is worth that figure. Furthermore, even if the service promised in return is worth much more than £50, the £50 is still regarded as a detriment — consideration need not be adequate — but see Atiyah's *An Introduction to the Law of Contract*, 5th ed., pp. 289–296, for some unorthodox but interesting views on this so-called rule.

Perhaps the most important point to note about the *Currie v Misa* definition, and the respect in which it is fundamentally incomplete, is that it makes no mention of *why* the promisee incurs a detriment (or confers a benefit). Take the case of *Combe v Combe* [1951] 2 KB 215, known to most students as the case where the Court of Appeal held that promissory estoppel could only be used as 'a shield and not a sword'. An equally significant feature of that case was the finding that there was no consideration for the defendant's promise to pay his ex-wife £100 per year even though in reliance on the promise she had not applied to the divorce court for maintenance and in that sense had suffered a detriment. The reason why this detriment did not constitute consideration was that there was no request by the husband, express or implied, that she should forbear from applying for maintenance. In other words, the detriment was not incurred in return for the promise, nor as part of a bargain, it merely resulted from the promise and thus was not consideration. This element of bargain, of consideration as the price of the promise, as something given in exchange or in return for the promise, is central to the classical notion of consideration. It is not apparent from the *Currie v Misa* definition which is one reason why some writers, e.g., Cheshire and Fifoot, prefer the view expressed by Pollock and adopted by Lord Dunedin in *Dunlop Pneumatic Tyre Co. Ltd v Selfridge & Co. Ltd* [1915] AC 847 that consideration is 'the price for which the promise of the other is bought'. The point is made even more clearly in the American Restatement of Contracts (1932) (the American Law Institute's attempt to distil the essence of the common law of contracts). The Restatement in its original form (s. 75) defined consideration as something 'bargained for and given in return for the promise' and is even more explicit in s. 71 of the more recent Restatement, Second, Contracts (1981) which states:

> (1)   To constitute consideration, a performance or a return promise must be bargained for.
> (2)   A performance or return promise is bargained for if it is sought by the promisor in exchange for his promise and is given by the promisee in exchange for that promise.

This notion of consideration as something bargained for, as the price of a promise, is a useful practical way of looking at consideration. When dealing with a problem it is a useful starting-point to ask: What did P do in return for the promise? It also helps to make sense of some of the traditional rules of consideration such as the past consideration rule — see below. You ought, however, to be aware that not everyone agrees that bargain is so essential to consideration and in particular Atiyah in *Consideration in Contracts: A Fundamental Restatement* (now helpfully reprinted and updated in *Essays on Contract*) argues that the fact that someone has foreseeably relied on a promise can be a consideration for the promise (in Atiyah's view, consideration means a good reason for enforcing) even though the reliance was not bargained for or requested by the promisor.

In order to assess this approach properly, it is necessary to say a little more about remedies for breach of contract. (If this is your first reading of this chapter you might wish to leave the next couple of pages for a later occasion.) The basic approach is that remedies are designed to put the plaintiff in the position as though the contract had been performed. This is clearly true of the remedy of specific performance, where the defendant is ordered to actually carry out his side of the contract (e.g., a vendor of land is ordered to complete, i.e., transfer ownership to the purchaser), and of the action for an agreed sum, e.g., for the price of goods sold and delivered. It is also true of the remedy of damages: if I contract to buy shares from you at 90p per share and you prove unable to sell me such shares and in the meantime the price per share has risen to £1.20, you will be liable to put me in the position as though you had sold me the shares. (A number of inexperienced investors apparently had their fingers burnt in this way in the first British Telecom share issue in 1984.) This will involve you paying me damages of 30p per share which I can then add to the 90p per share I was going to pay you and buy the shares elsewhere.

All the above remedies are said to protect the expectation interest — they protect what P expected to get under the contract — and it is significant that in most of the leading cases on consideration, the plaintiff was seeking this form of protection, often directly in the form of an agreed or promised sum of money — see, e.g., *Stilk* v *Myrick*; *Shadwell* v *Shadwell* (1860) 9 CBNS 159; *Combe* v *Combe*; *Tweddle* v *Atkinson* (1861) 1 B & S 393, to name but a few. It is, however, possible to give a more limited remedy for breach of contract which involves protecting not the full expectation interest but merely what has been dubbed the 'reliance interest' (see the incredibly influential article by Fuller and Perdue (1936) 46 Yale LJ 52), i.e., the extent to which the plaintiff is actually worse off as a result of relying on the defendant's promise. For example, as a result of your promise to pay me £500, I give £100 to charity. If you refuse to pay up, protection of reliance would merely involve £100 in damages whereas the protection of expectation would require an award of £500.

A possible way of accommodating Atiyah's views and perhaps of reaching a more appropriate solution in cases like *Combe* v *Combe* is to say that where a plaintiff wishes to enforce a promise in the sense of recovering his expectation interest, he must show that he has paid for those expectations, that he has a right to them because he has bought them with bargained-for consideration. Those expectations are just as much his as the car in his driveway for which he has paid the price (no doubt after a certain amount of haggling). Where, however, there is no bargain, as in *Combe* v *Combe*, but the plaintiff has in fact detrimentally relied on the promise, he ought to be able to recover compensation for that detrimental reliance though not for the loss of his expectations.

This would mean that the Court of Appeal in *Combe* v *Combe* was correct to refuse the claim for £600 arrears since this would have given the wife the full expectation value of the promise in the absence of bargained-for consideration. It would also involve, however, that the wife should have been able to recover compensation for her reliance, e.g., what she would have got if she had applied to the divorce court. This would certainly have been less than the £100 per year promised by her husband and indeed Denning LJ was of the opinion that she would have got nothing in which case there may have been no injustice on the facts (except that she may have relied on the promise in other ways, e.g., by spending more in anticipation of what she had been promised).

The implications of all this for the definition of consideration can be looked at in two ways. First, one could adhere to the orthodox view and say that (a) consideration must be given in return for the promise, i.e., must be bargained for, and that where such consideration is present you have an enforceable contract under which the expectation interest will be protected but that (b) there are other forms of liability, not strictly contractual and not supported by consideration, where promises are not bargained for but are reasonably relied on, where the courts ought to protect the reliance but not the expectation interest. English law has not yet overtly recognised point (b) of this approach but American law does so by virtue of the Restatement, Second, Contracts, s. 90, which provides a remedy for breach of promises unsupported by bargained-for consideration but which have been reasonably relied on, the remedy being in the latest version 'limited as justice requires', which often means limited to reliance rather than expectation damages. (Treitel, whose response to Atiyah is to be found in (1976) 50 ALJ 439, is clearly sympathetic to this approach — see his article at p. 441 and his textbook, 9th ed., p. 69.)

Alternatively, one could argue that consideration as bargain is too narrow a view and that mere unrequested reliance should be capable of amounting to consideration but that contractual liability does not or should not always involve protection of the expectation interest. This seems to be Atiyah's view (note the article (1978) 94 LQR 193 where he expresses his reservations about the justifications for imposing liability for expectation damages) but it is probably fair to say that this is more a view about what the law *should* be rather than what the law is. Nevertheless it is a view that you can usefully incorporate in an essay on consideration since the examiner is interested in your views about how the law might develop just as much as in your appreciation of what the law is (although Atiyah would defend his theory as much as a statement of what the law once *was* as well as a theory about what it *should* be).

Having merely dipped our toes into the sorts of controversies to which the doctrine of consideration can give rise (it gives rise to such controversies because at root what constitutes consideration is a question of policy about what sorts of promises the law should enforce and to what extent), it is now time to return to the traditional issues and problems around which most courses revolve. As will be seen, the wider controversies and policies about which I have already said a little are relevant when considering the following particular issues.

PAST CONSIDERATION

Most students are aware of the rule that past consideration is not sufficient as exemplified by cases such as *Re McArdle* [1951] Ch 669and *Roscorla* v *Thomas* (1842) 3 QB 234 but many unfortunately reveal that they do not fully understand it by being unable to distinguish properly between past and executed consideration. The keys here are to appreciate:

(a) that 'past' means past in relation to the *making* of the promise which is sought to be enforced, not past in relation to the time of seeking to *enforce* that promise, and

(b)   that the past-consideration rule can be seen as an application of the more fundamental rule that consideration is something given *in return* for the promise.

Thus if A promises B £50 if he finds A's lost dog, B can only enforce the promise once he has found the dog, when he has executed the consideration, but the consideration is clearly given in return for the promise since it is performed *after* the promise. Hence while it is past (executed) in relation to the time of enforcement, it is not past in relation to the giving of the promise and is good consideration. On the other hand if B, knowing that A has lost his dog, goes in search of it, finds it and returns it to A and A then, being naturally grateful, promises B £50 for his trouble, the promise would not be enforceable since finding the dog could not have been done in return for the promise as it was done *before* the promise was made. It was past in relation to the promise. This would be true even if A said expressly 'in consideration of your returning my dog' (see *Re McArdle* where the promise was stated to be in consideration of the plaintiff doing certain work but the work had already been done) since A is here using consideration in a loose sense as equivalent to motive (see *Thomas* v *Thomas* (1842) 2 QB 851) as opposed to something bargained for in return for the promise.

Any discussion of past consideration would be incomplete without mentioning the so-called exceptions to it but alas many students' accounts are incomplete in this sense. There are some statutory exceptions of rather narrow scope but the examiner is more likely to be interested in the common law rule traceable back in *Lampleigh* v *Brathwait* (1615) Hob 105 since this so-called exception is a means of examining whether you understand the rule itself. The necessary conditions for the modern version of this rule are, in the words of Lord Scarman in *Pao On* v *Lau Yiu Long* (1980) AC 614 that 'The [past] act must have been done at the promisors' request: the parties must have understood that the [past] act was to be remunerated either by a payment or the conferment of some other benefit: and payment, or the conferment of a benefit, must have been legally enforceable had it been promised in advance'. The facts of the above case are unfortunately not the simplest ones by which to illustrate the principle but if I return to my example of B finding A's lost dog, the point can be made quite simply. If A had *asked* B to go and look for the dog and there had been an understanding that B would be remunerated should he find it then A's later promise of £50 would be enforceable even though the consideration was apparently past. The explanation is that there is an *implied* promise to pay at the time of the request and in relation to that promise the finding of the dog is not past — indeed the finding of the dog is done in return for the implied promise. The later promise of £50 merely fixes the *amount* of the remuneration under the earlier implied promise. Of course the difficult question is whether there is an understanding that the benefit will be paid for: A might not have any intention to pay whilst B may only be acting on the assumption that he is to be remunerated. As usual, such issues have to be resolved by taking an objective approach and asking in the light of all the circumstances whether it was reasonable for the parties to assume that there would be some form of remuneration. If A and B are friends or neighbours then such an assumption would not normally be justified but if B is a professional dog-catcher, the reverse would be true.

EXISTING DUTIES

The question of whether a promise to perform, or the performance of, something which one is under an existing legal duty to do can constitute consideration for a fresh promise is a central issue in any theory of consideration. It is a question which can be answered on a fairly superficial level by drawing some rather arbitrary distinctions between different types of duties but which also raise some rather more fundamental issues about the nature of consideration. As a result of the Court of Appeal's decision in *Williams* v *Roffey Bros* [1991] 1 QB 1, the fundamental issues are becoming more and more explicit and difficult to avoid. Unfortunately, many examination candidates fail to deal with the question adequately at the superficial level and never even get near the more fundamental issues. I will look at these two levels in turn, and first at the superficial level.

The cases on existing duties can be separated into three types:

(a)   Those dealing with existing *contractual* duties owed to the *promisor*.

(b)   Those dealing with existing *contractual* duties owed to a *third party* (i.e., not the person whose promise it is sought to enforce).

(c)   Those dealing with existing *non-contractual* or so-called *public* duties (usually imposed by statute).

As to category (a), it is said to be fairly clear from *Stilk* v *Myrick* (1809) 2 Camp 317 that the mere performance of an existing duty is not good consideration. Although this rule has been criticised and can lead to inconvenience and absurdity it is supported by the notion that consideration has to be a *legal* benefit or detriment (see above p. 57) and does not merely rely on old obscurely reported cases such as *Stilk* v *Myrick* but has been affirmed (although significantly, evaded) in more recent cases such as *North Ocean Shipping Co. Ltd* v *Hyundai Construction Co. Ltd* [1979] QB 705 and *Williams* v *Roffey Bros*. It is equally clear (and note that this is true of all three categories) that if one does something beyond the scope of an existing duty, then that will constitute consideration since there is now clearly a detriment (doing something one needn't have done) and a benefit (getting something one wasn't already entitled to) in the legal sense. *Hartley* v *Ponsonby* (1857) 7 E & B 872 is usually cited for this proposition but *North Ocean Shipping* is in fact a more modern example where shipbuilders were held to have supplied consideration for the promise to pay them an extra 10%, by increasing their return letter of credit (the security provided by the shipbuilders for the advanced payment by the purchasers). It is noteworthy that Mocatta J was prepared to find this to be extra consideration 'though not without some doubt' since it is this ability to find, often on somewhat flimsy evidence, that the existing duty was exceeded that makes the rule in *Stilk* v *Myrick* tolerable, or rather, avoidable. (But see the Canadian case of *Gilbert Steel Ltd* v *University Construction Ltd* (1976) 12 OR (2d) 19 for an instance of the *Stilk* v *Myrick* rule being applied in its full rigour.) More recently, and more significantly, *Stilk* v *Myrick* was avoided by the Court of Appeal in *Williams* v *Roffey Bros* [1991] 1 QB 1. The court was at pains to stress that it was not overruling *Stilk* v *Myrick*, but nonetheless held that the defendants' promise to pay £10,300 if the plaintiff completed his obligations under the original contract was enforceable since the defendants would thereby get the benefit of actually having the work completed. This was important to the defendants inter alia, in order to avoid being liable under a 'penalty clause' to a third party. The court stressed the fact that the defendants had voluntarily made the promise of the extra £10,300, that it was not as a result of threats by the plaintiff and that it was agreed that the original contract was underpriced. The significance of *Williams* v *Roffey Bros* (which was applied at first instance in *Anangel Atlas Compania Noviera S.A.* v *Ishikawajima-Harima Heavy Industries Co. Ltd (No. 2)* [1990] 2 Lloyd's Rep 526) is further discussed below, p. 69.

Most students are aware of the *Stilk* v *Myrick* rule but many stop there and show little or no awareness of the rather different approach to category (b), existing duties owed to a third party. Here, by contrast, it is clear that the performance of an existing duty will be treated as good consideration. Again, the root authorities are 19th-century cases: *Shadwell* v *Shadwell* (1860) 9 CBNS 159; *Chichester* v *Cobb* (1866) 14 LT 433 and *Scotson* v *Pegg* (1861) 6 H & N 295. Of these, *Shadwell* v *Shadwell* is the easiest to understand on the superficial level since the nephew was under an existing duty (owed to his fiancée) to marry her (agreements to marry being legally enforceable at that time) and actually doing so was held to be good consideration for the uncle's promise of an annuity. Yet the majority judgment of Erle CJ never really discusses the question of existing duty and is concerned more with the question of whether the uncle *requested* the marriage and whether that *in fact* involved detriment and benefit. It was only the dissenting judgment of Byles J which expressly discussed the question of existing duty and, being in dissent, he felt that 'a promise, based on the consideration of doing that which a man is already bound to do, is invalid'.

The judgment of Wilde B in *Scotson* v *Pegg* is, however, much more explicit for he said:

I accede to the proposition that if a person contracts with another to do a certain thing, he cannot make the performance of it a consideration for a new promise to the same individual [the *Stilk* v *Myrick* rule]. But there is no authority for the proposition that where there has been a promise to one person to do a certain thing, it is not possible to make a valid promise to another to do the same thing.

This is significant because it expressly recognises that the seemingly arbitrary distinction between categories (a) and (b) is part of the law and if any doubts remained about the third-party rule, there is more modern authority in the shape of two Privy Council decisions: *New Zealand Shipping Co. Ltd* v *A. M. Satterthwaite & Co. Ltd* [1975] AC 154 and *Pao On* v *Lau Yiu Long* [1980] AC 614, where *Scotson* v *Pegg* was expressly approved and followed.

The third category to be considered is that of non-contractual or so-called public duties. *Collins* v *Godefroy* (1831) 1 B & Ad 950 is a case often cited by students for the proposition that mere performance of a public duty (in that case attending court as a witness in response to a subpoena) is not good consideration whereas going beyond an existing duty (as in *Glasbrook Brothers Ltd* v *Glamorgan County Council* [1925] AC 270) is good consideration. This would of course assimilate category (c) with category (a) but it should be at least pointed out that Denning LJ in *Ward* v *Byham* [1956] 3 All ER 318 thought that a promise to perform an existing duty was good consideration although the majority of the Court of Appeal in that case managed to find that the plaintiff, by promising to keep her child 'well looked-after and happy', had actually exceeded her statutory duty to maintain the child.

As we shall see, more can be made of these cases, but you should at least be able to give an accurate account of the case law at this superficial level and given the rather arbitrary approach which the law seems to take, not everyone finds this easy. It is here that the ability to reduce the case law to a simple plan comes in useful. Of course the best plan, the one that will mean most to you, is one that you have drawn up yourself but Table 4.1 might be a useful illustration of the way you might go about it.

	Mere performance	Exceeding duty
Existing duty to promisor	X *Stilk* v *Myrick* X *North Ocean Shipping Co. Ltd* v *Hyundai Construction Co. Ltd* ? *Williams* v *Roffey Bros*	* *Hartley* v *Ponsonby* * *North Ocean Shipping Co. Ltd* v *Hyundai Construction Co. Ltd*
Existing duty to 3rd party	* *Shadwell* v *Shadwell* * *Scotson* v *Pegg* * *New Zealand Shipping Co. Ltd* v *A. M. Satterthwaite & Co. Ltd*	* No particular authority but any other rule absurd
Existing public duty	X *Collins* v *Godefroy* *? *Ward* v *Byham* (Denning)	* *Glasbrook Brothers Ltd* v *Glamorgan County Council* * *Ward* v *Byham* (maj)

* = good consideration   X = not consideration   ? = debatable
Notice that in all cases, exceeding a duty is good consideration.

Table 4.1

The mere process of drawing up a scheme like Table 4.1 is likely to impress the relationships between the cases on your mind and the scheme itself will help you to recall them under pressure in the examination. Whilst this will certainly enable you to pass a question in this area, if you really want to *succeed* you ought to be able to go beyond this superficial arrangement of the cases and investigate some deeper issues.

Why, for example, does the law draw a distinction between category (a) and category (b)? One argument might be that in category (b) the promisor is at least getting the benefit of a legal right to compel the other party to perform his existing contractual duty, whereas prior to his promise only the third party had such a right. In category (a), by contrast, the promisor already has a right to enforce the existing duty. The problems with this argument though are twofold:

(a)   It is a circular argument — a bootstraps argument — the promisor only gets a right to sue if his own promise is binding, which is the very thing the argument is trying to establish.

(b)   Most of the existing-duty cases involve not a promise to perform an existing duty but the actual performance of it, i.e., they are unilateral contracts and the promisor never gets any right to sue since the other side never undertakes any obligation — the promisor merely gets the benefit of actual performance should the promisee choose to perform. Thus in *Shadwell* v *Shadwell*, for example, the uncle could not have sued the nephew if he had chosen not to marry his fiancée (although doubtless she would have had something to say about it!).

The truth is that there is no satisfactory reason for drawing hard-and-fast distinctions between the three categories and the category which needs explanation is not category (b), which appears at first sight to be out of line with the other two, but categories (a) and (c). Category (a) (the *Stilk* v *Myrick* rule) is really not based on lack of bargained-for benefit or detriment but on the risk of duress. There is a clear danger that in a situation like *Stilk* v *Myrick*, a crew might threaten that unless they are promised extra wages they will not complete the voyage, and no doubt much more serious threats are imaginable.

In an earlier case, *Harris* v *Watson* (1791) Peake 102, a similar decision to *Stilk* v *Myrick* was reached on the basis of public policy rather than lack of consideration and indeed in Espinasse's report of *Stilk* v *Myrick* itself (6 Esp 129) there is no mention of consideration. (It is only fair to say that Espinasse is not regarded very highly as a reporter — one judge is reported to have said 'I don't want to hear from Espinasse or any other ass'.) It is only in Campbell's report that lack of consideration is given as the reason for the decision in *Stilk* v *Myrick* (a good account of these matters is to be found in Gilmore, *The Death of Contract*, pp. 122-8, a short book which is well worth reading throughout) and it seems that the device of consideration was being used as a convenient tool for refusing to enforce a promise on policy grounds. It is this manipulation of consideration to serve policy ends in particular cases that makes the doctrine so difficult to state in logical and consistent terms and the emerging consensus today is that a promise to perform an existing duty of whatever sort can be good consideration but that the courts should refuse enforcement if there is duress, or perhaps other public policy reasons for denying enforcement, on the facts. The problem with the strict *Stilk* v *Myrick* rule is that it denies enforceability irrespective of whether there is duress or any other objectionable conduct on the facts. It is significant that whilst Mocatta J felt bound by *Stilk* v *Myrick* in *North Ocean Shipping Co. Ltd* v *Hyundai Construction Co. Ltd* [1979] QB 705 and found extra consideration to get round that case, he didn't let the rules of consideration dictate the result since he found that the promise of extra payment was voidable because of economic duress. In the third edition of this book it was stated that 'the recent expansion in the notion of duress is likely to lead to the formal demise of the rule in *Stilk* v *Myrick*'. *Williams* v *Roffey Bros* (discussed above, p. 66) is evidence of that process becoming further advanced as the court, in Glidewell

LJ's words, 'refined and limited' the principle in *Stilk* v *Myrick* so as not to apply it where the promisor obtains a factual benefit and has not been subjected to duress. It is not difficult to find a factual (as opposed to a legal) benefit in most of the existing duty cases so the key criterion is likely to be the presence or absence of duress. In *Atlas Express Ltd* v *Kafco Ltd* [1989] 1 All ER 641 a promise to pay more than the contract price in a road haulage contract was held to be unenforceable primarily because of economic duress. Right at the end of his judgment, Turner J then applied the *Stilk* v *Myrick* rule and held that there was 'in any event . . . no consideration for the new agreement'. This second ground for the decision is not really independent of the first ground, the finding of economic duress. It is interesting to speculate as to the likely outcome if there had been no finding of economic duress (which might have been the conclusion if the court had found, as in *Williams* v *Roffey Bros*, that the original contract was under-priced). The defendants certainly got a benefit in having their goods delivered to Woolworths, their principal customer, and under the *Williams* v *Roffey Bros* approach, consideration presumably would be found in such a case.

There is a further point to be made about *Stilk* v *Myrick*, and you may even be able to surprise your examiner with this one. If the original contract, under which the existing duty is owed, is rescinded or got rid of in some way then clearly the performance of any duty under it can be good consideration because it is no longer an existing duty. In *Raggow* v *Scougall & Co.* (1915) 1 TLR 564 (this is an English case but, as noted in Reiter and Swan, *Studies in Contract Law*, there almost seems to be a conspiracy to suppress it — though see Smith and Thomas, *A Casebook on Contract*) an agreement to accept less wages in return for continued employment was upheld even though the employers were already obliged to provide continued employment. Darling J justified his decision by saying that the parties had 'in fact torn up the old agreement and made a new one by mutual consent'. You may well ask why this analysis, of each party giving up its rights under the existing agreement in return for the other party doing likewise, cannot be applied to *Stilk* v *Myrick* itself. In fact this sort of argument was put to Mocatta J in *North Ocean Shipping Co. Ltd* v *Hyundai Construction Co. Ltd* but it was put forward on the basis of an American case (*Watkins & Son Inc.* v *Carrig* (1941) 21 A 2d 591) which his Lordship noted was cited by Treitel 'not as being the law of England'. This could hardly have been said about the King's Bench case of *Raggow* v *Scougall & Co.*, had that case been cited. Mocatta J went on to say, 'the facts here are in my opinion far removed from a case of rescission', no doubt because on the facts there was duress. Where there is no duress, there seems no good reason why you should not argue that *Raggow* v *Scougall & Co.* is another way round the apparent obstacle of *Stilk* v *Myrick*, should a court wish to use it. Moreover, it may be more appropriate and easier to use this analysis where the original contract has not set an economic price, as in

Williams v *Roffey Bros.* The mutual relinquishing of rights under a contract wihch was economically flawed at the outset is more legitimate and natural than in the situation where the original contract presented each party with potential benefits.

I have spent some time on *Stilk* v *Myrick*:

(a)   because it shows what you can do with seemingly well-established cases if you ferret around outside the standard accounts of them and

(b)   because it illustrates well the policy aspect of consideration, i.e., its role in identifying in a somewhat crude and clumsy way those promises which ought and those which ought not to be enforced.

Similar points are made rather more openly about category (c) as a result of Denning LJ's dicta in *Williams* v *Williams* [1957] 1 All ER 305 that 'a promise to perform an existing duty [he was speaking in the context of a statutory duty] is I think sufficient consideration to support a promise, *so long as there is nothing in the transaction which is contrary to the public interest'* (emphasis added). Thus a possible modern explanation of *Collins* v *Godefroy* is that it is against public policy to encourage a party to litigation to bargain about the compensation payable to a witness, since there is a very fine line between paying a person for attending court and paying him to say the right thing.

PART PAYMENT OF A DEBT

It is possible to view this as merely a subspecies of existing duties to the promisor in that the debtor is merely doing part of what he already has an obligation to the promisor/creditor to do. This is true up to a point but note that the issue here is not whether some *new* obligation is created (i.e., whether P can sue for what has been promised) but whether some previous obligation has been discharged. That is why the essentially defensive mechanism of promissory estoppel is able to help the debtor here because he is not suing to enforce a fresh promise but is merely trying to prevent a previous obligation (which he had been led to believe had been discharged) from being enforced against him.

Just as with the *Stilk* v *Myrick* rule, 'the rule in *Pinnel's Case*' (1602) 5 Co Rep 117a, that part payment of a debt does not discharge the whole, is generally regarded as unsatisfactory since, as Lord Blackburn pointed out in *Foakes* v *Beer* (1884) 9 App Cas 605 in reluctantly agreeing with the majority, 'all men of business, whether merchants or tradesmen, do every day recognise and act on the ground that prompt payment of a part of their demand may be more beneficial to them than it would be to insist on their rights and enforce payment of the whole'. Thus the Law Revision Committee in their report in 1937 (Cmd 5449) recommended the abolition of the rule but since nothing has yet been done about this by statute, your task is to be familiar with the exceptions that the courts recognise. Most of these are merely applications of the traditional consideration rules — e.g., payment in advance is clearly exceeding the obligation to pay on the due date, payment in kind may be worth more than the debt and the courts will not investigate the adequacy of the consideration — but others, such as those relating to part payment by a third party and composition agreements with creditors, are really policy based — the rule in *Pinnel's case* would be too inconvenient and unjust if followed in those situations.

It will be interesting to see what effect *Williams v Roffey Bros* might eventually have on the rule in *Pinnel's Case* although in *In re Selectmove Ltd* [1995] 1 WLR 474 (see also (1994) 110 LQR 353) the court was unwilling to countenance any modification of *Foakes v Beer* as a consequence of *Williams v Roffey Bros*. The company had offered to pay its arrears of taxes by instalments to the Inland Revenue who had said that it would come back if the arrangement was unacceptable. The company heard nothing for a time and paid some instalments and then received a threat of being wound up if the full arrears were not paid immediately. The Court of Appeal rejected the argument based on *Williams v Roffey Bros* that there could be consideration provided by the company in the form of benefits to the Inland Revenue in receiving partial payment in return for a promise by the Revenue to accept deferred payment by instalments. *Williams v Roffey Bros* was distinguished as being a case concerned with an obligation to supply goods and services as opposed to an obligation to pay a sum of money as in *Foakes v Beer* and the present case. The court was clearly not prepared to allow a rule laid down over a hundred years ago by the House of Lords in *Foakes v Beer* to be overturned by the side wind of *Williams v Roffey Bros*. Whether this will be the last word on the subject may perhaps be doubted. *In re Selectmove* was not the strongest case on its facts for challenging the rule in *Foakes v Beer*. In the first place, it is not clear that there was a genuine agreement to accept payment by instalments (cf the rule about no acceptance by silence although note that it was the Inland Revenue who appear to have introduced silence as the means for acceptance). Secondly, unlike *Williams v Roffey Bros*, it does not clearly appear that there was an absence of duress or that the original obligation was oppressive in any sense and the initative seems to have come exclusively from the debtor rather than partially at least from the promisor as in *Williams v Roffey Bros*. Given a more promising set of facts the courts may yet be more willing to use *Williams v Roffey Bros* as a means of modifying the principle in *Foakes v Beer* and the rule in *Pinnel's Case*.

Another potential way of avoiding the effects of *Pinnel's Case* is promissory estoppel, though it should be remembered that estoppel is capable of applying outside the sphere of part payment (see, e.g., *Brikom Investments Ltd v Carr* [1979] QB 467). There are three key elements you should look for in this doctrine:

(a)   A clear promise that existing legal rights (i.e., the debt) will not be enforced (cf. *Scandinavian Trading Tanker Co. AB* v *Flota Petrolera Ecuatoriana* [1983] QB 529 at pp. 534-7 where it was held that past conduct in allowing the hire under a charterparty to be paid late without forfeiture did not imply a promise to waive the right of forfeiture in future). The absence of a clear and express promise to accept payment by instalments was one reason promissory estoppel was not applicable in *In re Selectmove Ltd* (above).

(b)   Reliance on that promise by the debtor.

(c)   It being 'inequitable' for the creditor to go back on his promise (see *D & C Builders Ltd* v *Rees* [1966] 2 QB 617 where element was not satisfied). Neither was it satisfied in *In re Selectmove Ltd* where the debtor failed to comply with the revised payment schedule.

There are also two particular questions which are unclear about the doctrine in which you can therefore expect the examiner to be interested:

(a)   Whether the reliance must be to the debtor's detriment. Lord Denning, being in favour of giving estoppel a wide role, has said several times that in his view detriment is not necessary but other judges have been more cautious. The issue is concisely discussed in *Anson's Law of Contract*, 26th ed., pp. 103-4, and you should be prepared to show your awareness of the controversy. A possible compromise view that might be taken is that where it is clearly shown that the debtor has suffered no detriment the court may be reluctant to find that it is inequitable for the creditor to go back on his word.

(b)   Is estoppel suspensory or extinctive? Treating it as only suspensory is one way of reconciling the doctrine with the rule in *Pinnel's case* as confirmed by the House of Lords in *Foakes* v *Beer* — the part payment doesn't extinguish the debt because *Foakes* v *Beer* says it can't but promissory estoppel suspends the obligation and gives the debtor breathing space. This is hardly satisfactory because it robs promissory estoppel of most of its utility — the debtor usually has already *in fact* had the benefit of postponement of his liability. The better view would seem to be that promissory estoppel is *capable* of extinguishing a liability but that it will only be suspensory where the debtor can easily resume his original position or, obviously, where the promise was only to suspend in the first place. Again, there is a good discussion of the point in Anson, pp. 104-5 and note that in *Central London Property Trust Ltd* v *High Trees House Ltd* [1947] 1 KB 130 the instalments of rent due during the war were regarded as extinguished but the right to claim the full rent for future periods was only suspended. Thus in cases of periodic payments one has to ask very carefully what is being suspended or extinguished — the right to a *particular* instalment (or part thereof) or the right to such instalments *generally*.

There are two final points to make about promissory estoppel. First, the limitation of 'shield and not a sword' is necessary to prevent it from completely swallowing up the requirement of consideration (but see *Crabb v Arun District Council* [1976] Ch 179). This should be contrasted with the American approach whereby estoppel can create a cause of action but the remedy may be limited as compared with what will be awarded for breach of promise supported by consideration — see the earlier discussion of Restatement, Second, Contracts, s. 90.

Secondly, it is unclear what is the precise relationship between promissory estoppel and the doctrine of waiver. Lord Denning treated them as essentially the same thing but Roskill LJ in *Brikom Investments Ltd* v *Carr* specifically based his judgment on waiver as distinct from promissory estoppel although he did not make it clear exactly where the difference lay. It may be that Roskill LJ was merely trying to distance himself from the more liberal view of Lord Denning on the scope of promissory estoppel and considered the doctrine of waiver to have a more orthodox pedigree. Whatever the explanation, don't be misled into thinking that where a judge talks about waiver he is talking about something completely unrelated to promissory estoppel.

THE EXAMINATION

Clearly I have not looked at every aspect of the doctrine of consideration but I have looked at some of the most frequently examined areas which also raise most of the fundamental issues. You must of course be ready to deal with other issues such as how far compromises of invalid claims constitute consideration, the basic answer being that they are enforceable provided the claim is not known to be bad at the time of the compromise. The relationship between consideration and intention to create legal relations is also something which you should have thought about. The intention to contract is treated as a separate requirement in most of the textbooks but the two issues do have a habit of merging into one — given the objective test of intention it is often difficult to disentangle the question of whether the promise is one which was bargained for and ought to be enforced (the consideration question) from the question of whether the circumstances surrounding the promise suggest that the parties *intended* it should be enforceable. Note that in the supposedly leading case on intention to contract (*Balfour* v *Balfour* [1919] 2 KB 571) the wife never really promised anything in return for her husband's promise and count how many times the word 'bargain' was used in the judgment of Warrington LJ (as opposed to the more often cited Atkin LJ who based his judgment explicitly on lack of intention to create legal relations).

An issue closely related to that of intention to contract is the vexed question of agreements 'subject to contract' and the problem of combating 'gazumping' whereby a house seller accepts one offer 'subject to contract' but subsequently accepts higher offer(s) from other(s). *Pitt* v *PHH Asset*

Management [1993] 4 All ER 961 is a useful and important Court of Appeal case which picks up the suggestion in the earlier House of Lords case of *Walford* v *Miles* [1992] 1 All ER 453 that a 'lock-out agreement' whereby the vendor agrees not to consider offers from any one else for a fixed period can be an enforceable contract supported by consideration (as oppposed to a 'lock-in' agreement to continue to negotiate only with P which is unenforceable as being an agreement to agree or an agreement to negotiate). Various forms of consideration were found in *Pitt*, the one consisting of the dropping of a nuisance threat to seek an injunction of which there was no prospect of success being a somewhat debatable one (cf. *White* v *Bluett* (1853) 23 LJ Ex 36). More convincing is the consideration consisting of refraining from dropping out of the bidding and informing the other interested purchaser of that fact which would have caused the other's bid to fall and therefore was a clear benefit to the promisor/vendor.

The rule that consideration must move from the promisee (*Tweddle* v *Atkinson* (1861) 1 B & S 393) is more likely to arise in relation to a question on privity (see chapter 9) but the way that privity is handled varies from course to course so a study of previous examination papers is invaluable here. If your course is taught alongside the law of torts (as most contract courses are) and if the relationships between contract and tort are stressed (as they should be) then it makes sense to prepare yourself to talk intelligently about the finding of consideration in *De la Bere* v *Pearson Ltd* [1908] 1 KB 280 and the likelihood that such a case would now be dealt with under the *Hedley Byrne* principle (see, e.g., *Cheshire and Fifoot's Law of Contract*, 13th ed., p. 90). Indeed, given the wide-ranging and amorphous nature of the doctrine of consideration, there is no substitute for being alert to the particular themes that your own course and past papers seem to emphasise. There follows, therefore, a discussion of two questions which might be looked at in any course.

An Essay

'The law of contract is based upon bargain yet the rules of consideration fail to recognise economic reality.' Discuss.

The weak student, who has drudged away unimaginatively but nonetheless quite diligently for the past year, will often take this sort of question as an invitation to recite all he knows about consideration. He or she may even scrape a pass on this question as a result but will build up little credit to help out in the possibly even weaker answers to later questions or to climb up to the class of degree which is being hoped for. The examiner does of course wish to see that you have a good knowledge of the law on consideration but he also wants to see whether you understand and can evaluate it. By moulding your answer to the question asked you can show not only that you *know* the cases but that you understand them sufficiently well to be able to *manipulate* them. How can you do this?

One way is to dissect the statement which you are asked to discuss, e.g., (a) the law of contract is based upon bargain, (b) yet the rules of consideration fail to recognise economic reality. Be aggressive, attack the examiner's assumptions — the question may be deliberately provocative and anyway the examiner will be pleased to receive an answer that breaks the tedium of the majority. So as to the first portion of the statement, you could ask, is there a 'law of contract' and if so what are its limits? Does it or should it include the protection of mere reliance (see page 63 above) or are we talking purely about the protection of bargained-for expectations? If the latter, then the reference to bargain is obviously legitimate but you could point out that the protection of non-bargain promises is part of the American Restatement of *Contracts* (s. 90). However, you must make it clear that you appreciate that in English law mere unbargained-for reliance is not usually consideration (see the discussion earlier of *Combe* v *Combe* [1951] 2 KB 215) although it may raise the defence of estoppel and sometimes the courts are prepared to invent consideration where in truth there was really reliance rather than a bargain (*Shadwell* v *Shadwell* (1860) 9 CBNS 159 may be such a case as may the consideration for an auctioneer's promise to sell to the highest bidder, cf. *Warlow* v *Harrison* (1859) 1 E & E 309).

As to the second part of the statement: 'the rules of consideration fail to recognise economic reality', identify which rules this could refer to, most likely the rules about part payment of a debt, *Stilk* v *Myrick* (1809) 2 Camp 317 and the rule that an offer can be withdrawn at any time before acceptance since there is no consideration for any promise to keep it open. But don't agree too readily with the statement, point out the ways that *Stilk* v *Myrick* can be evaded by finding an excess over an existing duty, or a benefit to the promisor as in *Williams* v *Roffey Bros*, or perhaps by finding that the original contract has been discharged (as in *Hartley* v *Ponsonby* (1857) 7 E & B 872) or rescinded (as in *Raggow* v *Scougall & Co.* (1915) 31 TLR 564). Similarly, illustrate the ways around the part-payment rule, including promissory estoppel, perhaps mentioning in particular the rule about composition agreements with creditors since this appears to be *based* on economic realities rather than on consideration theory.

Further you can point out that not all the rules of consideration are unsympathetic to commercial reality. The well-established exception to the past-consideration rule is based on the economic reality that professional people (like the defendant in *Re Casey's Patents* [1892] 1 Ch 104) don't respond to requests for their services except on the basis that they are to be paid for them.

You should find that in discussing critically the words of the question in this way you have also given an *individualised* account of major areas of consideration without falling into the trap of routinely listing the standard rules in a way which neither answers the question nor distinguishes your answer from the majority of others.

Your conclusion will be dictated in part by the views which you have already expressed but it is usually prudent to acknowledge that there may be some truth in the examiner's quotation. (Examiners rarely set statements for discussion that are either completely true or completely untrue.) The extent to which the statement is true is of course a criticism of the law, therefore you should also discuss how the law could be improved. In the context of consideration, this must involve some reference to the Law Revision Committee's report of 1937 (see Hamson (1938) 54 LQR 233, for reaction to this at the time, and Treitel, *The Law of Contract*, 9th ed., pp. 148-149, for a discussion of the proposals and their present status). (See also Atiyah's *An Introduction to the Law of Contract*, for some thought-provoking comments about the future of consideration.)

A Problem

> Bildup plc has agreed with Blueburn Rovers, the Premier League Champions, to refurbish their sports stadium at a cost of ten million pounds, the work to be completed by 1 July. The stadium is to be used by the Football Association (FA) for the World Cup finals taking place early in August. In March, Bildup informs the Rovers that, due to bad weather conditions, the work is unlikely to be completed until the end of August. Hearing of this, the FA contacts Bildup and promises it one million pounds out of the profits of the World Cup if the work is completed on schedule. As a result, the stadium is completed early in June. The finals, however, fail to make as much profit as anticipated and in September the FA tells Bildup that as a result if can only pay it £600,000. Bildup accepts this 'as total discharge, in consideration of the complimentary tickets and facilities' provided by the FA for the directors of Bildup at the finals. In October the FA signs a lucrative sponsorship deal and Bildup, hearing of this, claims the balance of £400,000. Discuss.

You should be quite reassured on seeing a question like this for it is obvious that the examiner is a sports follower and has a sense of humour. His humour will be further improved if you set about answering the question in a clear and logical fashion and break it down into manageable chunks — manageable both for you and the examiner. The first real issue is the FA's promise of one million pounds — is it enforceable by Bildup, i.e., has Bildup given consideration by completing the stadium on schedule? The obvious difficulty is that they are already under a contractual duty to do just that so where is the detriment to them? However, it is clear that their existing duty is under a contract with Blueburn Rovers (a third party as far as this new promise of one million pounds is concerned, i.e., not the promisor) and thus the case falls conveniently within the *Scotson* v *Pegg* (1861) 6 H & N 295 line of authorities. You should not, however, leave it at that — take the opportunity to show your awareness of the rather arbitrary nature of the distinction on which you are relying and how the whole area of existing duty might be better approached (see below). In the light of *Williams* v *Roffey Bros*, you might want to discuss the question of factual benefit to the FA and whether Bildup has exerted any duress.

You could also make something of the point that the stadium is actually completed early in June. This is not only on schedule but ahead of schedule so you might argue that this is in fact a case of exceeding an existing duty (completing early) but this argument would ultimately have to be rejected since the FA did not *ask* them to complete early, just on schedule. Completing early is, rather like mere reliance, something done as a result of the promise but not something requested or bargained for (see *Combe* v *Combe* [1951] 2 KB 215, discussed above). You should nonetheless mention this argument, even if you go on to reject it, just to show that you are aware of the possibilities. It is clear, though, even without this argument, that the fact that the existing duty is owed to a third party means that the FA's promise of one million pounds is enforceable — i.e., there is a debt of one million pounds owed by the FA to Bildup.

The next issue is the effect of Buildup's agreement to accept £600,000 as full satisfaction. Is it binding on them as a contract supported by consideration? Of course you must recite the well-known rule in *Pinnel's Case* (1602) 5 Co Rep 117a as upheld in *Foakes* v *Beer* (1884) 9 App Cas 605 and perhaps say a little about its rationale. You could also mention *In re Selectmove* as showing that *Williams* v *Roffey Bros* is so far making little impact in this area. The part payment of a debt rule was applied again in *Ferguson* v *Davies* [1997] 1 All ER 315.

There is also the rather obvious point about the complimentary tickets and facilities as consideration. These are clearly past and thus do not constitute good consideration but make sure that you make it clear to the examiner that you are aware of the exception to the past-consideration rule even though there seems to be little scope for it on these facts — the tickets and facilities do not appear to have been requested and the word 'complimentary' seems inconsistent with any understanding that they should be paid for.

Finally, there is the question of whether promissory estoppel can come to the FA's defence (they only need a defence, they are not trying to sue on the agreement, the claim is against them). Go through the essentials of promissory estoppel systematically. The requirement of a clear promise is satisfied here. Is there reliance? This is more difficult. The only reliance that we are told of is that the FA actually pay £600,000 which perhaps they might not have done if Bildup had not agreed to discharge the whole debt. It is here that the earlier discussion of whether reliance has to be detrimental would be relevant. If it does have to be detrimental, a court might be unwilling to regard paying off part of an existing debt as a detriment, although this was really the only type of reliance in *Central London Property Trust Ltd* v *High Trees House Ltd* [1947] 1 KB 130. On the other hand it is likely, though we are not told this, that the FA has undertaken other financial responsibilities as a result of being told that this debt has been discharged.

Even if there is reliance in the required sense, is it inequitable for Bildup to go back on their word? The extent of any reliance will be relevant here, as will perhaps the fact that the FA appear to be back in funds. But on the other hand the agreement has not been obtained by the FA by improper means as in *D & C Builders Ltd* v *Rees* [1966] 2 QB 617 and indeed Bildup seemed quite happy to agree to the reduced payment because of the free tickets etc. which they had received. In assessing the equities of the situation it is also relevant to point out that the original debt was only incurred to encourage Bildup to perform *their* existing duty. In fact there is no substitute in this area for thrashing around in the facts of the problem because ultimately it is a question of fact whether it is inequitable to go back on the promise, and by your discussion of the facts you can show your understanding of the sorts of factors that might be relevant.

A concluding point is that the change in the FA's circumstances caused by the sponsorship deal is a clear signal and reminder to discuss what should always be mentioned in this context — the issue of whether promissory estoppel is suspensory or extinctive (see earlier). Even if it would originally have been inequitable for Buildup to go back on their word, if the doctrine is only suspensory, some may argue that it would not now be inequitable for Bildup to revive the debt. Personally, I am not attracted to this sort of argument which seems to leave a sort of sword of Damocles hanging over the debtor which will fall if he should be so foolish as to improve his position subsequently but the examiner will be interested in *your* view and your reasons for holding it. At the least you should make it clear that you are aware of the possibilities even if you cannot decide between them — this is true of almost any issue on which you can be examined but it is particularly true of consideration which, as noted at the outset of this chapter, is a topic in which there is no clear academic consensus on some quite fundamental questions.

5 TERMS OF THE CONTRACT

Up to this stage I have been considering the question of existence, that is, whether a binding contractual obligation has been *created*, and now it is time to turn to the *scope* of such obligations. This issue, the issue of what are the terms of the contract, can be faced from two directions: from the point of view of the positive obligations assumed by the parties, which will be the subject of this chapter, and from the negative point of view of the limitations or exclusions of liability the parties may have tried to incorporate, which, because of the special problems to which it has given rise, will be the subject of its own subsequent chapter. As far as positive terms are concerned, there are three key areas with which you need to be concerned:

(a) The distinction between terms and representations.
(b) The distinction between conditions, warranties and innominate terms.
(c) The nature of implied terms.

I shall look at each of these areas in turn before discussing how they are likely to be examined.

THE DISTINCTION BETWEEN TERMS AND REPRESENTATIONS

The first point to be aware of here is that this is not a distinction between real entities, like the distinction between birds and fish, but is merely two different ways of *classifying* what the parties have said. Thus one cannot recognise a term as opposed to a representation merely from the form of words used. The words, 'This car is a two-year old model' or 'This horse is sound' etc. are capable of being *either* a representation *or* a term and which one they constitute on any given occasion depends in classical theory on the intentions of the parties. This theory should not be allowed to disguise the fact that the reason for classifying statements as terms or representations is to decide what remedy, if any, should be available if the statement is unfulfilled. If the statement is classified as a term, then there is an automatic right at least to damages for its breach, whereas if it is 'merely' a representation which turns out to be untrue (a misrepresentation) there is no *automatic* remedy. As will be seen in chapter 7, there may be the remedy of rescission but that can easily be lost and there may be a remedy of damages but that depends basically on the representor being at fault. The remedies for misrepresentation have in fact been dramatically improved over the past 20 years or so (at some cost in complexity) and it is now rather easier to obtain damages for misrepresentation than it once was but the point remains that the remedies for misrepresentation are *different* from the remedies for breach of a term and are dependent on factors additional to the mere fact of breach.

Thus in *Oscar Chess Ltd* v *Williams* [1957] 1 All ER 325 the result of classifying the statement (that the car was a 1948 model) as a representation was that damages were not automatically available as they would have been had the statement been classified as a term. The purchaser (the motor dealer) instead had to rely on the remedies for misrepresentation which were of no avail (a) because it was too late to rescind and (b) because the seller was not at fault (which at the time meant was not fraudulent but which today, following the Misrepresentation Act 1967, would mean was not negligent).

If the sale had been the other way round, from the motor dealer to Williams, the chances are that precisely the same statement, 'This is a 1948 Morris', would have been regarded as a term of the contract (see *Dick Bentley Productions Ltd* v *Harold Smith (Motors) Ltd* [1965] 2 All ER 65). The dealer would then be liable for damages for breach of contract even if he was in no way at fault. It is worth remembering this very practical difference in result between a representation and a term when considering the more frequently discussed 'tests' for distinguishing terms and representations such as the 'relative degrees of knowledge' test relating to the *Dick Bentley* case, the 'interval' test of *Routledge* v *McKay* [1954] 1 All ER 855 or the 'importance attached' test of *Bannerman* v *White* (1861) 10 CBNS 844. No one pretends that these are really any more than helpful pointers towards the proper classification of the statement and there can be little doubt that the courts have one eye on the remedy which they feel to be appropriate in deciding on that proper classification.

This is not necessarily to belittle the test of the parties' intentions. If the courts can see that the parties clearly intend something to be a term, or to put the same thing another way, that one party clearly assumed full responsibility for his statement and undertook to make it good, then they will obviously give effect to that intention. The various tests come into play where it is not clear what the parties intended and of course in the absence of any clear intention the court will naturally be influenced by the fairness and appropriateness of the result of any given classification.

A word or two needs to be said here about collateral warranties. This is a label which is attached to a misleadingly wide variety of situations. These situations all have in common the fact that the remedies for breach of contract are made available to the innocent party, but there the similarities end. The device of finding a collateral warranty is in fact used for a variety of ends, usually to circumvent some rather inconvenient but unfortunately well-established rule of contract law. It is one of the unfortunate features of our law that unsatisfactory rules are not reformed but are evaded by devices like the collateral warranty, which themselves then add their own complexities to the law.

Thus the collateral warranty can be used to get around the privity rule as in *Shanklin Pier Ltd* v *Detel Products Ltd* [1951] 2 KB 854 where the decorators and the manufacturers were the parties to the main contract of sale of the paint but it was the pier owners who suffered the loss and who were able to recover it for breach of the collateral warranty given by the manufacturers to the pier owners. Similarly, in *De Lassalle* v *Guildford* [1901] 2 KB 215 the device was used to get around the parol evidence rule (the rule that a written contract contains *all* the terms of that contract, a rule which has so many exceptions that it is no longer sensible to refer to it as a rule except as a prima facie presumption) but in *Heilbut, Symons & Co.* v *Buckleton* [1913] AC 30, where a company in which the plaintiff subsequently bought shares was described as 'a rubber company', the House of Lords reversed a jury's finding that this amounted to a collateral warranty, there being 'an entire absence of any evidence to support the existence of such a collateral contract'. This decision, if rigidly followed alongside the rule that no damages were available for innocent misrepresentations, would have represented a fundamental defect in English contract law. However, in practice the courts were often prepared to treat statements as collateral warranties, as in the *Dick Bentley* case, and still provide a right to damages where that was appropriate.

The point to be understood is that in *Dick Bentley* the inconvenient rule that is being avoided is the rule that damages are not available for innocent misrepresentations. The way to provide a right to damages is simply to classify the statement as a warranty (i.e., a term) rather than as a representation and there is no need to label it as 'collateral'. Lord Denning MR recognised this in *Dick Bentley* when he said 'it is not necessary to speak of it as collateral'. Where, on the other hand, the rule being avoided means you cannot enforce the statement as part of the main contract, e.g., because the main contract is between two other parties as in *Shanklin Pier* or is illegal as in *Strongman (1945) Ltd* v *Sincock* [1955] 2 QB 525, it is necessary to speak of a separate collateral contract — the plaintiff can enforce the separate collateral contract even though he cannot enforce the main contract because it is illegal or because he is not a party to it (see Wedderburn [1959] CLJ 58 for a detailed discussion on this point).

Another use of collateral warranties which needs to be distinguished is illustrated in *Esso Petroleum Co. Ltd* v *Mardon* [1976] QB 801 where a collateral warranty was found — not that the estimated throughput of the garage would be 200,000 gallons of petrol — but that reasonable care and skill had gone into the estimate and thus Mr Mardon was compensated not for loss of his bargain but for reliance damages — the money thrown away on trying to run the business. One would expect this use of collateral warranty to wither away following the introduction of the Misrepresentation Act 1967 (the Act was inapplicable to *Esso Petroleum Co. Ltd* v *Mardon* because the facts arose before 1967) since the same result can be achieved directly under s. 2(1) (see chapter 7 below) but in fact the *Esso Petroleum Co. Ltd* v *Mardon* type of collateral warranty was utilised again at first instance in *Thake* v *Maurice* [1984] 2 All ER 513.

This case illustrates very well the differences between the different types of collateral warranty. Mr Thake contracted for a vasectomy to be performed on him but despite the operation's apparent success still managed subsequently to impregnate Mrs Thake (the couple already having five children). The explanation was that a vasectomy can in rare cases reverse itself naturally (male readers will appreciate it, and no doubt females will understand, if I do not go into any further technical details on what can be a rather sensitive point!). There was no question of the operation itself not being carried out skilfully but the complaint against the doctor was that he hadn't warned Mr Thake of the risk of natural reversal and the High Court judge, Peter Pain J, held that this meant that the doctor had in effect warranted that the operation would make Mr Thake *irreversibly* sterile, as opposed to the more normal warranty that the operation would be carried out with all due care and skill. Thus a full contractual warranty or promise of permanent sterility was the main basis of the decision (the Court of Appeal subsequently reversed the judgment on that point) but the judge also relied on *Esso Petroleum Co. Ltd* v *Mardon* and found a collateral warranty based on that case. This second warranty is perfectly understandable but it is of a different kind — it is not a promise about what the other party will get under the contract but a promise about how one party will conduct the negotiations leading up to it. And as recognised in *Esso Petroleum Co. Ltd* v *Mardon*, it will lead to a different measure of damages (not loss of bargain). It is at this point that Pain J's judgment is open to criticism since he assumed that on whichever warranty he based his decision the result would be the same. In fact, if one asks, 'What would have been the Thakes' position if the promise to advise carefully had been carried out?' the answer is they would have known about a remote risk but would have felt justified in ignoring it and Mrs Thake would still have ended up pregnant. Thus the breach of the *second* warranty didn't cause any damage, in the sense that the pregnancy was the damage. On the other hand, if the warning had been given, Mrs Thake would probably have realised rather more quickly that she was pregnant instead of regarding it as backache, fondly believing that it was impossible for her to be pregnant. In the Court of Appeal [1986] 1 All ER 497 liability was based on contractual negligence rather than warranty but the damages point was recognised and an allowance was made for the fact that the negligence had prevented the opportunity for an abortion and its consequent distress.

CONDITIONS, WARRANTIES AND INNOMINATE TERMS

Once having determined that something is a term, that will often be sufficient if the only remedy required is damages. But in some cases, it is not enough to claim damages. The breach may be such that the innocent party no longer considers it to be worth continuing with the contract — it may not be worth performing his own side given what he is going to get in return. The law recognises this by allowing the innocent party, in certain situations, to terminate the contract. The question is, though, *when* can the innocent party terminate a contract for breach, as opposed to merely claiming damages. One tradition is to make the right to terminate vary with the type of term broken — if the term is a condition, then breach gives rise to the right to terminate whereas if it is only a warranty, then damages only can be claimed. This approach is most clearly enshrined in the Sale of Goods Act 1979 (originally 1893) which designates certain terms as conditions or warranties and prescribes the remedies for these distinct classes. The point you must note is that the distinction is made, just like the distinction between terms and representations, for the purpose of deciding on the appropriate remedy. Designating terms as conditions and warranties is a way of prescribing in advance what the available remedies for breach of these terms should be. If everyone knows the rules of this particular game (a pretty big if, you might think) then at least this has the advantage of predictability and of letting the parties know where they stand. Conversely, it has the unfortunate effect that a party may be entitled to terminate a contract because a condition has been broken, even though that breach causes very little or no damage and there is no real justification for escaping one's own obligations under the contract. Thus in *Reardon Smith Line Ltd* v *Hansen Tangen* [1976] 3 All ER 570 an oil-tanker which was to be chartered was described as Osaka number 354 (i.e., the yard where it was built) when in fact it was Oshima number 004 (but was otherwise in every way exactly as specified). Because the market for oil-tankers had collapsed, the charterers sought to argue that the description of the tanker's origin was a condition which would enable them to terminate and so get out of what had become for them a bad bargain. The House of Lords rejected this absurd result and held the description was not a condition but an innominate term. Now the point about an innominate term is that the remedy is *not* prescribed in advance (thus any advantage of predictability is lost) but the actual remedy depends on the seriousness of the breach (thus improving the law's flexibility and ability to do justice). In a case like *Reardon Smith*, the answer is obvious, that the effects of the breach are trivial and do not justify termination but do not assume that this is always the result in innominate-term cases. If an innominate term is broken with a very serious effect, then the innocent party could be entitled to terminate — if, in the words of Diplock LJ in *Hongkong Fir Shipping Co. Ltd v Kawasaki KK Ltd* [1962] 2 QB 26, 'it deprives the innocent party of substantially the whole benefit under the contract'. Many students wrongly assume that an innominate term only ever leads to damages since this is what seems to have happened in most of the decided cases. The reason for this is that the decided cases are cases where the effects are *not* sufficiently serious which is precisely why the plaintiff is arguing that the term broken is really a condition which gives rise to the right to terminate irrespective of the effects of the breach. If one has a breach with obviously serious effects then the case is unlikely to go to the courts for classification because either way, whether it is a condition or an innominate term, it will give rise to the right to terminate. The litigated cases are by definition those where the effects do not justify termination and it is thus important to know whether the plaintiff can rely on the term being technically a condition in order to terminate. The *Hongkong Fir* case itself is rather borderline in that the effects were substantial — the ship was out of action for five months out of a two-year period — but not sufficiently so as to deprive the charterers of substantially the whole benefit, which is no doubt why they tried to argue the term was a condition in order to make the *effects* of the breach irrelevant.

Another prevalent misconception and over-simplification about innominate terms versus conditions and warranties is that the use of the condition-and-warranty approach always promotes certainty whereas the innominate-term approach promotes flexibility instead. In fact in some situations, designating a term as a condition will promote no more certainty than will designating it as innominate. Where one has a non-standard, one-off contract, a judicial decision that a term is a condition is not likely to help anyone. It won't normally promote certainty or predictability for the parties to the dispute since they don't know until the court pronounces its decision whether the term is a condition or warranty and as far as they are concerned the court might just as well say that the effects justify termination as say that the term is a condition. And saying it is a condition helps no one else since the contract is a one-off and thus the decision can't be an effective guide to others (quite apart from the fact that others are unlikely to know about the decision). The importance of realising this lies in the fact that it should help you to decide *when* to apply the condition/warranty approach — there is best reason for applying it where the contract you are considering is one in common use where a decision that a particular term *is* a condition can possibly help *other* parties in the future (although it does nothing for the present dispute) and there is some chance that others using that common form of contract will take the trouble to find out how the court has classified the particular clause. This should help you to understand *Bunge Corporation v Tradax Export SA* [1981] 2 All ER 513 where the House of Lords held that a standard clause in an international sales contract requiring 15 days' notice of readiness of shipping vessel was a condition. Commercial organisations using a standard clause can be expected to learn of and act on a judicial decision that a particular clause is a condition (see also *The Mihalis Angelos* [1971] 1 QB 164).

Yet another misconception in this area is that the innominate-term approach is essentially new and that it all originated in Diplock LJ's judgment in *Hongkong Fir* in 1961. In fact it is really only the name that is new. The courts were allowing or not allowing termination on the basis of the effects of the breach long before the condition/warranty distinction was canonised in the Sale of Goods Act 1893. Indeed in the cases of *Poussard v Spiers* (1876) 1 QBD 351 and *Bettini v Gye* (1876) 1 QBD 183, often cited as illustrations of the distinction between conditions and warranties, the courts looked in fact at the effect of the breaches rather than at the nature of the terms broken. The point is clearly and helpfully discussed in Smith & Thomas, *A Casebook on Contract*, 10th ed., p. 422.

One last point that can usefully be made at this stage and which can enable you to show that you fully understand the issues in this area concerns the question of whether it is really true to say that there are three types of terms — conditions, warranties and innominate — and whether the condition/warranty approach is really distinct from the innominate-term approach. The traditional classification of terms can be represented diagramatically as in Figure 5.1.

This is apparently a neat threefold classification of terms, but it appears to recognise that there are some terms, 'warranties', which, no matter how seriously or flagrantly broken, give no right to the innocent party to terminate. The potential injustice in this has led some writers to suggest that in reality there are not three types of term but only two (see Reynolds (1981) 92 LQR 541 and Treitel, *The Law of Contract*, 9th ed., p. 712). The first of the two types would be conditions, whereby any breach gives rise to the right to terminate, these terms being useful in recurrent contracts since it enables the injured party to know for sure that he can terminate. For all other terms, it matters not whether they be called warranties, innominate terms or even non-conditions, the remedy for breach would be at least damages but also possibly termination if the effects of the breach were sufficiently fundamental. There is no need on this view for a distinction between warranties and innominate terms because even for warranties the option to terminate should

Figure 5.1

Representations

Not part of the contract. No automatic right to damages. Damages only normally available if representor at fault. Primary remedy rescission but, being equitable, subject to limits (See chapter 7 on misrepresentation).

Terms

Part of the contract. D is effectively promising or guaranteeing that something is or will be so. Therefore automatic right to damages if not so.

Conditions

Important terms — other party's performance is conditional on this term being performed. Therefore remedy of termination available in addition to damages — this remedy available even if the breach does not have serious consequences.

Warranties

Less important terms 'collateral to main purpose' — no right to terminate, merely damages for actual loss.

Innominate Terms

Terms for which remedy not prescribed in advance. Termination allowed if effects of breach serious enough to deprive innocent party of substantially the whole benefit under the contract otherwise only damages available.

Figure 5.2

Representations	*Terms*
Not part of the contract. No automatic right to damages. Damages only normally available if representor at fault. Primary remedy rescission but, being equitable, subject to limits (See chapter 7 on misrepresentation).	Part of the contract. D is effectively promising or guaranteeing that something is or will be so. Therefore automatic right to damages if not so.

Conditions	*Warranties*
Important terms — other party's performance is conditional on this term being performed. Therefore remedy of termination available in additional to damages — this remedy available even if the breach does not have serious consequences.	All terms other than conditions — damages always available — termination available if effects of breach sufficiently serious or e.g., if breach shows D does not regard himself as bound by the contract.

be available for particularly bad or flagrant breaches. Ormrod LJ appeared to be of this view when in *The Hansa Nord* [1976] QB 44 he said:

> the court will be freer to regard stipulations, as a matter of construction, as warranties, if what might be called the 'back-up' rule of the common law is available to protect buyers who ought to be able to reject [i.e., terminate] in proper circumstances. I doubt whether, strictly speaking, this involves the creation of a third category of stipulations; rather, it recognises another ground for holding that a buyer is entitled to reject, namely, that, *de facto*, the consideration for his promise has been wholly destroyed.

On this view the diagram illustrating the different classes of terms would look like Figure 5.2.

Whilst this in many ways is an attractive way of looking at things it cannot really be said that it represents the current position although it is a possible way in which matters might eventually be resolved. It is therefore a possibility to which you should show the examiner that you are alert and, even better, it is a possibility which you should be prepared to evaluate. What are its drawbacks?

(a)   In terms of inconsistent authorities — cases like *Hongkong Fir*, where the courts clearly envisaged a threefold classification.
(b)   More importantly, in terms of policy. Isn't there an argument that to amalgamate innominate terms and warranties would be to deprive contracting parties of a distinction they might wish to utilise?

Just as it may be important in some contexts for the injured party to know for sure which are the terms for breach of which he can terminate, might it not be equally important for him (and even more important for the guilty party) to know the terms for breach of which he certainly can't terminate? Or, in a more interventionist spirit, should the law be prepared to say that the innocent party has the right to terminate for breach of any term if the effects of the breach are sufficiently serious? There are no easy answers to these sorts of questions but they are the sorts of questions that you should be prepared to ask and to which you should suggest tentative answers — it does not particularly matter what answer you give as long as you give your reasons.

IMPLIED TERMS

Another distinction between different types of terms is that between express and implied terms. This distinction cuts across the previous ones in that both express and implied terms may be conditions or warranties or innominate terms (in so far as there is a distinction between these last two). The distinction is also of a different type in that the distinction between express and implied terms has nothing to do with the remedies available for breach which, as I have said, is the whole *raison d'être* of the condition/warranty distinction. The issue in the area of implied terms is one of scope and existence — the scope of the contractual obligation, how far does it go beyond what has been expressly agreed on? The important thing to remember about implied terms is that, in accordance with the general freedom-of-contract approach, English law is sparing in the way it will imply terms which the parties haven't themselves seen fit to include expressly, and so as a general rule the courts will only imply terms that they feel the parties must, of necessity, have agreed to if they had thought about it. This *general* rule, often put in the form of the 'officious bystander' test (who for his officiousness is testily suppressed by a common, 'Oh, of course') is general in the sense that it can be applied to any contract (although the most frequent result is that no term is implied) and is supposedly a mere application of the parties' intentions. For this reason Treitel, in *The Law of Contract*, refers to this sort of implied term as a term implied in fact (one that the parties in fact intended) as contrasted with a term implied in law to which different rules imply. Because the rules for this latter category are quite different, Treitel's distinction is much more significant than the threefold distinction observed in other textbooks and unfortunately rather tediously repeated in many an essay, between terms implied by statute, by the courts and by custom. Thus you would do well to read the ten pages (pp. 185-195) of Treitel's *The Law of Contract*, 9th ed. on implied terms and note the principal distinctions between his first two categories, the most fundamental of which is that terms implied in law have nothing to do with the parties' intentions but are imposed on the parties as a matter of policy. Thus in contracts of employment, a term is implied that the employer will provide a safe system of work etc. even though such a term is of most use against an employer who doesn't regard his employees' safety to be of any consequence. The term is implied as a matter of policy even though it may be directly contrary to one party's intention. (See also the impact of the term implied in *Johnstone* v *Bloomsbury Health Authority* [1991] 2 WLR 1362 on the *express* terms of the contract.) Many terms implied in law have been adopted and confirmed by statute (e.g., those in the Sale of Goods Act 1979 concerning fitness for purpose, merchantable quality etc.) but the courts can recognise new ones.

   Liverpool City Council v *Irwin* [1977] AC 239 is an important modern example of this process where the question was whether a term could be implied into a tenancy of a flat in a tower block. The case is notable in the first place because in the Court of Appeal ([1976] QB 319), Lord Denning MR tried to liberalise the test for terms implied in fact and held that such a term could be implied wherever it was just and reasonable to do so. The majority, however, adhered to the traditional test of necessity and were upheld on this point in the House of Lords. However, in the House of Lords the argument switched to whether a term could be implied in law, as a legal incident of this type of tenancy, and it was found that a term could, on this basis, be implied. Students often find it difficult to understand why the tenant's appeal was dismissed (apart from allowing £5 damages for flooding cisterns!) if a term was implied, but a careful reading of the case shows that the tenants were arguing for a term imposing an *absolute* obligation on the council to keep the lifts working and the staircase lit whereas the term found to be *necessary* in this type of contract was one requiring the council to *take reasonable care* to keep them in reasonable repair and usability — and it was not proved that the council had failed to take such reasonable care so no breach was proved (cf. *Wilson* v *Best Travel* [1993] 1 All ER 353 for a similar result in a different context — but compare the result in *Wong Mee Wan* v *Kwa*

Kin Travel [1995] 4 All ER 745 where the implied term was that holiday services would be provided with reasonable care and skill even if actually provided by a third party. If the third party failed to act with reasonable care and skill, the defendants were, in effect, strictly liable for that failure.). Notice that the word 'reasonable' appears here not as the test for implying the term but as part of the description of the scope of the term implied. Having said that, Lord Cross of Chelsea did say in *Liverpool CC v Irwin* that for a term implied in law, 'the court will naturally ask itself whether ... the term in question would be one which it would be reasonable to insert'. Whilst by contrast for terms implied in fact: 'it is not enough for the court to say that the suggested term is a reasonable one'.

Thus when in a subsequent Court of Appeal case, *Shell UK Ltd v Lostock Garage Ltd* [1977] 1 All ER 481, Lord Denning MR takes up the distinction between terms implied in law (what he calls the first category) and terms implied in fact (his second category) it is not surprising that it is Lord Cross's speech that he cites for the proposition that the test for the first category (though not for the second) is one of reasonableness. In contrast, Lord Wilberforce in *Liverpool City Council v Irwin* (cited with approval by the Privy Council in *Tai Hing Cotton Mill v Liu Chong Hing Bank* [1985] 2 All ER 947 at p. 955) adhered to the test of necessity even for terms implied in law although even he at one point talked about 'what it is reasonable to expect of a landlord' and it is notable that in the end the House of Lords implied exactly the same term as Lord Denning in the Court of Appeal. Further support for Lord Wilberforce's view that the test of necessity is relevant to terms implied in law comes from the House of Lords decision in *Scally v Southern Health and Social Services Board* [1991] 3 WLR 778 where Lord Bridge endorsed again 'the clear distinction' between terms implied in fact and those implied in law. The distinction lay 'between the search for an implied term *necessary* to give business efficacy to a particular contract and the search, *based on wider considerations*, for a term which the *law* will imply as a *necessary* incident of a definable category of contractual relationship' (emphasis added). See *Phang* [1993] JBL 242 for further discussion of this case and for the argument that the word necessary must clearly mean something different in the two different types of term and that the key phrase in the second type (terms implied in law) is the phrase 'based on wider considerations' which imports policy considerations and, in effect, the notion of reasonableness. It is difficult to resist the conclusion that the courts are playing with words to avoid expressly adopting a test based on reasonableness which might introduce the degree of liberality probably favoured by Lord Denning and are retaining the reference to necessity even for terms implied in law to maintain an acceptable degree of control over their implication. As usual, what you have to do is to be aware of the different formulations and ways in which they can be manipulated to achieve the desired result.

THE EXAMINATION

I have now identified the three major issues in this area and the task now is to work out how this might be presented in an examination. This is not an area like consideration where there are a large number of little sub-issues, some of which might crop up and some of which might not. Happily the issues here are fairly large, central ones which are almost bound to crop up in some form or another. In particular, the distinctions between terms and representations and between conditions, warranties and innominate terms are so fundamental that they are guaranteed to arise in any examination. The question is, though, how? The condition/warranty/innominate-term issue is a good topic for a self-contained essay question, particularly perhaps where the subject is being examined at first-year level. If, on the other hand, you are being examined at second or third-year level, then you can perhaps expect the issues to be more mixed up — e.g., in a question about misrepresentation (particularly the term/misrepresentation/collateral-warranty distinction) or (for the condition/warranty distinction) in a problem concerning discharge of contract. Again, careful attention to past papers is likely to pay dividends, but it really shouldn't matter how the issues come up if you have the principles clear in your mind, and drawing up your own schematic diagrams, like the ones earlier in this chapter, is a good way of achieving this.

A Problem

> Tennis star, Nick Lobum, agreed to act as coach to Buster Slasher, the managing director of Slasher Rackets Ltd. The terms of the contract state that Lobum will not play in any tournament except as Slasher's partner in the 'doubles' and will use only equipment manufactured by Slasher Rackets Ltd. Lobum and Slasher entered the Kinky Cola International Tournament but on the day of the first round of the doubles, Slasher was taken ill and was unable to play. Lobum accepted an invitation to partner Rod Nastium and, by mistake, took on court a racket cover manufactured by Tinequip Ltd. Slasher has informed Lobum that he is repudiating the contract. Advise Lobum.

There are two immediate points to note about this problem:

(a)   The question clearly says 'the terms of the contract state' so one knows that they are terms, not misrepresentations and a discussion of that distinction would be irrelevant.

(b)   Slasher is said to be repudiating the contract so that the condition/warranty/innominate-term distinction is going to be important. Therefore, it would not be amiss to have a *short* introductory paragraph setting out the distinction between conditions and warranties and concluding that if either of the terms can be shown to be a condition and also be shown to have been broken, then Slasher will indeed be entitled to repudiate.

Having said that, and having shown the examiner that you are clear on that very basic point, you could then take each term in turn and examine its nature and whether it is broken. First of all, there is the term 'not to play in any tournament except as Slasher's partner in the doubles'. Is this a condition, does it go to the root of the contract? This question is usually easier to state than to answer but there is little evidence here that this term is central to the contract. One could argue from the opening sentence of the problem that the agreement is essentially about coaching and that the playing in tournaments is incidental to that. That of course might suggest that the term is only a warranty and its breach therefore only to be remedied by an award of damages. Indeed that might be the appropriate remedy in this case but of course you must show the examiner that you are aware of the third possibility, that the term is an innominate one. This wouldn't be likely to make any difference to the remedy on these particular facts but it would leave open the option of allowing a repudiation if the same term were broken in the future in a much more serious way (e.g., Lobum partners the managing director of Tinequip in a highly publicised tournament) or if the term is broken persistently and repeatedly. Furthermore, as the contract between Lobum and Slasher appears not to be a standard one, there is little utility in adopting the condition/warranty distinction — it is unlikely to further predictability for anyone else, as no one else is likely to use this form of contract, although it may possibly help Lobum and Slasher if the contract does continue and there is a further dispute about this term in future. On balance the term is likely to be classified as innominate but the effects of the breach are surely not such as to deprive Slasher of substantially the whole benefit of the contract. So, just as in *Hongkong Fir Shipping Co. Ltd* v *Kawasaki KK Ltd* [1962] 2 QB 26, the breach would justify merely an award of damages.

Before moving on to the second term, one ought also to ask, has the term been broken, because if not, there is no question of any remedy at all. At first sight it may seem obvious that this term is broken but it is here that the issue of implied terms might be worth mentioning. The term on the face of it is an absolute one — perhaps too absolute. (It might even be an unreasonable restraint of trade, for which see chapter 10.) Can it really be supposed that it was intended to apply when Slasher was ill? Could a term be implied that Lobum should be free to partner others when Slasher is unavailable? The answer to that question is not as important as being able to pose the question and to explain the approach that the courts will adopt in answering it. Since the contract is not one of common occurrence, the test for terms implied in law would not be applicable and it would be a question of applying the officious-bystander test of necessity. Would the parties have said, 'Oh, of course', if presented with this term at the outset? Is it necessary to give business efficacy to the contract? These are questions which permit of various answers but it is permissible, once having stated the correct tests, to use common sense in discussing the facts. So one could argue that without such an implied term, Lobum could end up playing no competitive tennis for two years if Slasher declines to enter any tournaments, a situation that is hardly in the business interests of either party since the provision for Lobum's use of Slasher's equipment would be of no value if Lobum is never on court. It is surely pointless from both parties' points of view to have Lobum off the court when Slasher can't play and this might be an argument for implying a term. Furthermore, without such an implication the contract is more likely to be regarded as an unreasonable restraint of trade. On the other hand the courts only rarely imply terms in fact and so a suitable note of caution should be left in your answer.

In respect of the second term, again the question is whether it is a condition, warranty or innominate term and again there would appear to be little utility in regarding it as a condition. However, it might be arguable that the contract could be seen as essentially about sponsorship and puiblicity rather than coaching so that the parties might have regarded this term as essential — as a condition — but there is no real evidence of this. It might be helpful to know what fee Lobum is being paid. If the fee is appropriate to coaching then the use of Slasher Racket's equipment may be seen as peripheral — but if the fee is a huge one that can only be justified on a sponsorship and advertising basis, then the second term may be more likely to be a condition. The point again is to discuss the alternatives and this involves discussing the facts in an intelligent way — posing questions like how much is Lobum being paid and stressing factors that are important and relevant such as the fact that the effects of the breach in this case are relatively trivial — it is only a racket *cover*, after all, which is taken on court. Although, as usual, your actual conclusion is not of itself important, it would be rash to conclude that this term is only a warranty as opposed to an innominate term because that would commit you to the view that Slasher would *never* be able to repudiate for breach of this term — even if, for example, Lobum went on court deliberately plastered from head to foot in Tinequip gear in a highly publicised match. The risk of a deliberate, flagrant, highly damaging breach is always there for most contractual terms so it is usually unwise to classify a term as a strict warranty.

Talking of deliberate breaches, it is worth saying something about the fact that Lobum's breach of the second term is 'by mistake'. Many students jump to the conclusion that, because the breach is not deliberate, Lobum can be excused altogether. This betrays a misunderstanding of the basis of contractual liability. You are bound in contract because you have promised and the normal rule is that if you fail to fulfil your promise you are liable — liability is strict. It is no defence not say that you did your best — that is not good enough when you have promised. Thus it is no defence for a retailer in breach of the implied term of merchantable quality to say that the goods came to him in a sealed container from the manufacturer and that it is the manufacturer who is at fault — the retailer is strictly liable for the quality of the goods that he sells. Similarly it would be no defence for Lobum to say that he didn't intend to take a Tinequip cover on court — he has promised only to use Slasher Rackets equipment and he is in breach of that promise.

That is not to say though that the accidental nature of the breach is totally irrelevant. If one is assessing how serious are the consequences of the breach, then the fact that the breach is accidental may be important for it shows that the breach is less likely to be repeated. It is more reasonable to expect the innocent party to continue to be bound by a contract where the other party is *trying* to perform faithfully than if the other party has shown himself to have a total disregard for the innocent party's rights. Note in this connection that in *The Mihalis Angelos* [1971] 1 QB 164 one reason for classifying the term as a condition was that a party breaking the term must have acted dishonestly or at least negligently.

Furthermore, it should be stressed that whilst contractual liability is *usually* strict, it does depend on the nature of the contract and the precise type of lialbity being assumed. Where the promise is to take reasonable care — as for example was found in *Liverpool City Council* v *Irwin* [1977] AC 239 — then clearly it *is* a defence to show that you did take such care. This is particularly true in contracts for professional services where, e.g., a doctor is not normally in a position to promise or guarantee a favourable result. The most he can do is to promise to exercise due care and skill in trying to bring about such a result. (Cf. the confirmation of this by the Court of Appeal in *Thake* v *Maurice* [1986] 1 All ER 497 where they reversed Peter Pain J's ruling that the surgeon had promised not only to use due care and skill in carrying out a vasectomy but had further promised that Mr Thake would become irreversibly sterile.)

It is also worth mentioning that, particularly in business contexts, there is unlikely to be any action taken where a breach is non-deliberate or without fault. The potential damage to the plaintiff's reputation generally, not to mention his future business relationship with the defendant, if he should sue for every technical breach of contract will, in most cases, outweigh any temporary advantages to be gained by suing. (See the influential article by Macaulay, 'Non-contractual relations in business', *American Sociological Review*, vol. 28 (1963), pp. 55–66, an abridged version of which is more accessible in Aubert, *Sociology of Law*, pp. 194–209.) Of course, it is different where the breach is deliberate or there is unlikely to be any future relationship anyway or where the defendant can pass on the liability to someone else who is at fault, as in the case of the retailer of negligently manufactured goods.

You may feel that I have now digressed somewhat from the question, but this is not a model answer and it is only by understanding these sorts of issues that you can discuss a problem of this nature properly and display the sort of 'feel' for the area that the examiner will be looking for. The rules in this area are fairly general and unspecific and problem questions demand a sympathetic discussion of the facts rather than the recital of elusive rules of law.

An Essay

'The manner in which the law of contract determines and classifies the contents of a contract is not rational, nor precise, nor helpful.' Discuss.

An all-too-common reaction to this sort of question, indeed to any essay question, is to write down all you know about the contents of a contract, rather than trying to discuss the opinion stated in the question. This tactic is mistaken for a number of reasons.

First, it will annoy the examiner, who could easily have said 'Write all you know about . . .' if that is what he wanted.

Secondly, having annoyed him, it will bore him and if there is one thing meaner than an annoyed examiner, it is a bored one.

Thirdly, it will leave him wondering whether you really understand the material you are reciting or whether you are merely repeating it parrot fashion.

Finally it may mean that you fail even to mention important points that need discussion.

Taking this last point first, the question does not merely refer to how the contents of a contract are classified but also how they are determined so it would be wrong to talk only about the terms of the contract without discussing how they are to be distinguished from representations, which are not part of the contents of the contract.

The proper technique for answering this or any other question is to *answer the question* and *discuss*:

(a) How *does* the law of contract determine and classify the contents of a contract?

(b) Does the answer to (a) reveal a rational or precise or helpful way of going about it?

Under (a) you need first of all to explain differences between terms and representations, mentioning the standard tests like relative degrees of knowledge etc. (see the earlier discussion) and illustrating the difference by referring to one or two cases, such as *Oscar Chess Ltd* v *Williams* [1957] 1 All ER 325. You could also mention the parol evidence rule and the use of collateral warranties. At this point there is a choice to be made. You can either *now* pose question (b) about the distinction between terms and representations — i.e., is the distinction drawn in a rational or precise or helpful way? — or you can postpone that question until you have dealt with the whole of part (a) of your answer, i.e., until after you have explained how the law classifies the terms of the contract. The latter is probably the softer option since it enables you to spend the whole of the first half of your answer merely expounding the law as it is which should not be too difficult if you have learnt it properly in an organised way. The first option is probably the more impressive if you can manage it since it emphasises to the examiner throughout that you are answering the question that he has set. So, if you adopt the first option you will now have to ask whether the distinction between terms and representations is rational, precise or helpful. Your own views are what counts but one view might be that:

(a)   Yes, it is *rational*, there is some logic to the distinction based on what the parties intend and what they don't intend to be contractually bound by.

(b)   No, it is not *precise* because it is very difficult in a particular case to know what the parties intended — hence the standard objective tests, which don't always yield obvious answers — contrast the case of *Hopkins* v *Tanqueray* (1854) 15 CB 130 and *Schawel* v *Reade* [1913] 2 IR 64 for example.

(c)   Yes, on balance it is *helpful* because once you have made the admittedly difficult classification you have a convenient and succinct way of distinguishing those cases where the applicable remedies are those for breach of contract from those where the applicable remedies are those for misrepresentation.

You may well feel that you would wish to answer the above three points in the opposite way and that is perfectly acceptable provided that you back up your views with sensible arguments.

Next you will have to return to part (a) of the question and explain how the law classifies terms into conditions, warranties and innominate terms and what are the consequences of classifying a particular term in a particular way, again illustrating your answer with cases such as *Hongkong Fir Shipping Co. Ltd* v *Kawasaki KK Ltd* [1962] 2 QB 26; *The Mihalis Angelos* [1971] 1 QB 164; *Bunge Corporation* v *Tradax Export SA* [1981] 2 All ER 513 and *The Hansa Nord* [1976] QB 44. Of course you need not, indeed must not, recite all the facts of these cases. The knack is to extract from them in a pithy manner sufficient material to indicate that you know them thoroughly and understand their significance (even if your acquaintance with them is in fact rather brief, although closer encounters are to be recommended). Thus you might say of *The Hansa Nord* that 'The Court of Appeal was even prepared to apply the innominate (or, as Denning dubbed it, intermediate) term approach in that bastion of the condition/warranty dichotomy, the contract for the sale of goods, the goods in this case being citrus pulp pellets to be used as cattle food.'

Having explained and illustrated the distinctions you then need to ask whether they are rational, precise or helpful. There doesn't seem to be anything *ir*rational about enabling the parties to distinguish:

(a)   Those terms breach of which will automatically entitle the other party to escape his own obligations and repudiate.

(b)   Those terms where the appropriate remedy for breach will vary, depending on the actual effects of the breach.

(c)   Those terms (no doubt comparatively rare these) where the breach will never justify repudiation, but only damages.

As far as the second issue, precision, is concerned you might make the following points. The word 'condition' itself is notoriously ambiguous, sometimes being used in its more natural sense of something which is *not* a term at all (in the sense that anyone will be *liable* for its breach) but on which the creation or continuation of the contract is dependent, i.e., conditions precedent and subsequent. It was this ambiguity that helped the House of Lords in *L. Schuler AG* v *Wickman Machine Tool Sales Ltd* [1974] AC 235 to conclude that a term described in the contract as a 'condition' was not a condition (as opposed to a warranty or innominate term) in law. Given that sort of ambiguity one might legitimately ask whether there is any utility in having the expression 'condition' at all and whether it might be better to refer, more long-windedly but less ambiguously, to terms which automatically give rise to the right to repudiate if broken. Certainly, for anyone drafting a contract, it would be safest to define condition expressly in this way.

Quite apart from the ambiguity of the terminology there is the difficulty of being able to predict when the courts are going to treat something as a condition and when they are going to take the innominate-term approach. This relates to the third issue, of whether the present classification is helpful or not, as much as to the issue of precision. There is little point in having precise terminology if no one knows when or to what circumstances that terminology will be applied. You could make the point here that the apparent certainty fostered by the condition/warranty approach is something of an illusion where the term is not one in common use.

It is useful if you can end your essay with a brief conclusion which reminds the examiner that you have been tailoring your discussion to the question asked. The examiner usually will not and should not be looking for any specific 'correct' conclusion but nevertheless, just in case he is, it is not a bad idea to hedge your bets and conclude that, e.g., the law's approach is fairly rational but lacks precision (which is perhaps to some extent inevitable) and is therefore not as helpful as one might wish for. Again, the actual conclusion you reach is not as important as the way you reach it and the essential thing is to explain *why* you have reached it. Thankfully, there is now one conclusion that you have reached for certain — the conclusion of this chapter!

6 EXEMPTION CLAUSES

In order to understand any area of law fully it is not enough to have a static picture of the law as it stands at the moment unless you also have an appreciation of the way in which the law has developed in the past in order to arrive at its present position. Only by knowing where it has come from can you hope to have any real understanding of where it might go to in the future and so an insight into its historical perspective is necessary in order to see how it is likely to develop. In the context of exclusion clauses where there have been important changes in recent years and the law is in a state of transition it is particularly important to be able to see the law in its historical perspective in order to understand properly the current trends. Thus this chapter will commence with a historical survey before analysing the key issues in the current situation and investigating how to deal with these in the context of an examination.

HISTORICAL DEVELOPMENT

The Industrial Revolution and the consequent growth of the railways and other large monopolistic suppliers of goods and services provided the opportunity for undertakings like the railways to standardise the terms on which they were willing to do business and include within those terms clauses excluding or limiting liabilities that would otherwise be imposed on them. Any disputes arising from these standard-form contracts came before judges who, in the 19th and early 20th centuries, were still steeped in notions of *laissez-faire* economics and freedom of contract and who were consequently reluctant to interfere with the terms under which the parties had apparently contracted (even though economic and political theory had by now moved on from the *laissez-faire* ideal, this had not yet percolated through to the legal profession who, like most professions, are usually a generation behind in their knowledge of theories from other disciplines). That is not to say that exemption clauses are always a bad thing and that the courts should have cut them down indiscriminately. It may be in the consumer's interest on occasions for a supplier to exclude a certain type of liability if that enables the service to be provided at a lower charge, particularly if the consumer is already likely to be insured against that sort of loss. This is even more true in contracts between two businesses but the courts' attachment to freedom of contract meant that they regarded themselves as powerless to interfere even where the exemption clause was imposed unfairly and oppressively on someone who had no real choice about whether to contract or who lacked real knowledge of the terms. As late as 1930, a clause excluding liability for personal injury to an illiterate railway passenger, which was only available on page 552 of a timetable costing 6d (the railway tickets having cost 2s 7d) was held to be effective by the Court of Appeal: *Thompson* v *London, Midland & Scottish Railway Co.* [1930] 1 KB 41. Despite decisions such as these (which Atiyah explains as the judiciary's attempt to protect the railway companies against juries over-sympathetic to passengers, see The *Rise and Fall of Freedom of Contract,* p. 732) the courts had already started to realise the dangers in allowing exclusion clauses to operate without any controls at all and were beginning to do what they could, within their conceptual apparatus of freedom of contract, to keep clauses within reasonable bounds. Thus in 1894 in *Richardson, Spence & Co.* v *Rowntree* [1894] AC 217 the House of Lords actually upheld a jury's finding that a steerage passenger on a ship (who belonged to a class of persons who one would not expect to read small print) had not been given reasonable notice of an exemption clause, on a folded-up ticket, partly obliterated by a stamp. But control by denying that the clause was a term of the contract was doomed to fail as it was already accepted that precise knowledge of the actual terms of the clause was unnecessary (see *Parker* v *South Eastern Railway Co.* (1877) 2 CPD 416) and a supplier could ensure that his terms were incorporated by getting the customer to sign a document containing them (albeit in small print) as in *L'Estrange* v *F. Graucob Ltd* [1934] 2 KB 394. Therefore, the courts turned to the interpretation of clauses as a means of controlling them (Lord Denning MR calls this 'the secret weapon' in his own readable, historical survey in *George Mitchell (Chesterhall) Ltd* v *Finney Lock Seeds Ltd* [1983] 2 AC 803) and a series of cases in the first half of this century show this approach's early success but ultimate ineffectiveness.

In *Baldry* v *Marshall* [1925] 1 KB 260 a Bugatti car was sold in breach of the implied condition that it was fit for its purpose (touring) but there was a 'guarantee' against defects of manufacture which expressly excluded 'any other guarantee or warranty, statutory or otherwise'. These words were held not to exclude the liability for breach of the implied condition since this was a condition and not a warranty. Those responsible for drafting exclusion clauses no doubt took this reverse to heart for a few years later in *Andrews Brothers Ltd* v *Singer & Co. Ltd* [1934] 1 KB 17 the Court of Appeal was faced with a rather more explicit clause which referred to conditions as well as warranties: 'all conditions, warranties and liabilities implied by common law, statute or otherwise are excluded'. The court still managed to evade the exclusion clause by pointing out that the term broken was an *express* one rather than implied and was thus not covered by the clause. The draftsman responsible for the clause in *L'Estrange* v *F. Graucob Ltd* had, however, been more percipient since the clause in that case excluded 'any express or implied condition, statement or warranty, statutory or otherwise'. Faced with such clear all-embracing words there was apparently little the courts could do to control a determined excluder with the power to impose his terms on those who dealt with him.

Nevertheless, the courts did continue to develop interpretative devices such as *the contra proferentem* rule and the rule that clear words are needed to exclude liability for negligence. But again, these devices were of no use against a person who did use clear words and so the courts developed a doctrine in the 1950s and 60s that no exclusion clause could protect against a fundamental breach (such as in *Karsales (Harrow) Ltd* v *Wallis* [1956] 1 WLR 936 where the purchaser was shown a car in good condition and agreed to buy it but the car later delivered had had many parts substituted by old ones and was incapable of self-propulsion). This doctrine was itself rejected by the House of Lords in *Suisse Atlantique Société d'Armement Maritime SA* v *NV Rotterdamsche Kolen Centrale* [1967] 1 AC 361 which re-emphasised the intention of the parties and held that there was no rule of law that an exclusion clause could not cover a fundamental breach although as a matter of construction a clause would not be held to cover a very serious breach in the absence of clear words.

The judicial instinct to intervene against exclusion clauses had, however, become so strong by now, especially in the Court of Appeal, that in the 1970s the doctrine of fundamental breach started to reappear, most notoriously in *Harbutt's 'Plasticine' Ltd* v *Wayne Tank & Pump Co. Ltd* [1970] 1 QB 447 where Lord Denning MR seized on some ambiguous dicta of Lord Reid in *Suisse Atlantique* to support the proposition that once a contract had been terminated as a result of a fundamental breach, the exclusion clause can no longer apply. The result was that a doctrine originally invoked to protect consumers against unscrupulous businesses was applied to a contract between two commercial organisations whose insurance was based on the exclusion clause being valid. The plaintiffs, who were insured, got £146,000 in damages (which would go straight to their insurance company who had been paid a premium to carry that very risk) and the defendants had to pay up even though they themselves were not covered by their primary insurance (see *Wayne Tank & Pump Co. Ltd* v *Employers Liability Assurance Corporation Ltd* [1974] QB 57).

Quite apart from the unfortunate effects of the decision in the *Harbutt's 'Plasticine'* case, the decision was theoretically unsound for when a contract is terminated for breach it is only the future obligations which are discharged and the terms of the contract remain relevant for the purpose of measuring damages etc. There is no reason why the exclusion clause should be treated any differently from other terms and suddenly cease to be relevant, and thankfully the House of Lords unequivocally recognised this 10 years later in 1980 in *Photo Production Ltd v Securicor Transport Ltd* [1980] AC 827 when *Harbutt's 'Plasticine'* was overruled (and s. 9(1) of the Unfair Contract Terms Act 1977 confirms that an exemption clause can be effective despite the termination of the contract) and it was made clear that there is no rule of law that an exclusion clause cannot cover a fundamental breach although it was recognised that clear words would be necessary in order to do so.

The reason that the House of Lords was able to dispense so clearly with the fundamental breach rule was that in the meantime Parliament had given the courts a much more direct weapon to use against exclusion clauses in the form of the Unfair Contract Terms Act 1977 (although this was inapplicable to *Photo Production*, the facts of which occurred before 1977). This Act gives to the courts the power to intervene openly in the contractual relationship and invalidate unreasonable exclusion clauses, a power which, with one exception, they had consistently denied to themselves since it would have meant interfering with the parties' freedom of contract. (The exception was, predictably, Lord Denning who argued that the courts had a power at common law openly to disallow reliance on an unreasonable clause. In *Levison v Patent Steam Carpet Cleaning Co. Ltd* [1977] 3 All ER 498, whilst the Bill that became the Unfair Contract Terms Act 1977 was before Parliament he said: 'I do not think we need wait for that Bill to be passed into law. You never know what may happen to a Bill.')

Of course the Unfair Contract Terms Act 1977 was not the first Act to give the courts powers to disallow exemption clauses. As early as 1854 the Railway and Canal Traffic Act itself actually disallowed certain exemption clauses and gave the courts powers to *validate* fair and reasonable ones. Much closer to date, the Misrepresentation Act 1967 gave the courts power to disallow reliance on clauses which excluded liability for misrepresentation and the Supply of Goods (Implied Terms) Act 1973 did the same thing for clauses excluding the implied terms in contracts for the sale of goods or hire-purchase. However, the Unfair Contract Terms Act 1977 does it in respect of a much wider range of situations. The real significance of this is not only the existence of the powers themselves but the impact they will have on the older common law techniques, such as the *contra proferentem* rule, for controlling exemption clauses. There are already signs that the courts will not apply their older techniques as strictly as they would once have done now that they have the powers provided by statute (see *Ailsa Craig Fishing Co. Ltd v Malvern*

Fishing Co. Ltd [1983] 1 WLR 964 and *George Mitchell (Chesterhall) Ltd v Finney Lock Seeds Ltd* [1983] 2 AC 803). Indeed in *Phillips Products Ltd v Hyland* [1987] 2 All ER 620, the trial judge completely ignored the question of construction and went straight to the position under the Act.

As has already been said, the Unfair Contract Terms Act 1977 was not the first instance of statutory intervention in the field of exclusion clauses and it is now clear that it is not to be the last. The European Community has now adopted a Directive on Unfair Terms in Consumer Contracts (OJ 1993 L95/29) to be implemented by member states by the end of 1994. The Directive is clearly inspired by legislative controls originally introduced in West Germany (Allgemeinen Geschäfts bedingungen) in the same year ironically as the enactment of our own Unfair Contract Terms Act 1977. Unlike our misleadingly entitled legislation, the German legislation and the Directive do apply to a wide range of unfair contract terms and not just to exclusion clauses (however widely defined). However, one of the main difficulties with the Directive is likely to be the overlap with UCTA caused by the fact that the definition of 'unfair terms' in the Directive (which has now been implemented more or less *verbatim* via statutory instrument — (SI 1994/3159)) clearly does include exemption clauses within its scope.

Given that the regulations implementing the Directive only come into force on 1 July 1995, it is a little premature to comment in too much detail on the effects of the Directive but the following key points can perhaps be made:

(a)   the Directive only applies to terms in 'consumer contracts';

(b)   it applies only to terms that have not been 'individually negotiated' (cf. 'written standard terms' under s. 3 of UCTA);

(c)   the test of unfairness is whether the term '... contrary to the requirement of good faith, ... causes a significant imbalance in the parties' rights and obligations arising under the contract, to the detriment of the consumer'. It will be interesting to see how this differs from the UCTA test of reasonableness and what the courts make of the singularly continental notion of the 'requirement of good faith'. Schedule 2 of the Regulations gives guidelines some of which echo *some* of the guidelines in Schedule 2 of UCTA.

Having seen how the law has developed historically and is still developing, the task now is to identify those issues that are still important today. Fundamental breach, I would suggest, despite the space still devoted to it in some quarters, is not one of them except in so far as it is important as providing historical background. The three key issues that you will probably need to discuss in most questions on exemption clauses are:

(a)   Incorporation (common law).

(b)   Interpretation (common law).

(c)   The effect of the UCTA (and the EC Directive).

INCORPORATION OF EXCLUSION CLAUSES

It is still necessary, if one wishes to rely on an exclusion clause against a person with whom one is in a contractual relationship, to show that the clause has become part of the contract. (Non-contractual exclusion clauses can take effect where there is no contract between the parties, e.g., where a landowner erects a notice excluding his liability to visitors or indeed where gratuitous advice is given subject to a disclaimer as in *Hedley Byrne & Co. Ltd* v *Heller & Partners Ltd* [1964] AC 465.) There are three main ways in which incorporation into the contract can be achieved:

(a) *By signature*, as in *L'Estrange* v *F. Graucob Ltd* [1934] 2 KB 394 where it matters not that the signer is unaware that the document he or she is signing contains exemption clauses (although the effect of any such clauses must not be misrepresented to him as in *Curtis* v *Chemical Cleaning & Dyeing Co.* [1951] 1 KB 805). The document must, however, be a contractual document (see below) — i.e., one which purported to be a contract or to have contractual force and not merely an administration or accounting document recording one party's performance as in *Grogan* v *Meredith Plat Hire, The Times,* 20 February 1996.

(b) *By notice.*

(c) *By course of dealing.*

(a) is relatively straightforward but (b) and (c) require further discussion.

Incorporation by Notice

The basic test is whether reasonable steps have been taken to bring the existence and whereabouts of the clause to the attention of the other party before or at the time of contracting. Within this test a number of more specific points can arise.

The question of timing

Notice given after the contract is formed as in *Olley* v *Marlborough Court Ltd* [1949] 1 KB 532, is clearly ineffective but when is a contract formed? The courts do not seem to worry about split seconds so that where exclusion clauses are referred to on tickets, the issue of the ticket will be regarded as sufficiently contemporaneous with the contract even though technically the contract may have been formed a split second before the ticket was handed over. The theory is that if on seeing that the ticket refers to conditions the customer immediately decides he doesn't want to contract, he would still be able to return the ticket and get his money back. This theory is clearly inapplicable where one is dealing with an automatic machine as in

Thornton v *Shoe Lane Parking Ltd* [1971] 2 QB 163 where as Lord Denning MR pointed out, the customer 'may protest to the machine, even swear at it, but it will remain unmoved. He is committed beyond recall.' Thus the contract was already formed before the machine issued the ticket and the exclusion clause on the ticket did not form part of the contract. Thus in any exclusion clause problem which you are given, it is worth asking at what point is the contract formed?

Contractual and non-contractual documents
A separate but not totally unrelated issue is whether the document containing the clause is a contractual one. This relates not only to the type of document (is it one on which the reasonable person would expect to find contractual terms?) but also to the time when it is supplied. Both aspects can be seen in *Chapelton* v *Barry Urban District Council* [1940] 1 KB 532 where the deck-chair ticket was only regarded as a receipt to prove payment rather than as something on which one would expect to find contractual terms. This was no doubt reinforced by the fact that frequently the customer could have been sitting in the deck-chair for a number of hours before the ticket was actually issued. Beware, however, the question that tells you that a ticket or document is a 'receipt' — it does not automatically follow that it is not a contractual document in law — you must still ask whether in the light of all the circumstances it could reasonably be expected to contain the terms of the contract.

Notice of existence or of contents
The general rule is that reasonable notice of the existence of terms is required, not of their detailed contents. For example, in *Parker* v *South Eastern Railway Co.* (1877) 2 CPD 416 Mellish LJ talked about 'reasonable notice that the writing contained conditions' not notice of what those conditions actually were and in *Thompson* v *London, Midland & Scottish Railway Co.* [1930] 1 KB 41 it was sufficient that there was an indication of where the details could be inspected rather than it being necessary to set out the full terms at the scene of the contract. However, this seems only to apply where the term is of a sort that is usual or to be expected in the particular type of contract. Where the terms are unusual or objectionably wide, a higher degree of notice is required as was pointed out by Lord Denning MR in *Thornton* v *Shoe Lane Parking Ltd*, referring to a clause excluding not only liability for damage to property, which might be expected, but also for personal injury. This was an example of the sort of clause which Denning LJ had said in an earlier case, *J. Spurling Ltd* v *Bradshaw* [1956] 1 WLR 461, 'would need to be printed in red ink on the face of the document with a red hand pointing to it' in order to be sufficient. Most students are able to recite that particularly lurid quotation but the point to be understood is that what constitutes reasonable notice will vary according to the type and acceptability of the exclusion clause.

The principle has been more recently applied by the Court of Appeal in *Interfoto Picture Library Ltd* v *Stiletto Visual Programmes Ltd* [1988] 1 All ER 348, a case which also demonstrates that the principle is applicable to contractual terms generally, not just exclusion clauses.

Blind or illiterate plaintiffs
The question is whether reasonable steps have been taken by the defendant, not whether the plaintiff has actually read the clause, so in principle it is irrelevant that, the plaintiff cannot read the clause. That principle only applies, however, if the contract is made in such circumstances that the defendant can reasonably expect the plaintiff to be able to read and is thus inapplicable if it is known that the plaintiff cannot read the clause, as in *Geier* v *Kujawa* [1970] 1 Lloyd's Rep 364 where the plaintiff was known not to speak English, or if the notice is aimed at a class of people which is known to be likely to include illiterate persons, as in *Richardson, Spence & Co.* v *Rowntree* [1894] AC 217.

Incorporation by Course of Dealing

This is a method of incorporation often neglected by students but is none the less important with its own subtleties and controversies. A notice which could be insufficient in a one-off contract, because it is introduced only after the contract has been formed, may still be effective if the parties have contracted on previous occasions and the same procedure has always been followed, as in *J. Spurling Ltd* v *Bradshaw* [1956] 1 WLR 461. The important issues to be aware of here are that:

(a)   The previous course of dealings must be regular and consistent (which was not the case in *McCutcheon* v *David MacBrayne Ltd* [1964] 1 All ER 430).

(b)   The courts will require much more in the way of previous dealings where the contract involves a consumer rather than two businesses — compare *Hollier* v *Rambler Motors (AMC) Ltd* [1972] 2 QB 71 with *British Crane Hire Corporation Ltd* v *Ipswich Plant Hire Ltd* [1975] QB 303.

(c)   There is a question mark as to whether on the previous occasions the plaintiff must have actually been made aware of the contents of the clause or whether it is sufficient that he knew that some conditions existed. One would expect the latter to be the correct position in line with the rule for incorporation by notice but in *McCutcheon* v *David MacBrayne Ltd* Lord Devlin thought that the previous dealings were insufficient because actual knowledge of the details of the terms was not shown and this was followed by Lord Denning MR in *Mendelssohn* v *Normand Ltd* [1970] 1 QB 177. However, the balance of authority is to the effect that actual knowledge of the details of the terms on the previous occasions is not necessary, see, e.g., Salmon LJ in *Hollier* v *Rambler Motors (AMC) Ltd* although perhaps the best view is that, just as with incorporation by notice, it depends on the extent to which the clause is an unusual one. Irrespective of what is the best view, the important thing is for you to be aware of the different possibilities and to be able to express your own views on the matter if the opportunity should arise in the examination.

INTERPRETATION OF EXCLUSION CLAUSES

Having identified the major ways in which an exclusion clause can be incorporated in the contract, the next issue is to examine how the courts will interpret such a clause. The short and simple answer is narrowly, although as already mentioned, their attitude is likely to be perhaps less severe today than was the case before the advent of the Unfair Contract Terms Act 1977.

Some examples of strict construction have already been given earlier in this chapter but one which I think is particularly illustrative and memorable and yet which is not as well known as some is *Houghton* v *Trafalgar Insurance Co. Ltd* [1954] 1 QB 247 where a car insurance policy excluded liability if the car was carrying an excess 'load' and this was held not to be applicable to a situation where the car was carrying too many passengers, load being artificially restricted to baggage etc. rather than passengers. (It is interesting to note that the main provisions of the Unfair Contract Terms Act 1977 do not apply to contracts of insurance and if the Act results in a less strict construction of exclusion clauses generally, one wonders whether the strict approach will be reactivated for contracts falling outside the Act.) Whatever the implications of the Act for the interpretation of exemption clauses, there are three particular aspects of interpretation which still deserve special mention:

(a)   Exclusion of liability for negligence.
(b)   Fundamental breach.
(c)   Differential treatment of limitation clauses.

Exclusion of Liability for Negligence

Clear words are necessary to exclude liability for negligence because whilst it is perfectly understandable for a person to say, 'I am not liable for things that happened due to no fault of mine', it is less legitimate (and less to be expected) for someone to say, 'I am liable even if I have failed to take reasonable care'.

Smith v *South Wales Switchgear Ltd* [1978] 1 All ER 18 is a case which is often misunderstood and misquoted in this connection. The House of Lords did *not* say that to exclude liability for negligence the word 'negligence' or a synonym must *always* be used, as some students seem to think. The House was discussing the threefold test laid down by Lord Morton of Henryton in *Canada Steamship Lines Ltd* v *The King* [1952] AC 192 for determining whether a clause covers negligence:

(a)   does the clause expressly exempt from negligence, in which case it is effective, or

(b)   are the words wide enough in their ordinary meaning to cover negligence, in which case the clause may still be effective, unless

(c)   there is some head of damage other than negligence which the words could be construed as applying to rather than to negligence.

All that the House was saying was that to come within the first limb of the test, as an *express* examination of negligence, the word 'negligence' or a synonym was necessary and that words such as 'any damage whatsoever' did not amount to an express exemption of negligence. (The House was actually dealing with an indemnity clause, i.e., a clause whereby A agrees to reimburse B if B is found liable to C, but made it clear that the same principles applied to an exemption clause.) The decision does not mean that words like 'any loss or damage howsoever caused' are not capable of covering negligence under the second limb of the test — they clearly are so capable but if the words are only effective under limb (b) then one has to go on to limb (c) to see if there is any other liability which they could reasonably be intended to cover in which case they will not be applied so as to cover negligence. This is borne out by a subsequent Court of Appeal case, *The Raphael* [1982] 2 Lloyd's Rep 42, where the words 'not liable for ... any act or omission' were held to cover negligence even though there was no express reference to or synonym used for negligence since the words were wide enough in their ordinary meaning to cover negligence and there was no other liability, 'not fanciful or remote', which they could reasonably be supposed to be intended to cover. It is worth noting that this was a contract between two commercial concerns (see also *EE Caledonia Ltd* v *Orbit Value Co. Europe* [1994] 1 WLR 1515) and the same result will not necessarily be achieved where the party is obviously in a weaker bargaining position as in *Hollier* v *Rambler Motors (AMC) Ltd* [1972] 2 QB 71 where even though there was no liability other than negligence which the clause could be intended to cover, the Court of Appeal held that the clause did not cover negligence and so deprived the clause of any real effect, save as a warning to customers that the garage was not liable in the absence of negligence. This is a rather extreme solution which perhaps today would be effected by applying the Unfair Contract Terms Act 1977 and it is unnecessary where there is another type of liability, as in *White* v *John Warwick & Co. Ltd* [1953] 2 All ER 1021, where there was strict liability under the contract to which the exclusion clause could be applied and thus be given some effect, as well as liability for negligence which the clause did not cover. Furthermore, the *Hollier* v *Rambler Motors (AMC) Ltd* argument *can't* be applied to a *limitation* clause as opposed to an exclusion clause. A limitation clause must limit something, it can't be construed merely as a warning, and if the only liability possible is liability for negligence, then it must be effective to limit that liability. See Smith and Thomas, *A Casebook on Contract*, 10th ed., p. 454, question 2.

It is easy to get confused amongst the above rather complex rules, which it should be stressed are really only prima facie guides to construction rather than hard-and-fast rules to be rigidly adhered to, and you may find the algorithm in Figure 6.1 a helpful aid in picking your way through the mire. (The uses of algorithms and helpful advice on how to construct them are given in Twining and Miers, *How To Do Things with Rules*.)

The conclusions in this particular algorithm (which are boxed in double lines) are only as strong as the rules of construction themselves but the algorithm does indicate the sorts of questions which are relevant and the significance of the possible answers to such questions.

Figure 6.1 — Algorithm

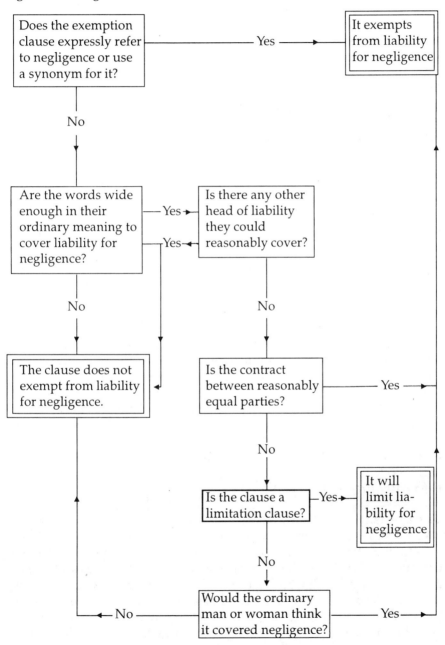

Fundamental Breach

Although there is clearly no longer any substantive rule of law concerning fundamental breach, it is still said that there is a rule of construction that, rather like liability for negligence, clear words are necessary to protect against a fundamental breach. However, it is equally clear, as illustrated by the facts of *Photo Production Ltd v Securicor Transport Ltd* [1980] AC 827 that if sufficiently clear words *are* used, a breach that appears to be fundamental will be covered by such an exclusion clause. It is probably best to avoid attaching any significance to the question of whether a breach is or is not fundamental because the notion of what counts as a fundamental breach has never been very clear either in theory or in application. (Lord Diplock in *Photo Production* was prepared to countenance the expression if it was restricted to a breach of an (innominate) term which is serious enough to give rise to the right to terminate, but as noted in chapter 5, it is notoriously difficult to know when a breach is of such a nature.) Even if it was possible to say with confidence that a particular breach is fundamental, it would still be a matter of construction as to whether the exemption clause applies. The only sensible thing one can really say is that an exemption clause will not normally be interpreted so as to remove the whole of the other party's obligation under the contract because that would mean there was no contract at all. That proposition can be stated without referring to the concept of fundamental breach and so I think you need worry no further about that concept and need only be aware of its historical role in the development of controls on exclusion clauses. (See *Anson's Law of Contract* and beware Yates, *Exclusion Clauses in Contracts*, ch. 6, which was written at a time when it was conceivable that *Photo Production* might suffer the same fate as *Suisse Atlantique Société d'Armement Maritime SA v NV Rotterdamsche Kolen Centrale* [1967] 1 AC 361 whereas *Photo Production* has since been confirmed in spirit in this respect by *George Mitchell (Chesterhall) Ltd v Finney Lock Seeds Ltd* [1983] 2 AC 803.)

Differential Treatment of Limitation Clauses

This is a fairly recent phenomenon, having been brought to the fore by yet another House of Lords decision in this area, *Ailsa Craig Fishing Co. Ltd v Malvern Fishing Co. Ltd* [1983] 1 WLR 964. This is a distinct point to the one made earlier in relation to *Hollier v Rambler Motors (AMC) Ltd* [1972] 2 QB 71, i.e., that a limitation clause can be hardly construed as a warning that the defendant is not liable *at all* in the absence of negligence. The point being made in *Ailsa Craig* was rather that the strict rules of construction of exclusion clauses are not as rigidly applied to limitation clauses since it is not as improbable that a person would agree to a limitation clause which is more likely to be justified on the basis of what remuneration the defendant receives under the contract, the risk to which he is exposed and the plaintiff's opportunity to insure. One has to agree with Palmer (1982) 45 MLR 322 that it is difficult to see why these factors should be relevant to limitation clauses but should not be relevant to exclusion clauses as well, especially when one sees how close to zero in percentage terms the limitation of liability can actually become (1.8% in *Ailsa Craig* and 0.33% in *George Mitchell (Chesterhall) Ltd v Finney Lock Seeds Ltd* [1983] 2 AC 803). Nevertheless the distinction in this context was approved of by the House of Lords in *George Mitchell (Chesterhall) Ltd v Finney Lock Seeds Ltd* so it is a distinction which you have to reckon with and be prepared to comment on. Despite this distinction, the more recent House of Lords decision in *Bovis v Whatlings Construction, The Times,* 19 October 1995 shows that limitation clauses are still construed with a degree of strictness even if not to the same extent as exclusion clauses. Thus a clause limiting damages for delay to £100,000 did not cover delay which amounted to a repudiatory breach leading to complete non-performance.

UNFAIR CONTRACT TERMS ACT 1977

This may be the first time in your course that you have had to look in detail at an Act of Parliament as opposed to case law. To deal successfully with a major Act like this you need first of all to understand what it was that prompted the Act and what its principal aims were. You then need to develop a picture of the overall structure of the Act, how it fits together and which are the important sections before going on to consider the meaning of the important sections in more detail and looking at the interpretation they have received.

As far as the background to the Act is concerned, you already have part of it in your knowledge of the common law rules for exemption clauses and of their inadequacies but there is a more specific source which you can turn to in the Law Commission Report, No. 69 (1975) on which the Act was based. If you look at that report, you will see that the Law Commission recognised that all exemption clauses are not of the same type and that the situations in which they occur vary significantly and that the need for control is more pressing with some types and situations than with others. This in fact is the key to understanding the Act because the Act is based on a number of significant distinctions and definitions (not all of them the same distinctions that the Law Commission had recommended) which form the basis of the statutory control of exemption clauses. Identifying these distinctions and definitions and understanding their rationale will enable you to remember the important provisions of the Act and to apply them in a sensible manner.

The first thing to note about the Act comes appropriately enough in s. 1 — the main provisions of the Act only apply to business liability and therefore not, in the main, to any exclusions of liability made by a private individual not acting in the course of a business. The main reasons for this are that such exclusions are comparatively rare and even where they occur there is not likely to be any opportunity to impose an unfair term on a weaker party. However, the restriction to business liability is subject to exceptions, i.e., s. 6 controlling clauses excluding liability for breach of the terms implied by statutes into contracts for the sale or hire-purchase of goods (although this exception is more apparent than real since many of such terms can only arise on a sale in the course of a business and the more drastic part of the section dealing with consumer contracts can only effectively apply to business liability) and s. 8 dealing with the exclusion of liability for misrepresentation. It is not easy to state precisely why these sections are not restricted to business liability except to say that they are largely re-enactments, with minor modifications, of provisions initially found in earlier statutes, namely the Supply of Goods (Implied Terms) Act 1973 and the Misrepresentation Act 1967.

The next thing to notice about the Act is that some exclusions of liability are rendered completely ineffective, whereas others are only effective 'in so far as they satisfy the test of reasonableness'. Generally speaking those singled out for total ineffectiveness are those which are most objectionable or which are most likely to result from inequality of bargaining power etc. Thus the main examples of total ineffectiveness likely to be relevant to a contract course are s. 2(1) dealing with exclusion of liability for *death or personal injury* caused by *negligence* and s. 6(1) and (2) dealing with the implied terms in sales and hire-purchase of goods. These latter are singled out partly because the exclusion is of a liability which is implied in law, i.e., one which the law as a matter of policy ordains *ought* to be imposed but even here (apart from the implied terms as to title) the ineffectiveness of the exclusion of liability depends on a further distinction, i.e., whether the purchaser is 'dealing as a consumer'. One then has to go to s. 12 to find out what this expression means (and, as will be seen, it has a significance beyond s. 6 alone) and there one finds a threefold test of:

    (a)   the purchaser not contracting in the course of a business,
    (b)   the seller *is* contracting in the course of a business,
    (c)   the goods are of a type ordinarily supplied for private use and consumption.

Again this test is designed to single out those cases where the exclusion is likely to be particularly objectionable and where there is most likely to have been an abuse of a superior bargaining position. Most of the other exclusions of liability which the Act affects are not made totally ineffective but merely subjected to a reasonableness test. However, even these are selected on various criteria because the Act doesn't apply to all exclusion clauses and the Act only imposes the reasonableness test in those situations where control is likely to be necessary. Again, understanding why the Act selects certain criteria for its own application will help you to remember the criteria themselves.

Thus s. 2(2) subjects clauses excluding liability for *negligently* caused loss or damage *other than death or personal injury* to the reasonableness test, reflecting the well-established concern at common law about clauses excluding liability for negligence. Similarly, s. 3 imposes a reasonableness test on clauses excluding contractual liability (not all contractual liability for there are often good reasons for excluding such liability especially where it is strict) but only where the person affected by the clause is either:

(a)   dealing as a consumer (see above, although the third limb of the test is inapplicable here) or

(b)   dealing on the other's written standard terms (where the probability that he has had little choice about accepting them is obvious).

Thus far the provisions of the Act identifying the main types of terms and contracts to which the Act is applicable have been considered and that has involved looking at ss. 1, 2, 3, 6, 8 and 12. The main issue that remains is that of the application of the reasonableness test itself to which s. 11 and sch. 2 are relevant but before dealing with that I should say something about the meaning of the term 'exemption clauses' under the Act.

It is relatively easy, and certainly not unknown, for a contracting party to disguise what might otherwise look like an exclusion clause as a term positively defining the extent of his liability, e.g., compare contract (a) — an agreement to deliver a hire car at 9.00 a.m. tomorrow subject to a clause stating that the supplier will not be liable for any loss suffered if the car is delivered no more than three hours late — with contract (b) — an agreement to deliver a hire car at 9.00 a.m. tomorrow morning subject to a clause stating that the delivery times are guaranteed to within three hours.

The effect of (a) and (b) is precisely the same but (a) obviously involves an exclusion clause while (b) may appear not to do so. To deal with this sort of deviousness, s. 13 of the Act gives a fairly wide definition to exclusion clauses to start with although s. 13 is not itself applicable to the particular situation I have outlined — see *Stewart Gill Ltd* v *Horatio Myer & Co. Ltd* [1992] 2 All ER 257 for a case where s. 13 was applicable. However, in relation to the situation outlined above, s. 3(2)(b) prevents (where it applies) a person by reference to *any* contract term claiming to be entitled to render a performance substantially different from that reasonably expected of him. Thus if one supposes that the customer in (b) was dealing as a consumer or that the contract was on written standard terms and that therefore s. 3 is applicable, and one further supposes that the car is not delivered until 11.59 a.m. the question would be whether that is a performance which is substantially different from that reasonably expected. The answer to that question might turn on factors such as how much was being paid and how long the hire was for — if it was only for the rest of the afternoon then the section is perhaps more likely to apply than if the hire was to last for another week because in the latter case the loss of the morning is proportionately less significant. Even if the Act does apply (i.e., if the performance was substantially different from what was *reasonably* expected that is not the end of the matter) — one then has to ask whether the term itself was reasonable. (You may think the word 'reasonable' is being rather overworked, not to mention the similar concept of 'substantially different'.)

The Reasonableness Test

The stock criticism of tests of reasonableness in any branch of the law is the uncertainty and unpredictability that they can introduce and so it is important to know how far the Act provides guidance as to the application of the reasonableness test (always remembering that it is not all terms to which the test is applicable).

The principal section providing such guidance is s. 11 which itself refers to specific criteria in sch. 2 (these latter, however, are only strictly applicable to exclusions of implied terms in contracts under which goods pass but there is no doubt that they will also be relevant factors for all types of contract).

The first point to note about s. 11 is its last subsection, subsection (5), which puts the burden of proving reasonableness on the person relying on the clause. This can be a crucial factor in practice (see *St Albans City and District Council* v *International Computers Ltd, The Times*, 11 November, 1994) especially when the clause is on the borderline between reasonable and unreasonable and it represents a change from the original provision in the Act's predecessor, the Supply of Goods (Implied Terms) Act 1973.

The next point arises in s. 11(1) and again marks a potentially significant change from the law introduced in 1973. The question is now whether the clause is a fair and reasonable one to have included at the time of entering the contract rather than whether it is fair and reasonable to allow reliance on it now. This shifts the emphasis from the particular damage actually suffered and from the circumstances of the breach, and clearly emphasises instead the fairness of the bargain when it was struck and this could have quite significant effects on whether a clause is likely to be upheld. For example, it might be fair and reasonable to allow reliance on a clause given the actual damage suffered and the liability actually excluded on the particular facts but the clause may not have been a fair and reasonable one to include in the contract because of its *potential* width and its potential to be relied on in other fact situations which could not be regarded as fair. There is a possible analogy here with the law on restraints of trade where, *pace* Lord Denning MR in *Shell UK Ltd v Lostock Garage Ltd* [1977] 1 All ER 481, reasonableness has to be judged by reference to the time the contract was entered into, otherwise, per Ormrod LJ, 'many more covenants would pass the normal test at the time they were entered into'. Conversely, if a clause is fair and reasonable having regard to what the parties knew at the time of the contract, the fact that it is later found to operate harshly will be in principle irrelevant.

The significance of the formula used in s. 11(1) has now been expressly recognised by the Court of Appeal in *Stewart Gill Ltd v Horatio Myer & Co. Ltd* [1992] 2 All ER 257 where Lord Donaldson MR stated that:

> The issue is whether 'the term' [the whole term and nothing but the term] shall have been a fair and reasonable one to be included. This has to be determined as at the time when the contract is made and without regard to what particular use one party may subsequently wish to make of it.

As a result, whilst anyone drafting an exclusion clause has to ensure it is sufficiently widely worded to cover the damage to be excluded, care has to be taken at the same time not to make the clause wider than is necessary since that will increase the risk of it being judged unreasonable whereas a narrower clause would have been reasonable and still sufficient to protect the defendant.

These consequences of the way s. 11 is drafted were in fact foreseen by the English Law Commission in its Report (1975) and to avoid these consequences they recommended sticking to the reliance formula already contained in the 1973 legislation but the Scottish Law Commission disagreed and it was the Scottish Law Commission's formulation which was eventually embodied in the 1977 Act. If you wish to pursue the pros and cons of this argument further (and it is the sort of point which will distinguish your paper in the eye of the examiner) take a look at paras 170 to 183 of the Law Commission's Report and note that *George Mitchell (Chesterhall) Ltd v Finney Lock Seeds Ltd* [1983] 2 AC 803 was decided under the old formula.

Ironically, the House of Lords was again concerned with the 'old formula' in *Smith v Bush* [1989] 2 WLR 790 since that is the test imposed by s. 11(3) for *non-contractual* exclusion notices (one cannot apply a test of 'fair and reasonable to include in the contract' where there is no contract!).

A further point to note about the test of reasonableness is that the question is merely whether the particular term was a reasonable one to include in *this* contract, not whether the term would be reasonable in any *other* circumstances. Coupled with the observations of Lord Bridge of Harwich in *George Mitchell (Chesterhall) Ltd v Finney Lock Seeds Ltd* [1983] 2 AC 803 to the effect that appellate courts will be reluctant to interfere with the findings of trial judges as to whether a clause is reasonable, this means that decided cases are going to be of relatively little help in predicting how the same clause might fare in a different set of circumstances before a different trial judge. This can clearly be illustrated if one looks at *Waldron-Kelly* v *British Railways Board* [1981] CLY 303 and compare it with *Wight* v *British Railways Board* [1983] CLY 424. In the former case a clause limiting liability for lost luggage by reference to its weight rather than its value was held to be unreasonable but in the latter case the same clause was held to be reasonable on the particular facts in a different county court.

More specific criteria are provided by sch. 2 for clauses excluding liability for the implied terms in contracts involving the supply of goods and these will no doubt also be relevant to other situations so you should understand them and be able to summarise them. Again, they have been selected for a reason and understanding their rationale will help you to remember them.

Paragraph (a), in referring to relative strength of bargaining power is fairly obvious and 'alternative means by which the customer's requirements could have been met' is geared to the question of how far the supplier is a monopolist (but note that there is a fair amount of scepticism about how well equipped the courts are to recognise inequality of bargaining power — see Nicol and Rawlings (1980) 43 MLR 567 at p. 571 and Trebilcock and Dewees, 'Judicial control of standard form contracts', in Burrows and Veljanovski (ed.), *The Economic Approach to Law*, pp. 93-119, especially pp. 98-102, or Trebilcock (1976) 26 UTLJ 359).

Paragraph (b) — inducements to agree to the term. If you are charged a lower price in return for the exclusion, that is likely to make the clause reasonable. This was an important factor under the 1854 Railway and Canal Traffic Act as interpreted by the courts and cf. *R. W Green Ltd* v *Cade Brothers Farms* [1978] 1 Lloyd's Rep 602 where a limitation clause in relation to uncertified seed potatoes was upheld because the purchaser could have bought certified seed for a higher price. This paragraph also talks about the 'opportunity of entering a similar contract with other persons, but without having to accept a similar term: — i.e., was it effectively a take it or leave it situation or did the customer have a choice?

Paragraph (c), whether the customer ought to have known about the existence and extent of the term. This is the common law incorporation test coming back in again and most clauses which are actually incorporated will probably be reasonable under this criterion but it could be useful where the incorporation test operates harshly, e.g., in cases of signed documents like *L'Estrange* v *F. Graucob Ltd* [1934] 2 KB 394.

Paragraph (d) is fairly self-explanatory and refers to, e.g., a clause whereby liability is excluded unless a complaint is made in writing within seven days. Such a clause was held to be unreasonable in *R. W. Green Ltd* v *Cade Brothers*

Farms [1978] 1 Lloyd's Rep 602 since the defect was not capable of being easily detected until much later.

Paragraph (e) reflects the fact that where the supplier is complying with a special order it may be perfectly reasonable to exclude all obligations save conformity with the specification. The purchaser can hardly complain that a product is not fit for its purpose if it complies with the specifications which he himself has laid down.

Finally, s. 11(4) specifies two factors which are particularly relevant to limitation as opposed to exclusion clauses:

(a)   the resources available to the party excluding the liability — obviously the smaller his resources the more understandable is the limitation of liability — and

(b)   the availability of insurance, again the less the opportunity to insure against the liability the more understandable that he should seek to limit that liability.

Note that these factors were not decisive and were outweighed by other factors justifying a limitation clause in *Singer* v *Tees & Hartlepool Port Authority* [1988] 2 Lloyd's Rep 164.

THE EXAMINATION

Clearly you need to understand the historical development of the law in this area and to be thoroughly familiar with the three key areas of incorporation, interpretation and statutory control which I have already identified. In addition, there are a number of other issues which you need to be conscious of which might crop up in a question on this topic. (See chapter 2 for an overall plan of this area.) In particular you need to be able to deal with the issues of privity and whether a third party can take the benefit of an exemption clause, to which the answer is basically no but the courts have ways of holding that an apparent third party is not a third party by finding consideration provided by him as in *New Zealand Shipping Co. Ltd* v *A. M. Satterthwaite & Co. Ltd* [1975] AC 154.

A further issue that you ought to be prepared to discuss is the question of what amounts to an exemption clause and what is its relationship with the other terms of a contract (cf. the earlier discussion of s. 3(2) of the Unfair Contract Terms Act 1977). Is an exemption clause something which merely provides a defence to a breach (the most prevalent attitude in the case law) or is it merely a negative term but nonetheless a term like all the others in the contract, which defines the extent of the obligations? This latter type of view is expounded in Professor Coote's *Exception Clauses*, published in 1964, the classic work in the field and Lord Diplock's speech in *Photo Production Ltd v Securicor Transport Ltd* [1980] AC 827 is probably the judgment most sympathetic to his views (although Lord Diplock nowhere refers to Coote's work). If you wish to pursue this point there is a good discussion in Yates, *Exclusion Clauses in Contracts,* 2nd ed., pp. 123-33 and you may cope better with Lord Diplock's speech if I tell you that:

> 'Primary obligations' means the express (or implied) promises made by the parties.
>
> 'The general secondary obligation' means the obligation to pay damages for actual breach of a primary obligation.
>
> The 'anticipatory secondary obligation' is the obligation to pay damages for non-performance of future primary obligations once the contract has been terminated (either for breach of condition or breach, going to the root of the contract, of an innominate term).

If you can understand all that and get the opportunity to demonstrate it to the examiners then, whilst you may be dubbed along with Lord Diplock as having a penchant for 'gratuitous philological exhibitionism' — cf. Diplock LJ in *United Dominions Trust (Commercial) Ltd* v *Eagle Aircraft Services Ltd* [1968] 1 WLR 74 (the expression could be regarded as having an element of self-fulfilment about it) — you will undoubtedly obtain and deserve useful marks!

Besides being prepared to discuss the theoretical basis of exclusion clauses you should be prepared to discuss the not unrelated issue of how far the law is currently taking an appropriate attitude to exclusion clauses. Again, Yates, *Exclusion Clauses in Contracts,* chs. 1 and 7 this time, is a useful source of ideas on this subject and particularly if you are given an essay question you ought to show an awareness of the different uses, both legitimate and illegitimate, to which exemption clauses are put. Further inspiration may be gained from an article by Adams and Brownsword in 104 (1988) LQR 94 where the authors regret the unduly interventionist but unpredictable approach being adopted by the courts in relation to exclusion clauses in *commercial* contracts. (Contrast the EC Directive which is only concerned with consumer contracts.)

However, many examiners cannot resist the opportunity to draft exemption clauses themselves and you are quite likely to get a problem question in this area so a specimen problem will now be considered.

> Bob regularly hires a rubbish skip from Tidy Skips. On each of the last five occasions, the invoice, received afterwards, has had the following printed on the reverse.

> Tidy Skips shall not be liable for any loss or damage howsoever caused to customer's premises and if notwithstanding the foregoing, any

liability for damage to customer's property should arise, that liability shall be limited to a total of £100.

Bob telephones Tidy Skips and orders a skip to be delivered to his home on the following day. Syd, an employee of Tidy Skips, negligently drives the delivery vehicle into Bob's garden wall causing it to collapse on to Bob's new car. The wall costs £500 to rebuild and the repairs to the car cost £800. Advise Bob.

There is a fairly simple technique which one can apply, with slight modifications where appropriate, to almost any problem on exclusion clauses and that involves asking whether the clause clears the three major hurdles (our three key issues) of incorporation, interpretation and statutory control. This problem is no exception and the only major modification required is that one has to be careful to distinguish the two parts of the exemption clause, one of which totally excludes, and the other of which merely limits, liability. Other questions you may get may require different sorts of modification to this plan, e.g., you may be told 'the terms of the contract state', which would mean the issue of incorporation need not be discussed and you are expected to concentrate on interpretation and the effect of the statutory controls.

Rather than wasting time on a long introduction, much of which might be irrelevant, you could start a question like this with an introduction which clearly signals to the examiner the logical route you are going to follow in answering the question. For example:

Prima facie, both Syd and Tidy Skips are liable for the damage caused by Syd's negligence. In order to assess whether Bob will be able to recover compensation for the damage to his garden wall and car from either of them it is necessary to investigate how far the clause on the invoice excludes or limits any claim he might wish to make. This will involve looking at:

(a) Whether the clause has been incorporated into the contract which Bob makes.

(b) If so, whether the clause on its true construction is effective to exclude or limit Tidy Skips' (or Syd's) liability for the damage.

(c) Whether the clause, if incorporated and aptly worded, is affected by the Unfair Contract Terms Act 1977.

Each of these three issues will be looked at in turn before attempting an overall conclusion.

You could then start looking in more detail at issue (a). Since the contract is made over the telephone and no notice of the clause is given on this occasion there is no need to discuss incorporation by signature or by notice. The invoice is clearly too late on this occasion, but there is an issue concerning previous course of dealing. The significant factors which you might want to extract from the given facts include the fact that Bob appears to be a consumer and Tidy Skips a business so that *Hollier* v *Rambler Motors (AMC) Ltd* [1972] 2 QB 71 may be in point as contrasted with *British Crane Hire Corporation Ltd* v *Ipswich Plant Hire Ltd* [1975] QB 303. This would militate against incorporation but on the other hand the question says that Bob 'regularly' hires a skip and the clause has been on the invoice on 'each of' the last five occasions so the course of dealing is fairly regular and consistent. Contrast *McCutcheon* v *David MacBrayne Ltd* [1964] 1 All ER 430 where the risk note was not always signed. The question doesn't say whether Bob was actually aware of the clause on the previous occasions so you could also discuss Lord Devlin's views in *McCutcheon* v *David MacBrayne Ltd* (as discussed earlier in this chapter) and whether this matters.

You are unlikely to be in a position to say positively one way or another whether the clause is incorporated so the correct thing to do is to explain the alternatives — *either* the clause is not incorporated, in which case it can't possibly defeat or limit Bob's claim *or* it is incorporated in which case one has to go on to issue (b), the construction or interpretation of the clause.

Perhaps the first point to make here is that the clause does not even purport to protect Syd, the driver, and so there is no question of the clause being found to exempt Syd (contrast the clause in *New Zealand Shipping Co. Ltd* v *A. M. Satterthwaite & Co. Ltd* [1975] AC 154 which did purport to protect the stevedores), quite apart from the difficulty that Syd does not appear to be a party to the contract. It is also worth showing an awareness of the realities of the situation by pointing out that Bob would probably not be very keen on suing Syd anyway since the prospects of being able to enforce any judgment against him in a satisfactory way are much slimmer than against Tidy Skips.

Having narrowed the issue down to whether the clause protects Tidy Skips, you can then start looking at the wording more closely and comparing it with the damage suffered. It makes sense to cut this clause into two parts, the first purporting to exclude liability completely, the second merely limiting it. As far as the first part is concerned, you could perhaps make a few remarks about the traditional strict interpretation of exclusion clauses and the possibility (discussed earlier) that that strict approach will be followed less religiously now, given the advent of statutory controls. Having said that, the courts are not going to go to the other extreme of giving a wide construction to exclusion clauses and so you ought to identify the ways in which the clause may not be sufficiently clear.

First of all the liability here is for negligence. (You should find that the algorithm set out earlier in this chapter, is helpful here.) There is no express reference to negligence (see *Smith v South Wales Switchgear Ltd* [1978] 1 All ER 18) but the words 'any loss or damage howsoever caused' are wide enough to cover negligence in their ordinary meaning. The question then becomes whether there is any other liability they could cover besides negligence and the answer is probably no, since it is difficult to see how any damage to premises is likely to occur other than by negligence or if it did on what basis Tidy Skips could be liable for it. So the clause *may* cover liability for negligence but bear in mind that Bob is a consumer as was the plaintiff in *Hollier v Rambler Motors (AMC) Ltd*, and the court might take the view that the clause should merely be treated as a warning that Tidy Skips are not liable in the absence of negligence.

Even if the clause does cover negligence, are there any other ambiguities in it? The first part of the clause only covers damage to *premises* not property generally so it can hardly cover the damage to the car. A few years ago one might even have tried to suggest that premises could be interpreted to cover buildings and not to include garden walls etc. but that would be to adopt the highly artificial and strained construction that is now going out of fashion. So your conclusion on the first part of the clause might be that it is at least *capable* of excluding the damage to the wall.

When one turns to the second part of the clause, the immediate point to make is that it is a limitation clause and therefore, following the decisions of the House of Lords in *Ailsa Craig Fishing Co. Ltd v Malvern Fishing Co. Ltd* [1983] 1 WLR 964 and *George Mitchell (Chesterhall) Ltd v Finney Lock Seeds Ltd* [1983] 2 AC 803, it will be given a less strict interpretation than the exclusion clause. It would not be out of place to offer some comment at this point about whether the distinction between the two types of clause is an adequate basis for adopting a different approach to interpretation. Given the more benign interpretation, the clause will probably be held sufficient to limit liability for negligence (what other meaning could the clause have?). Again, you might once have been tempted to argue that the word 'property', especially as contrasted with the word 'premises' in the first part of the clause, refers only to movable property and doesn't apply to the damaged wall but this argument is untenable following the *Ailsa Craig* case. (The limitation clause will apply to the damage to the wall, of course, only if the exclusion clause is held not to cover negligence.)

The net result is that at common law, Tidy Skips may well have effectively limited their liability to £100. The remaining question concerns the effect of the Unfair Contract Terms Act 1977.

What are the applicable sections, if any, and what is their effect on these facts? You should have a checklist of questions to ask about the Act (based perhaps on a chart like the one in Figure 2.2).

Is the liability being excluded business liability? Answer obviously yes.

Is it liability for negligence? Yes, so s. 2 applies.

Death or personal injury? No, so the clause is not totally deprived of effect under s. 2(1) but it is only effective under s. 2(2) 'in so far as' it satisfies the test of reasonableness.

In addition you could point out (just to show you fully understand the Act in detail) that, since the negligence also amounts to a breach of a term of the contract (to perform the contract with reasonable care) and since Bob is dealing as a consumer under s. 12, the reasonableness test would also be applied by virtue of s. 3. (Quite apart from Bob dealing as a consumer, he is also dealing on Tidy Skips' written standard terms, so that is another reason for s. 3 being applicable.)

The real question then is how the reasonableness test will be applied in this particular case. There is an interesting analysis of some decisions on the application of the reasonableness test in Adams and Brownsword's article 104 (1988) LQR 94 but note that they are essentially concerned with contracts between two commercial parties. Our problem concerns a business excluding its liability to a consumer to which *Smith v Bush* [1989] 2 WLR 790 might be thought equally relevant even though the House of Lords was here concerned with a non-contractual notice and s. 11(3) rather than s. 11(1).

The basic question in our problem is whether the clause is a fair and reasonable one to have included in the contract under s. 11(1). One difficulty is whether the clause should be regarded as a single term or whether it can be separated into its two constituent parts. Should the question be whether the clause as a whole was a fair and reasonable one to be included or whether the two separate parts are reasonable. If the former is the correct approach, the clause might fail, e.g., because the first part is not reasonable even though the second part is. (See the *Stewart Gill case* above, p. 117.) This might be a sensible approach on the basis that it would encourage those drafting clauses to keep them short and simple and to resist the temptation to draft them too widely. (A wide but unenforceable clause can have great effects in making the other party *think* his rights are less than a court would actually adjudge them to be.) However, this policy could easily be evaded by the drafter creating a series of short, separate clauses which together add up to the same thing as one very long, all-embracing clause. Since the clause in the problem, unlike that in *Stewart Gill*, could quite easily be separated into two independent clauses you could legitimately discuss whether *either:*

    (a)   the first exclusionary part of the clause *or*
    (b)   the second, limiting part, were fair and reasonable to have included.

As far as (a) is concerned you should refer to the guidelines in sch. 2 (whilst pointing out that strictly they are only applicable to ss. 6 and 7 of the Act) and ask whether, e.g., Bob could have hired a skip anywhere else at the same sort of price without having to agree to a similar exclusion. Factors other than those mentioned in sch. 2 are also obviously potentially relevant such as whether Bob is likely to be, or ought to be, insured (his car probably will be insured but should he be expected to lose his no-claims bonus, and his house insurance may well not cover damage to garden walls in these circumstances). There is a limit to how much you can be expected to say about reasonableness in a problem which inevitably gives you few details about the background to the contract but you should be prepared to discuss the factors that have been found relevant in decided cases. *Phillips Products Ltd v Hyland* [1987] 2 All ER 620 is particularly relevant to this problem in that it concerned the negligence of an employee of the defendants (and also in that it was decided under the Unfair Contract Terms Act) and one factor in that case found to be significant was that the customer had no control over the employee whose negligence caused the damage. Additionally, the Court of Appeal stressed that the issue was the reasonableness of the term in this particular contract, not in other contracts, so stress that here and also mention the fact that an appeal court would be reluctant to interfere with any finding of fact by the trial judge. Since it is, to say the least, feasible that the exclusion clause will be found unreasonable, you must go on to examine (b) the reasonableness of the limitation part of the clause.

The same sort of factors will be relevant here but it is probably easier to justify a limitation clause than an exclusion clause, so Tidy Skips have more chance of success here. In particular, under s. 11(4) the court is directed to take account of Tidy Skips' resources and opportunity to insure. If Tidy Skips are a relatively small firm then the resources point may be in their favour but the sort of damage which could have been foreseen at the time of the contract (and, indeed, which actually occurred) is likely to arise from driving the delivery vehicle and Syd is by law compelled to be insured. However, we are considering Tidy Skips' liability, not Syd's (he is clearly not protected by the clause as mentioned earlier) so the question is whether Tidy Skips will be insured. The most you can be expected to do is to point to the considerations specifically mentioned in s. 11(4) and discuss how you think those considerations might be applied.

What you clearly cannot say is, e.g., that it is reasonable for Bob to recover the whole £500 for the wall but that the clause can be used to limit the liability for the car to £100 since Bob can claim on his car insurance. That would involve not just severing the clause into two parts (which I have already said is probably legitimate) but applying the second part to some of the losses but not to others. Even in *George Mitchell (Chesterhall) Ltd v Finney Lock Seeds Ltd* [1983] 2 AC 803 where the question was to what extent it was fair and reasonable to allow reliance on the clause, Lord Bridge of Harwich expressed the view that this was not possible and on the wording of the Unfair Contract Terms Act 1977 the point is even clearer since the test is now 'except in so far as the *term*' is reasonable.

Having discussed the above points in detail, it would be as well to end with some sort of conclusion that shows you can see the wood for the trees, e.g., by concluding that whilst the clause may just manage to clear the incorporation hurdle by course of dealing and may possibly be effective at common law to exclude the liability for the damaged car and, more probably, to limit overall liability to £100, whether Bob will be able to recover more than that amount depends on whether the limitation clause in particular is regarded as reasonable under the Act. It is always a good idea to show that you are thinking critically about the subject so you might also want to express a view as to whether it is desirable for the law to be such that you have to advise Bob (the question does ask you to advise Bob) that much depends on the attitude of the trial court as to whether the clause was a reasonable one to have included. Of course, if you are going to criticise the way in which the law is moving, you ought also to be prepared to suggest some constructive alternatives. (The chapter on exemption clauses in Miller and Harvey, *Consumer and Trading Law, Cases and Materials,* contains some useful material on alternative techniques of control and on the drawbacks that these alternatives have themselves.) It would also be advantageous to speculate on the impact of the EC Directive on Bob's case. Bob would probably also be able to rely on this in addition since he is a consumer and the clause is not individually negotiated. However, whether a court would regard the clause as 'contrary to the requirement of good faith etc.' is probably at the moment an even more unpredictable question than that relating to reasonableness under the 1977 Act.

CONCLUSION

Exemption clauses is an area where a considerable body of law has accumulated, some of it quite complex, with the additional problem of a new statute with as yet relatively little explanatory case law. (At least one hopes for explanatory case law, although what one often gets is added complications!) However, it is as a result a stimulating area to study which is given added interest by the fact that it is currently going through a period of change. Although it can be complex at the level of detail its overall structure is relatively easy to grasp and it is an area that will amply repay careful study.

7 MISREPRESENTATION

Just as in the previous chapter on exclusion clauses, it is important to see misrepresentation in its historical perspective, not so much because it is going through a transitional period — the dramatic changes in the law of misrepresentation took place in the 1960s, a decade earlier than those relating to exclusion clauses — but because the older cases would be misleading if it were forgotten that they were decided in a quite different context from that which is applicable now. In particular, until the 1960s there were only two main categories of misrepresentation, fraudulent and innocent, and the concept of negligent misrepresentation was not separately recognised in English law. As a result one needs to ask oneself repeatedly in relation to any older authorities about innocent misrepresentation whether the same rule would apply (a) to a negligent misrepresentation or (b) to a wholly innocent misrepresentation, today. Furthermore one needs to bear in mind that statements which might formerly have been classified as contractual terms (because no damages were available for innocent misrepresentations, see chapter 5) might now be treated as negligent misrepresentations, given the introduction of damages as a remedy for these in the 1960s. It might well be that a consequence of this could be the expansion of the importance of the law on misrepresentation as opposed to breach of contractual terms. This seems increasingly to be the case, underlining the fact that the area is an important one in the syllabus and it will be examined by first looking at the basic essentials of a misrepresentation and then at the different types of remedies available for each of them.

BASIC REQUIREMENTS

A misrepresentation is defined in *Anson's Law of Contract* as:

A false statement/of existing or past fact/made by one party before or at the time of making the contract/which is addressed to the other party/and which induces the other party to enter into the contract.

Anson then goes on to discuss four aspects of this definition corresponding to four out of the five sections in which the above definition has been divided. The one which he misses out is the third section, the requirement that the representation be made by a party to the contract, which perhaps is fair enough on the grounds that it is rather obvious. However, it should be borne in mind that a statement made by someone *other* than a party to the contract can be actionable under the *Hedley Byrne* principle (as in *Hedley Byrne & Co. Ltd* v *Heller & Partners Ltd* [1964] AC 465 itself) or as a collateral contract (as in *Shanklin Pier Ltd* v *Detel Products Ltd* [1951] 2 KB 854). Such liabilities are subject to their own appropriate rules and are properly distinguished from liability for *misrepresentation*. But they are obviously liabilities related to misrepresentation which you should be aware of.

As far as concerns the other four sections of the definition, which are discussed in *Anson*, there would be little point in merely reiterating what is said there, but it perhaps would be useful to highlight a number of key points.

A False Statement

The main point here is that silence or non-disclosure does not normally give rise to liability but there are a number of exceptions to this. Most of these concern particular types of contract (especially insurance contracts) and few contract courses examine these in detail but the situation exemplified in *With* v *O'Flanagan* [1936] Ch 575 of a statement true when made but false by the time of entering the contract is one with which you should be thoroughly familiar. Issues arising from that case (this did not arise on the actual facts because only rescission was claimed) include the question of whether the failure to disclose counts as a fraudulent misrepresentation. Anson suggests that it does and cites *Davies* v *London & Provincial Marine Insurance Co.* (1878) 8 ChD 469 at p. 475 but it is difficult to see how that case supports Anson's proposition. The question is probably largely academic anyway, as you can point out to the examiner, because s. 2(1) of the Misrepresentation Act 1967 gives a right to damages unless, *inter alia*, the representor 'did believe up to the time the contract was made that the facts represented were true'. (See Treitel, The *Law of Contract*, 9th ed., p. 372, for a discussion of this latter point.)

Statements can of course be implied by conduct, e.g., a person who purchases goods by cheque impliedly represents (even if nothing is said) that the cheque is a valid order for the amount stated on it, and furthermore one express statement may imply another. In particular it may imply that there are no other facts known to the speaker which make his statement misleading. This is probably the best way of looking at what Treitel calls 'statements literally true but misleading' or so called partial non-disclosure as in *Dimmock v Hallet* (1866) LR 2 Ch App 21 where a vendor of land said that all the farms on the land were fully let. The vendor was falsely representing that he knew of no other facts which made that statement misleading since he knew that the tenants had given notice to quit.

Existing or Past Fact

Facts have to be distinguished from 'mere puffs', from statements of belief or opinion, from statements as to the future including statements of intention, and from statements of law. It is quite common for students to recite these propositions, as though they were engraved in stone without any evidence of any understanding of why such statements do not constitute misrepresentations. This is a pity since not only does this mean they have missed the opportunity to see the real basis of liability for misrepresentation, but it also means they will also be unable to distinguish the rules in the appropriate situations.

The basic rationale underlying the requirement of a statement of fact is that only facts are true or untrue at the time the statement is made and that one is only justified in relying on facts, not on honestly and reasonably held opinions and beliefs etc. The 'wrong' or breach of duty in misrepresentation occurs when the statement is made (whereas in breach of contract it occurs when the promise is broken). There is nothing wrong in stating one's belief or opinion or what one intends to do in the future (assuming one is not negligent in making the statement — note that *Hedley Byrne* liability is not restricted to statements of fact) and there is no justification for a person relying on such a belief etc. (or indeed on a mere puff, the essence of which is that it is obviously intended not to be taken literally or seriously). Furthermore, a statement about the future cannot be wrong at the time of being made (unless one is an out-and-out determinist), it only becomes wrong at the relevant future time. In contrast, there is a justification for imposing some liability on a person who states as a *fact*, as opposed to merely expressing an opinion, something which the other party then relies on when entering the contract and which is capable of being true or false at the time of the statement being made. The question of whether the statement is one on which it is reasonable to rely is of course a factor in deciding whether to class it as a statement of opinion or of fact.

Thus in *Bisset* v *Wilkinson* [1927] AC 177, the statement that the land would support 2,000 sheep was merely an expression of an opinion partly because the seller was not in any better position than the purchaser to know its true capacity. Similarly in *Hummingbird Motors* v *Hobbs* [1986] RTR 276, a statement about the mileage of a second-hand car was not treated as a statement of fact because it was qualified as being correct 'to the best of my knowledge and belief' and again the seller was in no better position to know the truth than the purchaser. In contrast, in *Esso Petroleum Co. Ltd* v *Mardon* [1976] QB 801, the statement about the capacity of the petrol station could have been treated as one of fact (it was not found necessary to do so because liability was based upon *Hedley Byrne* and upon contractual warranty) since, given the expertise of Esso, Mr Mardon was justified in relying on it as such. This reveals the ultimate basis of the law on misrepresentation — justified reliance on verifiable statements of the other party to the contract.

In addition, this points the way to the apparent exceptions to the requirement of statements of fact:

(a)   A statement of opinion may imply that the speaker is aware of reasonable grounds for his opinion (this would be an alternative way of implying a factual statement in *Esso Petroleum Co. Ltd* v *Mardon*) and that he is not aware of facts which clearly invalidate the opinion — as in *Smith* v *Land & House Property Corporation* (1884) 28 ChD 7.

(b)   A statement as to one's intention clearly is capable of being true or false in the sense that one either has that intention or one does not. The fact that someone acts differently in the future from his previously stated intention does not make the statement of intention a misrepresentation of fact — we can all change our minds, some more than others — but there is clearly a misrepresentation (indeed a fraudulent one) if the intention was not actually held when the statement was made — as in *Edgington* v *Fitzmaurice* (1885) 29 ChD 459. A more recent example can be found in *East* v *Maurer* [1991] 2 All ER 733 where the vendor of one of a pair of hairdressing salons fraudulently misrepresented that he did not intend to continue to work in the other salon retained except in emergencies.

(c)   A wilful misrepresentation of law constitutes misrepresentation since it is a misrepresentation of the fact of what is the speaker's belief as to the law. The justification for excluding misrepresentations of law in the first place is probably that, unless the speaker is a lawyer, such statements are really analogous to opinions, on which the other party is not justified in placing any reliance and as to which the other party is equally capable of forming an opinion. This perhaps explains why statements of private right and statements about the contents of a private Act, as in *West London Commercial Bank Ltd* v *Kitson* (1884) 13 QBD 360, are treated as statements of fact, since the speaker can be expected to know about laws particularly applicable to him. If this is correct then the rule that a statement *of foreign* law is a representation of fact is perhaps too bald a statement. If the speaker is obviously in no better position than the representee to know the foreign law, such a statement could be treated merely as a statement of opinion.

Addressed to the Other Party

There is little that needs saying in the present context other than this has to be understood in the usual objective sense so that if A makes a misrepresentation to B which he ought to know will be passed on to C and on the faith of which C is then likely to contract with A, A is liable as though he directly misrepresented the fact to C. (Cf. the position of the assignees in *Brikom Investments Ltd* v *Carr* [1979] QB 467 where, however, the representation was not one of fact.)

Induces the Contract

This is really another way of saying that the representee must have relied on the statement. I have already mentioned the fact that this reliance must be justified (which Treitel deals with by postulating a separate requirement of materiality) and that this is in effect dealt with by the way in which the courts apply the distinction between statements of fact and statements of opinion. The point here is that the reliance must actually take place. Thus if the representee makes his own enquiries, as in *Attwood* v *Small* (1838) 6 Cl & F 232, which shows that he does not rely on the statement, he cannot claim relief for misrepresentation but if, as in *Redgrave* v *Hurd* (1881) 20 ChD 1, the representee does not take advantage of opportunities to check the truth of the statement, even if he is negligent in failing to do so, he can still obtain relief. The fact that he has not checked for himself reinforces the inference that he has relied on the statement, rather than weakens it and there would be little point in the parties to a contract exchanging information about the subject-matter if they were each under a duty to check each other's statements. Nevertheless, one should be wary of applying the decision in *Redgrave* v *Hurd* too mechanically and the point made at the start of this chapter about the law formerly not distinguishing between negligent and wholly innocent statements is relevant here. The representor in *Redgrave* v *Hurd* was found not to be fraudulent, but was at least negligent. If you are faced with a problem where the representor is wholly innocent and the representee is in fact negligent it may be more just to conclude that rescission should not be available. (Cf. Treitel, *The Law of Contract*, 8th ed., p. 304 and note the suggestion that even if the representor is negligent and damages are being claimed, as now they could be, the negligence of the misrepresentee might be a ground for reducing them under the Law Reform (Contributory Negligence) Act 1945.) This possibility has been confirmed in theory by the Court of Appeal in *Gran Gelato Ltd* v *Richcliff (Group) Ltd* [1992] 1 All ER 865. However, no reduction was made on the facts because, although the plaintiffs could have made their own enquiries, they had relied, as they were intended to do, on the defendant's representations as in *Redgrave* v *Hurd*. Since reliance is always required before liability can arise in the first place, this approach makes the possibility of a reduction in damages for contributory negligence largely theoretical.

Treitel also says that if the representation is fraudulent, even if the representee takes steps to check the statement, the right to rescind should not be lost. This view can perhaps be justified on the basis that fraudulent statements are usually *calculated* to be strong inducements and the independent investigation will not mean *no reliance at all* is placed on the fraudulent statement, but if the view means that rescission should still be available even where it is quite clear that no reliance whatsoever is placed on the statement, then it is a view which can only really be justified on deterrent grounds. Of course, it is normally sufficient merely to refer to the views of someone like Treitel, but life is so much more interesting if you can offer your own thoughts about those views.

Even for non-fraudulent misrepresentations, it is not enough to negative reliance to show that the misrepresentation was not the *sole reason* for entering the contract and that the representee also relied on other statements (see *Edgington* v *Fitzmaurice*) but if it is shown that the representee placed no reliance at all on the false statement, then obviously no action would lie. Treitel here says that if the representee would still have entered into the contract even if the misrepresentation had not been made, then there would be no liability. This is consistent with the case he cites (*JEB Fasteners Ltd* v *Marks, Bloom & Co.* [1983] 1 All ER 583) but it is difficult to reconcile with *Barton* v *Armstrong* [1976] AC 104 (which was in fact a duress case but the House of Lords accepted that the same principles would apply to misrepresentation) where the House of Lords allowed rescission even though it was admitted that Barton may well have still entered into the contract without the duress. The point is that a misrepresentation can still be an inducement even though without it there would still have been sufficient other inducements to enter the contract and rescission should still be available. Perhaps the explanation of *JEB Fasteners* (apart from saying that it is wrongly decided and that the first-instance decision of Woolf J is preferable — note that *Barton* v *Armstrong* was not cited in the Court of Appeal) is that it was a damages case where the 'but for' test of causation has to be satisfied whereas in claims for rescission, the question is one of inducement rather than causation. The point is not an easy one but it is of the type for discussion of which you can gain considerable credit. Perhaps to make the point clear a simple diagram might help.

Suppose that in situation A, to enter a contract P requires reasons to a value of 6, that the misrepresentation by D constitutes a reason valued at 2 and P has other reasons for entering the contract valued at 7.

A

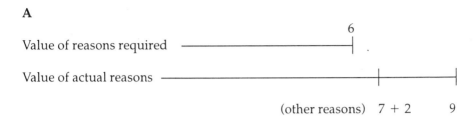

Value of reasons required

Value of actual reasons

(other reasons) 7 + 2   9
                 (Misrep)

Further suppose a situation B, exactly the same as A, except that the other reasons are only to the value of 5.

B

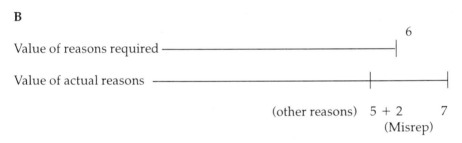

Value of reasons required

Value of actual reasons

(other reasons) 5 + 2   7
                 (Misrep)

In situation A, P would still have entered the contract if the misrepresentation had not been made, and according to Treitel and *JEB Fasteners* this negatives reliance. In situation B, there clearly is reliance — without the misrepresentation P would not have entered into the contract even though equally the misrepresentation on its own would not have been a sufficient reason. My argument, based on *Barton v Armstrong*, is that there is also reliance, or at least inducement, in situation A if P takes account of the misrepresentation as an *additional* reason — e.g., if it helps him to enter the contract much more confidently. On the other hand, if he takes no account at all of the misrepresentation, e.g., his reasoning is 'I have reasons 1 to 7 for entering the contract and I really don't care whether D's statement is true or false', then clearly he hasn't in any sense relied on the statement or been induced by it and he cannot rescind.

REMEDIES FOR MISREPRESENTATION

So far I have been looking at the requirements common to all misrepresentations. To identify the remedies available in any particular case one has to distinguish between fraudulent, negligent and innocent misrepresentation. However, before examining those distinctions, it ought to be stressed that, for *any* misrepresentation, the remedy of rescission is *in principle* available, although it may in actual practice not be allowed due to the various limits on the right to rescind. The question of the type of misrepresentation is primarily important in deciding what remedies in *addition* to rescission are available and it can also have a bearing on whether one of the limits on rescission is applicable. It therefore makes sense to look first of all at the general remedy of rescission before examining the various different types of misrepresentation.

Rescission

The first point to note is that rescission is not necessarily a remedy that one has to obtain from the court. A purchaser can rescind a contract for the sale of goods merely by returning the goods and cancelling his cheque, if in a position to do so, although of course if he rescinds when he has no right to do so, he will then be in breach of contract himself. Furthermore, if you are being sued for failing to perform a contract, you can use 'rescission' as a defence by asserting that the contract was induced by a misrepresentation. Where, however, you have partly or fully performed your own side of the contract, you will normally need to approach the court for an order of rescission i.e., an order which undoes or dissolves the contract *ab initio* and which involves the return from each party to the other of anything which has passed under the contract. It is important to distinguish this remedy clearly from so-called 'rescission for breach' (which in this book is referred to as 'termination') which does not dissolve the contract *ab initio* but merely terminates it from the date of the breach. The distinction is important, *inter alia*, because the limits on the right to rescind for misrepresentation do not necessarily apply to the right to terminate for breach and also because one can clearly both terminate and claim damages for breach but one cannot rescind *ab initio* and still claim damages for breach.

An ancillary order which can also be made along with rescission (even for innocent misrepresentation) is the award of an indemnity. This is a monetary award but should not be confused with damages as it is much more limited. It only covers expenditure which the representee is *obliged* to incur under the terms of the contract which is being rescinded. If money has been paid directly to the other party then of course it will be returned as part of the remedy of rescission itself so that it is payments made under the contract to third parties that the indemnity is concerned with, as in, e.g., *Whittington v Seale-Hayne* (1900) 82 LT 49, where the indemnity included money paid out in rates and to do repairs which the tenant was obliged to do under the lease, but did not extend to removal and medical expenses which, although foreseeable, were not incurred under an obligation contained in the lease. (These latter, and other items claimed, would only be recoverable if a right to damages could have been established, which at the time would have meant proving fraud — the increased availability of damages today would mean that the limited right to an indemnity is less commonly relevant.)

Despite the limited nature of the indemnity, rescission is still, given that it dissolves the contract *ab initio,* a fairly drastic remedy and for that reason as well as because of its equitable origins, is subject to a number of limits or 'bars'.

Restitution impossible   Some such limit can hardly be avoided. The courts can hardly order what is not possible and if a crate of whisky falsely represented to be Scotch has already been consumed, rescission is clearly impossible. The problems arise where the subject-matter of the contract can literally be returned but it has significantly deteriorated or improved in condition. The court may still in these circumstances order rescission and order one party to pay some allowance to the other to take account of the improvement or deterioration and the discretion will obviously be influenced by factors such as the culpability of the representor and the reasons for the improvements or the deterioration.

Third-party rights   Rescission is a personal right against the representor and the plaintiff cannot claim the return of property so as to defeat rights acquired by a bona fide third party. The timing of rescission is important here, since if rescission can be effected before the third party acquires any rights, it will in fact prevent any such rights being obtained — see *Car & Universal Finance Co. Ltd* v *Caldwell* [1965] 1 QB 525 where the Court of Appeal held, rather generously, that the rescission was effected by notifying the AA and police of the fraud, even though the representor could not be traced and this was held to prevent an innocent third-party purchaser getting a good title from the rogue. The decision has been criticised and probably only applies to cases of fraud.

Affirmation   The representee cannot play fast and loose with the contract. Once he discovers the falsity of the misrepresentation he must take action to avoid (rescind) the contract or he is in danger of being regarded as affirming it as in *Long* v *Lloyd* [1958] 1 WLR 753. Affirmation can only occur once the plaintiff has discovered the falsity of the misrepresentation, but once this occurs the court may draw the inference of affirmation very quickly especially in contracts where the value of the subject-matter fluctuates rapidly (such as share purchases) since otherwise the representee could speculate at the expense of the representor with no risk to himself.

Lapse of time   This is often confused by students with affirmation but the difference is that here time can start to run from the date of the contract even though the truth (i.e., the falsity of the misrepresentation) has not yet been discovered. The amount of time allowed depends on the subject-matter and on how long the reasonable man would take to discover the truth and the bar is based on the need to limit the time for which an innocent misrepresentor is at risk of having his contract rescinded. Thus this bar does not apply to fraud. It probably does apply to negligence but probably the courts would require a longer period to elapse before they would hold the right to rescind for a negligent misrepresentation to be barred through lapse of time.

Misrepresentation Act 1967, Section 2(2)   This is not so much a bar on the right to rescind as a qualification to it. As noted before, the remedy of rescission is quite drastic, it is an all-or-nothing remedy, and in some cases, particularly where the misrepresentation is innocent and the detriment to the representee small in proportion to the value of the contract as a whole, it may be rather unfair to order rescission. Section 2(2) recognises this by giving the court discretion to award damages *instead of* rescission (contrast the rights to damages for fraud and negligence, discussed below, which are available in addition to rescission). *William Sindall* v *Cambridgeshire County Council* [1994] 1 WLR 1016 is an example where the court would have restricted the plaintiff to damages instead of rescission had it found that there had been an actionable misrepresentation in the first place.

There are two key issues in relation to s. 2(2) which you should be prepared to discuss:

(a)   Is the court's power under s. 2(2) available where rescission is barred anyway?

(b)   What is the measure of damages in the subsection?

As far as (a) is concerned, it is difficult to see why, as a matter of policy, the bars on rescission ought to prevent an award of damages under s. 2(2), but the subsection only applies where the representee 'would be entitled ... to rescind'. This wording is not entirely clear and perhaps a middle way which you might suggest would be that s. 2(2) is not applicable where the right to rescind has been *lost* through affirmation or lapse of time (where there is perhaps less justification for giving the representee damages) but can be applied where restitution 'would be' available but is impossible or barred in favour of third-party rights. This was effectively the position in *Thomas Witter* v *TBP Industries* [1996] 2 All ER 573 where the Court of Appeal said (*obiter*) that damages under s. 2(2) did not depend on the right to rescind still being in existence.

As to (b), the measure of damages, although there were some peculiar *obiter* statements in the *William Sindall case* referring to the contractual measure, the obvious solution is to make an award which would put the representee in as good a position as if the contract had been rescinded (and any indemnity awarded). Suppose then that X buys from Y a car for £2,500, £500 of the purchase money to be paid to Z, but due to a misrepresentation about the car's age, the car is only worth £2,200. If X rescinded, he would return the car worth £2,200 and get his £2,500 back from Y (£500 of it, strictly speaking, as an indemnity). So he has £2,500 back in his hands. If the court decides to award damages in lieu of rescission under s. 2(2), such damages would have to achieve the same result. Since no rescission is being ordered, X keeps the car worth £2,200 so he needs another £300 to bring him up to the £2,500 he could have got under rescission. What these damages should not cover, however, is any other items of loss, e.g., suppose X has purchased £100 of accessories which only fit models of the year he thought he was purchasing and which are now useless to him. Such losses would have been left equally uncompensated if rescission plus indemnity had been awarded and they can only be recovered if X establishes some other right to damages, e.g., under s. 2(1), which is considered below.

A final point to note is that s. 2(2) only applies to a misrepresentation made 'otherwise than fraudulently'. If the misrepresentation is fraudulent, the court has no power to substitute damages and the victim of fraud can insist on rescission (provided none of the other bars to rescission is applicable). If the victim of fraud actually *wants* damages instead of (or indeed in addition to) rescission he has a right to damages anyway, independently of s. 2(2), as will be seen. Other representees may actually prefer damages under s. 2(2) to rescission but it would be wrong, quite apart from the fact that the power under s. 2(2) is discretionary, to talk about them *claiming* damages under s. 2(2). Although most discussions assume *either* party can take advantage of s. 2(2) the only possible way a representee can do so under the terms of the subsection is to *claim* that 'the contract has been or ought to be rescinded' and then, rather contrarily, to invite the court to exercise its discretion to award damages instead (or hope that it does so of its own accord). Again, this is not the sort of point made in the standard textbooks, it is the sort of point that you can work out for yourself by looking carefully at the words of the subsection. The point is not merely an exercise in semantics but is fundamentally one of whether s. 2(2) is merely intended to provide relief to representors from the drastic effects of rescission, or whether in addition it is meant to give representees an extra option. Even if the points you make can ultimately be shown to be misconceived (as no doubt it is possible to show about some of the points made in this book) you will get credit for trying as long as you put forward reasonable grounds in support.

Damages (Other Than In Lieu Of Rescission)

Fraud   The law of torts has long recognised through the tort of deceit that damages should be available for fraudulent misrepresentations, whether or not they lead to a contract. As far as fraud leading to a contract is concerned (which is the concern of a contract course) there are two main issues to be aware of: (a) the meaning of fraud and (b) the assessment of damages for fraud. As to (a) *Derry* v *Peek* (1889) 14 App Cas 337 is *the* case where a clear distinction was drawn between fraud and negligence (and a right to damages for negligent misrepresentation denied) and the essence of fraud was defined as an absence of a genuine belief in the truth of one's statement. Thus if you have a belief in the truth of what you say, no matter how negligent or unreasonable you are in holding that belief, you are not fraudulent, just as the directors were found, perhaps rather charitably, not to have been fraudulent in *Derry* v *Peek*. Of course if a belief is unreasonable, you will have difficulty in establishing that you held it, but the burden of proof is on the plaintiff and fraud is a serious allegation not lightly found to be proved by any court and likely to be penalised in costs if not made out. As to (b), it is now clear since *Doyle* v *Olby (Ironmongers) Ltd* [1969] 2 QB 158, despite some earlier doubts, that the measure of damages is not the contractual one of putting the plaintiff in the position as if the representation had been true, but the tortious one of restoring him to the position he would have occupied had the misrepresentation not been made, i.e., the extent to which he is worse off as a result of entering the contract. It is now clear that, as Lord Denning MR stated in *Doyle* v *Olby (Ironmongers) Ltd*, such losses are not subject to the requirement of being reasonably foreseeable (the remoteness test). See *Royscot Trust Ltd* v *Rogerson* [1991] 3 All ER 294. Further points to note about damages for fraud are that damages for injured feelings can now be awarded (see *Shelley* v *Paddock* [1979] QB 120) in an appropriate case and that possibly exemplary damages can be awarded (see *Archer* v *Brown* [1984] 2 All ER 267 for judicial opinion on this).

Given the availability of the next type of damages and the rather slight potential differences between the two types, it will rarely be worth the trouble of proving fraud although the ways in which fraudulent misrepresentation is treated differently for the purposes of rescission (especially under s. 2(2)) should be borne in mind.

Negligence   *Derry* v *Peek* was as significant for its denial of a remedy for negligent misrepresentation as for its definition of fraud and it was not until the 1960s that a general right to damages for negligent misrepresentation was established. When it came there was a certain amount of irony and overkill in that both the courts and Parliament each provided an independent right at about the same time.

The common law right   The House of Lords in *Hedley Byrne & Co. Ltd* v *Heller & Partners Ltd* [1964] AC 465 recognised a right to damages for negligent *misstatements* where there was a special relationship between the parties. It is not immediately clear whether this would be applicable to pre-contractual statements by one party to another but it is now clear from *Esso Petroleum Co.*

Ltd v *Mardon* [1976] QB 801 that it can be so applicable. It does not follow that a negligent misrepresentation inducing a contract would always give rise to liability under *Hedley Byrne* for in each case it has to be established that there is a special relationship. In *Esso Petroleum Co. Ltd* v *Mardon* this was not too difficult given the expertise of the oil company as compared with the inexperienced Mr Mardon but in *Howard Marine & Dredging Co. Ltd* v *A. Ogden & Sons (Excavations) Ltd* [1978] QB 574 all three members of the Court of Appeal expressed different views as to whether there was a special relationship. Shaw LJ thought there was, Lord Denning MR thought there wasn't and Bridge LJ was undecided. However, as this case itself illustrates, the question is no longer likely to be a crucial one since the plaintiffs are now much more likely to rely on the more favourable right given by the Misrepresentation Act 1967.

The statutory right   The Misrepresentation Act was based on the tenth report of the Law Reform Committee (Cmnd 1782) published in 1962, i.e., before *Hedley Byrne* was decided in 1963, and so quite naturally included a provision, s. 2(1), to remove the long-standing lack of a remedy for negligent misrepresentation. It is a sad comment on our system of law reform that Parliament acted so swiftly (in the Directors Liability Act 1890) to undo the narrow effects of *Derry* v *Peek* but left its more general influence to distort the law for seven decades and only provided a more general remedy three years after the House of Lords had itself at last recognised liability for negligent statements at common law.

Whatever ironies you see in that and whatever conclusions you wish to draw, the fact remains that s. 2(1) is *the* important provision today as far as damages for misrepresentation are concerned, largely because the plaintiff has only to prove that he has entered into a contract as a result of a misrepresentation by the other party thereto, i.e., he has to prove no more than he would for even innocent misrepresentation. (The section also requires that he proves loss, but that is always true when claiming more than nominal damages.) The burden then passes to the representor to show that he had reasonable grounds for believing and did believe up to the time the contract was made that the facts represented were true and if he fails to do so he is liable in damages 'notwithstanding that the misrepresentation was not made fraudulently' provided that he would have been liable 'had the misrepresentation been made fraudulently'.

It is unfortunate that such an important provision should be expressed in such convoluted language, even more so because it has led to some rather odd applications of the section, but one thing is clear: the section is a much easier right to rely on than either common law negligence or fraud. This is amply illustrated by *Howard Marine & Dredging Co. Ltd* v *A. Ogden & Sons (Excavations) Ltd* [1978] QB 574 where the plaintiffs were held not to have discharged the burden of showing that they had reasonable grounds even though Bridge LJ thought that if there was a duty of care at common law, it was doubtful whether the evidence established a breach of it. The only advantage that *Hedley Byrne* liability might have over s. 2(1) (assuming that a contract with the representor has resulted) is that *Hedley Byrne* is not limited to statements of fact but can cover negligent advice or opinions. However, where an opinion is given negligently there is usually an *implied* misrepresentation of fact that the opinion is based on reasonable grounds so that is no real problem (although it might lead to the defendant trying to show under s. 2(1) that he had reasonable grounds to believe that he had reasonable grounds on which to base his opinions).

Students, and, as will be seen, the courts, sometimes get confused by the reference to fraud in s. 2(1) and the best course initially is to read the section by excluding the references to fraud and reading the words 'so liable' as 'liable in damages'. (The reference to fraud was probably only put in to make it clear that the basic requirements of liability for misrepresentation, which are also requirements of deceit, such as a statement of fact, reliance etc. have to be satisfied although it was admittedly an obscure way of doing this and it perhaps also shows how deeply ingrained until the 1960s was the notion that damages were only available for fraudulent misrepresentation.) Thus modified the subsection would read like this:

> Where a person has entered into a contract after a misrepresentation has been made to him by another party thereto and as a result thereof he has suffered loss, then the person making the misrepresentation shall be liable in damages unless he proves that he had reasonable grounds to believe and did believe up to the time the contract was made that the facts represented were true.

Whilst this amended version of the subsection is still not exactly child's play, I think you will agree that it is rather easier to understand. However, the courts have not been content to ignore the fiction of fraud in this way and it has had a curious effect on the way in which damages have sometimes been measured under the subsection. The general consensus is that the section does not impose liability for damages on a contractual, expectation basis, i.e., as though the misrepresentation had been true, but on a tortious or reliance basis — as though the misrepresentation had not been made. (See chapter 4 for an explanation of the difference between these two bases.) If it were otherwise there would be very little, although admittedly still some, point in distinguishing terms and representations and you would be treating someone who has merely misled you on a matter of present fact as though he had actually promised you something.

After flirting with the contractual measure in *Watts* v *Spence* [1976] Ch 165 and one or two subsequent cases (see (1982) 45 MLR 139), the courts have now unequivocally acknowledged that the appropriate measure is a tortious one in *Royscot Trust Ltd* v *Rogerson* [1991] 3 All ER 294. In reaching this desirable conclusion however, the Court of Appeal has perhaps gone farther than is warranted in giving effect to the fiction of fraud in s. 2(1). It was held in *Royscot* that the same test of remoteness applied as was laid down in *Doyle* v *Olby* [1969] 2 QB 158 for the tort of deceit i.e., all the loss directly flowing from the fraudulent inducement with no limitation as to foreseeability.

Since the Court of Appeal in *Royscot* took the view that the damages were in fact foreseeable anyway, their view about the applicability of the deceit remoteness rule could perhaps be regarded as *obiter*. Indeed in *Smith New Court* v *Scrimgeour Vickers* [1996] 4 All ER 769, the House of Lords, whilst confirming the special remoteness rule for deceit, pointedly declined to express a view on the correctness of *Royscot* in this respect. It is however worth investigating the way the courts apply the deceit rule (whether under s. 2(1) or for fraud) since there is a danger that if some of the more recent cases are misunderstood, the unjustifiable recovery of expectation losses will be reintroduced into the law of misrepresentation. The key to understanding these cases is to appreciate that damages for 'loss of profits' do not always represent loss of expectation and that they can sometimes quite properly be recovered under the tortious reliance measure. Thus in *East* v *Maurer* [1991] 2 All ER 733 the plaintiffs recovered (in a fraud case) £10,000 lost profits that they could have earned by investing in a *different* hairdressing business and not the £15,000 that the trial judge had found they would have earned from *this* business if the defendant's representation had been true. They were entitled not to the profits that they *expected* under *this contract* but the profits from some *other* contract which they had lost the opportunity to enter in *reliance* on the defendants representation which led them into this contract. *East* v *Maurer* was quite rightly distinguished in the case of *Davis* v *Churchward* (but see the criticism in (1994) 110 LQR 35 by Chandler) where the evidence was that even if the plaintiff had invested in an alternative business, there would still have been no profits and so no lost profits were awarded by the Court of Appeal. With respect to the criticism by Chandler, this seems correct in principle and to hold otherwise on these facts would be to re-introduce recovery for loss of expectation for deceit, a course firmly rejected by *Doyle* v *Olby* in the first place.

Another pair of interesting cases relate to whether the plaintiff can recover for the further significant depreciation of the property he has purchased due to other causes or events not directly caused by the defendant's misrepresentation. In *Naughton* v *O'Callaghan* [1990] 3 All ER 191, the plaintiff was allowed to recover (under s. 2(1)) the further drop in value of a racehorse due to it being unplaced in all six races it ran in the two years after purchase. A similar result was reached ultimately by the House of Lords in *Smith New Court v Scrimgeour Vickers* [1996] 4 All ER 769 where the plaintiffs recovered (in an action for fraud) not merely the losses based on the open market value at the date of the purchase of the shares but also substantial further losses which became evident when further facts about the shares subsequently emerged which had not affected the valuation of the shares at the date of purchase. Part of the justification may lie in the fact that as Waller J noted in the first case, '[the horse] was not a commodity like, for example, rupee paper, which it would be expected the defendants would go out and sell'. In the second case, the subject-matter, shares, was such a commodity but the number of shares purchased and the reason for purchasing them precluded early disposal without adversely affecting the price.

Before concluding this survey of the different rights to damages, it should be remembered that there is one more potential right to damages which is easily overlooked — damages for breach of contract. That of course is not damages for misrepresentation as such, it is damages for breach of a term, but a statement can be both a representation and a term — the representor can both *state* something as a fact which the other party relies on (a misrepresentation) and also *promise* in the contract that the statement is true (a term), i.e., promise to put the other party in as good a position as if it were true. In such a situation, the representee can choose whether to claim damages for breach of contract (to which it will be no defence to show that the representor had reasonable grounds for thinking the statement was true) or to claim damages for misrepresentation (where it will be a defence under s. 2(1) to show the statement was based on reasonable grounds). Given the possible defence under s. 2(1), and the fact that contractual damages will be higher if the bargain would have been a good one had the statement been true, contractual damages will normally be preferred. If, however, the bargain is a bad one (even had the misrepresentation been true) the representee would want to rescind and/or claim damages for misrepresentation (note that a representee cannot both rescind for misrepresentation and claim damages for *breach* and that if he rescinds and claims damages for misrepresentation his damages will be reduced to take account of the fact that he has rescinded).

If you did not get lost in this superabundance of remedies some time ago, you are probably lost now and so the chart in Figure 7.1 outlining the various possible remedies may be helpful (you might be able to devise an improved one for yourself).

Figure 7.1

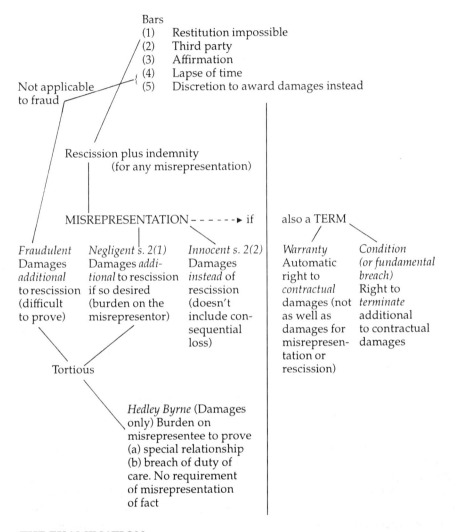

```
                        Bars
                        (1)    Restitution impossible
                       /(2)    Third party
                      / (3)    Affirmation
                     /  (4)    Lapse of time
Not applicable ____ /  {(5)    Discretion to award damages instead
to fraud
```

Rescission plus indemnity
         (for any misrepresentation)

MISREPRESENTATION - - - - - - ▶ if | also a TERM

Fraudulent	*Negligent* s. 2(1)	*Innocent* s. 2(2)	*Warranty*	*Condition*
Damages	Damages *addi-*	Damages	Automatic	*(or fundamental*
additional	*tional* to rescission	*instead* of	right to	*breach)*
to rescission	if so desired	rescission	*contractual*	Right to
(difficult	(burden on the	(doesn't	damages (not	*terminate*
to prove)	misrepresentor)	include con-	as well as	additional
		sequential	damages for	to contractual
		loss)	misrepresen-	damages
			tation or	
			rescission)	

Tortious

Hedley Byrne (Damages only) Burden on misrepresentee to prove
(a) special relationship
(b) breach of duty of care. No requirement of misrepresentation of fact

THE EXAMINATION

Your main task for the examination is to have clear in your mind the basic requirements of a misrepresentation, the different remedies available for the different types of misrepresentation and the various prerequisites for each particular type. Since it is in itself a fairly complex area of law, examiners will often be content to set a self-contained question on misrepresentation but, as usual, the safest course is to have regard to previous examination papers.

If other issues are going to be mixed in, the most obvious contenders include exclusion clauses (cf. s. 3 of the Misrepresentation Act 1967 as amended by s. 8 of the Unfair Contract Terms Act 1977) and the whole question of remedies, in particular the distinctions between the various ways in which damages can be available to a contracting party.

Both essay and problem questions are equally likely in this area so I shall discuss one of each type in turn.

A Problem

> Ann is considering purchasing a burglar alarm system from Bert who tells her that it will still operate even if the mains electricity supply fails. Bert genuinely believes this to be so and a week later Ann signs a contract which makes no mention of what would happen in the event of a power failure. During that week Bert discovers that the system will not operate during a power cut but, having forgotten that he ever discussed the matter with Ann, doesn't say anything more about it. Having paid £400 for the system, Ann is burgled two weeks later during a power cut and £2,000 worth of jewellery is stolen. There are other systems on the market which are not dependent on the mains supply but all cost over £600.
>
> Advise Ann as to any remedies she may have against Bert.

The question asks you to advise about remedies but you could start by pointing out that the available remedies will vary according to how the statement about the burglar alarm would be classified by the courts. The first point to note is that the contract is silent on the question of the effect of a power failure and there does not appear to be any breach of a contractual term unless one could find some sort of collateral contract but there seems to be little ground for this on the facts. Thus the question becomes one of whether Bert's statement amounts to an actionable misrepresentation. You could here briefly outline the main requirements of a misrepresentation discussed earlier in this chapter, such as, it must be a statement of fact made by Bert which induces Ann to enter the contract. There appears to be no difficulty with it being a statement of fact — Bert can hardly argue that a statement about his own product is merely a statement of opinion — but the more difficult issue is whether the statement induces the contract. There is nothing in the problem to suggest that Ann attaches any special significance to the question of what would happen in the event of a power cut but it is no doubt something that would influence the reasonable man (or woman) and the point to make is that this means that the burden is on Bert to show that the statement did not influence Ann. The earlier discussion of *JEB Fasteners Ltd v Marks, Bloom & Co.* [1983] 1 All ER 583 could be relevant here and you could discuss the issue of whether Bert could escape liability by showing that Ann would still have entered the contract even if this statement had not been made. As indicated earlier, personally I don't think that should be of itself a sufficient excuse for Bert unless he can show further that Ann regarded the statement as completely insignificant, which would be a very difficult thing to prove.

Whatever conclusion you come to on this issue it is clearly possible, to say the least, that the contract was induced by the misrepresentation. The issue then becomes, what remedies are available to Ann? The two possibilities are rescission and damages.

Taking rescission first, this is prima facie available whatever the type of misrepresentation, whether innocent, negligent or fraudulent. It would involve Ann receiving her £400 back and taking out the burglar alarm. It may be that Ann would not wish to do this, given that a better system would cost her more money, but the point to make is that she must make up her mind whether she wishes to rescind because if she delays too long, now that she knows the true position, she may be held to have affirmed. Apart from that, none of the other bars to rescission seems applicable here, so if she decides to claim rescission, she is likely to get it subject to the court's discretion to award damages in lieu of rescission under s. 2(2) of the Misrepresentation Act 1967 (there is no evidence of fraud on Bert's part which would remove the court's discretion to do this). There doesn't appear to be any compelling reason why the court should want to award damages in lieu of rescission here and if it did it is rather difficult to see what those damages would consist of unless it could be shown that the system was not worth the £400 which Ann paid for it. None the less you should demonstrate your awareness of the possibility.

Ann's concern, however, is more likely to be with the question of whether she can obtain damages for the stolen jewellery. This would certainly not be covered by any award under s. 2(2) and she needs to establish an independent right to damages. Historically, of course, she would have had to prove fraud, of which there is no evidence, as I have already mentioned, but she may be able to recover damages for negligent misrepresentation, either under *Hedley Byrne & Co. Ltd v Heller & Partners Ltd* [1964] AC 465 at common law or under s. 2(1) of the Misrepresentation Act 1967.

As far as the common law is concerned, you need to point out the requirement of a special relationship which is quite possible on the facts, and of a breach of the duty of care by Bert and that the burden of proving both of these matters lies on Ann. There is an additional problem on the facts that we don't know why Bert originally believed his statement was true. If he had reasonable grounds for the statement originally, the statement is not negligent at that stage and it is not clear whether *Hedley Byrne* can be applied to a negligent failure to correct an earlier innocent misstatement.

A claim under s. 2(1) will be a much better bet. Ann would only have to show that she has suffered loss as a result of entering the contract and the burden is then on Bert to show that 'he had reasonable ground to believe and did believe up to the time the contract was made the facts represented were true'. Thus Ann would be relieved of the need to prove a special relationship or breach of a duty of care and it would be irrelevant for Bert to show, even if he were able, that he had reasonable grounds for making the statement as he did not 'believe up to the time the contract was made' that the facts represented were true.

Thus, liability under s. 2(1) would appear to be established, and the remaining issue would be as to what items of loss it would cover. If the burglar alarm was actually worth less than £400 then clearly the difference can be recovered under s. 2(1) (unless of course Ann also rescinds or recovers damages under s. 2(2) in lieu of rescission). However, as already stated, she is more likely to be concerned with the £2,000 loss represented by her stolen jewellery.

It is easy to jump in here and say, of course she can recover it. Clearly, if the statement had been a term of the contract, she would be entitled to be put in the position as though the statement had been true, i.e., as though the burglar alarm worked despite the power cut. Even then it would not automatically follow that she could recover for the lost jewellery, since the thieves might still have been able to steal the jewellery despite the burglar alarm (see *Davis & Co. (Wines) Ltd* v *Afa-Minerva (EMI) Ltd* [1974] 2 Lloyd's Rep 27 at p. 33). Much depends on the determination and sophistication of the particular burglars. However, as pointed out earlier, the measure of damages under s. 2(1) is different from the contractual one and is based on the position as though the misrepresentation had not been made or the contract not entered into. On this basis there is the additional problem of whether Ann would, if she hadn't purchased this alarm system or thought it operated independently of the mains, have purchased a different one or taken any other precautions that would have been effective against this particular burglar. Would she have been prepared, e.g., to pay the extra £200 to get a system which would operate during a power cut? On the other hand, would she have taken any other precautions in respect of her jewellery, like insuring it, had she realised the fallibility of her burglar alarm? Perhaps on this basis she has *relied* on the misrepresentation and can recover the £2,000 under s. 2(1). It is analogous to the award in *East* v *Maurer* [1991] 2 All ER 733 based on the missed oppportunity to invest in another business because of reliance on misrepresentation.

There is no easy answer to these sorts of issues and the more one thinks about the measurement of damages in these sorts of cases, the more complex the issues seem to become, but even if you merely show your awareness of the controversies and the difficulties you will get considerable credit for doing so.

A final point to note about this particular problem is that many students will leap into it and start talking about *With* v *O'Flanagan* [1936] Ch 575 and the duty to disclose a change of circumstances. Whilst that case is not completely irrelevant, it is not directly in point since the issue there concerned a statement which was initially true when made, but which became untrue or misleading in the light of later developments. The issue in our problem is rather one of a statement which is untrue right from the beginning but which is innocently (or at worst negligently) made, the representor only learning the true position later on. In other words the change here is not one of the facts represented but of the representor's state of mind. The ability to see the differences between a problem and a leading case is as important as the ability to see the similarities and will often be precisely the point which the examiner is looking for.

An Essay

'Whilst the remedies for misrepresentation have improved dramatically in the past 20 years, the resultant law in this area is something of a conceptual muddle.'
    Discuss.

The quotation which you are asked to discuss makes two assertions which you can deal with in turn.

(a)   That the remedies for misrepresentation have been improved in the past 20 years, but
(b)   That the resultant law is a conceptual muddle.

You need to illustrate how far each of these propositions is true and/or how far you would disagree with them. Taking (a) first, you must show the examiner your awareness of the developments in the law since the 1960s, in particular the changes made by the Misrepresentation Act 1967 and the impact of the decision in *Hedley Byrne & Co. Ltd v Heller & Partners Ltd* [1964] AC 465. Don't forget that the Act not only introduced a right to damages for 'negligent' misrepresentation under s. 2(1) but also improved the remedies for misrepresentation in other respects. In particular s. 1 of the Act removes two former quite serious limitations on the right to rescind, i.e., where a misrepresentation has become a term of the contract and where the contract has been performed. It would be wise to link any discussion of this point with a comment about s. 2(2) actually qualifying the remedy of rescission (which can be particularly drastic where the contract has been performed and the representation is innocent) so that the court can award damages in lieu of rescission.
    You could then turn to the remedy of damages and point out the big improvement effected by the introduction of a right to damages for negligent

misrepresentation, which means that the courts no longer need to distort the law on contractual warranties in order to do justice (although you might also note that the courts still seem to be attached to the process of finding a warranty rather than relying on misrepresentation — see *Esso Petroleum Co. Ltd* v *Mardon* [1976] QB 801 and *Thake* v *Maurice* [1986] 1 All ER 497 in Chapter 5).

Having set out the major improvements, you then need to deal with part (b) of the statement and discuss whether the law is now a 'conceptual muddle'. Again, tackle the question in an orderly way, breaking it down into manageable components, first of all the changes to the remedy of rescission, then the new rights to damages. On rescission, the Act probably simplified more than anything by removing, in s. 1, two former anomalous restrictions but you can point out that it can lead to a situation which is rather odd at first sight, namely, that where a representation is repeated as a term of a contract (and is only a warranty and not a condition) there is no right to terminate for breach of contract but there may well be a right to rescind for misrepresentation. One way of resolving this point might be to say, e.g., that there is no conceptual muddle here provided one remembers that the right to rescind for misrepresentation is quite a different sort of right to the right to terminate for breach. In particular the right to rescind is subject to various bars, is subject to the court's discretion to award damages in lieu, and if one exercises the right to rescind for misrepresentation, one cannot also claim damages for breach of contract.

You could also point out that there are various aspects of the law introduced in the 1967 Act which are still unclear (Atiyah and Treitel (1967) 30 MLR 369 is an exhaustive description of the uncertainties created by the drafting of the Act) such as whether the power to award damages in lieu of rescission applies where the right to rescind is already barred, and also what exactly is the measure of damages under s. 2(2).

Similarly, with the new rights to damages themselves, whilst they have no doubt improved the available remedies, there is now almost a problem of a surfeit of available remedies with the attendant problem of knowing which one to claim and understanding the relationship between the different ones. More fundamentally, there is the issue of whether the increased availability of damages for misrepresentation in effect destroys the distinction built up with such care, between terms and representations (cf. the New Zealand Contractual Remedies Act 1979 which effectively abolishes the distinction). Again, one way of dealing with this point (and of adhering closely to the question asked) might be to say that whilst there may be the appearance of a conceptual muddle, the distinction between terms and representations can still be maintained since normally fault is not necessary for breach of a term whereas it is for damages for misrepresentation and that the measure of damages is different for breach of contract as opposed to misrepresentation where damages will be assessed on tortious principles.

You could then end with a conclusion along the lines that yes, the remedies have improved but the result is not so much a conceptual muddle as an area of great complexity and that perhaps what is needed is a restatement which clearly distinguishes the possible different remedies both for misrepresentation and breach of contract, their relationship to one another and the appropriate measure of damages for each type of claim. The important thing is to express your view in your conclusion and to relate it in some way to the statement you have been asked to discuss.

CONCLUSION

The law on misrepresentation occupies a pivotal position in the law of obligations. It provides not only defences to breach of contract but positive rights to damages which are essentially tortious in nature and it can also give rise to restitutionary rights. It is thus a complex but important area of law, a good understanding of which can help provide you with the ability to link different branches of the law together and to see their relationships with one another. It can thus help you not only to be successful in your contract course but will stand you in good stead in torts if you are also studying that subject at the same time.

8   MISTAKE AND FRUSTRATION

This chapter deals together with two topics, mistake and frustration, which you might expect to be treated separately but dealing with them together should enable you to see certain themes and ideas which are common to both areas and which are capable of illuminating either. Having said that, there are obviously some types of mistake which have very little to do with frustration and there are aspects of the law on frustration which have little to do with mistake and so a separate section of the chapter will be devoted to each topic before looking at a question which straddles both areas.

MISTAKE

It is with some trepidation that I venture to say anything at all about mistake since it is an area ripe with confusing terminology and conflicting views but it is no doubt for that reason all the more imperative that I say something about it. The key point to understand is that the cases traditionally lumped together under the heading of mistake do not really all belong together and to try to identify or impose rules applicable to all of them will inevitably lead to confusion and distortion. One way of separating the cases is to adopt Cheshire and Fifoot's classification into unilateral, mutual and common mistake. Unilateral is where A is mistaken and B knows of A's mistake (i.e., only one party is mistaken as in *Smith v Hughes* (1871) LR 6 QB 597). In mutual mistake each party mistakes the other's intention, as in *Raffles v Wichelhaus* (1864) 2 H & C 906, where the parties were mutually mistaken as to which ship called *Peerless* the other intended. In common mistake, both parties make exactly the same mistake, as in *Solle v Butcher* [1950] 1 KB 671 where the mistaken belief that the flat was not subject to the Rent Acts was common to both parties.

Under this analysis, common mistake is fundamentally different from the other two types of mistake (although the judges frequently refer to mutual mistake (as does Anson) when they mean common mistake), since in common mistake the parties are in agreement whereas in the other two cases they are not. Further distinctions are then drawn between the effects of mistake at law and in equity and between fundamental and non-fundamental mistakes and between mistakes that render a contract void and those which make it merely voidable.

If you think you can follow and apply all these distinctions then all well and good but if you find, e.g., the distinction between fundamental and non-fundamental mistakes somewhat elusive and the task of reconciling the so-called common law position with that in equity rather a difficult one then you may prefer to consider some additional issues which are in reality more significant. These include:

(a)   The question of who is alleging that there is a mistake and for what purpose.

(b)   The question of whether the 'contract' has been executed or not.

(c)   The question of whether the rights of third parties are involved.

(d)   The question of whether either party is responsible for or could have been expected to discover the mistake.

It can be shown that the so-called mistake cases are merely a rag-bag of cases at the borderline of a number of other doctrines like offer and acceptance, warranty and misrepresentation and that one has to look at a variety of legal rules in order to resolve the various types of cases that arise. Appeal to a single rather unwieldy doctrine of 'mistake' is unlikely to be helpful. I will take a number of the leading cases in turn to see if more sense can be made of them in the light of these and other factors.

Unilateral Mistake Cases

Hartog v Colin and Shields [1939] 3 All ER 566, where the purchaser knew that the seller had mistakenly offered to sell hare skins by the pound rather than by the piece, is a classic case of unilateral mistake allegedly making the contract void. But it is important to note that it was the purchaser who was suing for breach of a contract to sell at a price per pound. Treitel, in *The Law of Contract*, 6th ed., suggests that if the *seller* had wanted to enforce the contract at so much per pound, he would have been able to do so, which makes one wonder what notion of voidness is being used here. If the seller had actually delivered the skins, there could surely be little doubt that he would be entitled *at least* to the price per pound actually agreed and more probably at the price per piece he thought he was selling, provided in this latter case he believed that the purchaser intended to buy at the price per piece. Saying that the mistake is fundamental or that the contract (which contract?) is void doesn't really help and the case can quite satisfactorily be worked out using the techniques of offer and acceptance discussed in chapter 3 (and see the discussion there of *Smith* v *Hughes*).

The notion of voidness doesn't do much actual harm in cases like the last one but in other cases where a third party is involved it can cause a lot of mischief, because if, as in *Cundy* v *Lindsay* (1878) 3 App Cas 459, a contract of sale which has been executed is held to be void for mistake, the goods can be claimed back from an innocent third party. In order to avoid unduly prejudicing third parties in this way, the law had to restrict the situations in which mistakes, particularly of identity, could make the contract void. The result was the distinction between mistakes as to identity and mistakes as to attributes which, like that between fundamental and non-fundamental mistakes, is merely one of degree and thus of no help in deciding hard cases. This is why Lord Denning MR in *Lewis* v *Averay* [1972] 1 QB 198, along with thousands of law students, found it impossible to distinguish *Phillips* v *Brooks Ltd* [1919] 2 KB 243 from *Ingram* v *Little* [1961] 1 QB 31. In any case the question of what type of mistake the seller has made is quite immaterial from the point of view of the third party who acquires the goods from the fraudulent purchaser which is why the Law Reform Committee in 1966 recommended that mistakes as to identity should render a contract only voidable as far as third parties are concerned. The point to note is that in this type of case, the contract is voidable anyway, i.e., it can be rescinded, not because of mistake, but because of misrepresentation and that to classify a contract that has actually been carried out as void for all purposes flies in the face of common sense.

Again in *Boulton* v *Jones* (1857) 2 H & N 564, the defendant Jones ordered goods (a hose-pipe) from Brocklehurst against whom he had a set-off (and who would not therefore require payment) but who, unknown to Jones, had just transferred his business to Boulton, his former foreman. On the assumption that Boulton knew Jones only wanted to deal with Brocklehurst because he would not need to pay him (this assumption is not unrealistic given that Boulton was formerly employed by Brocklehurst) there clearly was no contract between Boulton and Jones because Boulton could not accept an offer that he knew was addressed to someone else. There is no need to muddy the waters by classifying the case as a 'mistake' case. Equally, if Boulton did not know about the set-off and had no reason to suppose that the order was not addressed to whoever was presently carrying on the business, then the normal objective approach to offer and acceptance should have applied and Jones should have been liable. (The really difficult issue thrown up by the case is, given that Jones did not have to pay for the hose-pipe, what should happen to his set-off against Brocklehurst? Thankfully you will not be required to answer that question in an undergraduate course on contract.)

An alternative way of looking at *Boulton* v *Jones* would take note of the fact that the 'contract' was executed and that the hose-pipe had been 'consumed' (the report doesn't specify how — presumably it was destroyed or disposed of). It is rather unrealistic to say there is no contract in these circumstances and the alternative approach would involve recognising that there was a contract (created by Jones taking delivery of the hose-pipe and thereby accepting a counter-offer from Boulton) but there was an implied misrepresentation by Boulton that he was Brocklehurst (implied from the conduct of tendering the hose-pipe without disclosing the fact that he was not Brocklehurst). If Jones had discovered this before 'consuming' the hose-pipe, he could have rescinded but of course recission became barred once consumption made rescission impossible. If, however, Boulton knew or ought to have known of the set-off, Jones could claim damages for fraud or negligent misrepresentation which damages would be equal to the price he had made himself liable for under this contract with the result again that he would not have to pay. Although Bramwell B at one point said 'the plaintiff misled him by executing the order unknown to him' it did not occur to the court at the time to classify the case in terms of misrepresentation because the remedies for misrepresentation were so underdeveloped then. Of course if Boulton had no reason to suppose Jones only wanted to deal with Brocklehurst, there would be no grounds for implying a representation by Boulton that he was Brocklehurst or indeed for denying that Jones's original offer had been accepted by Boulton. The case can be much better dealt with by the rules of offer and acceptance and misrepresentation than under the rather nebulous doctrines of mistake.

The phrase 'unilateral mistake' is also, somewhat confusingly, used for cases where only one party makes a factual mistake about the terms of the contract and the actual subject-matter but this mistake is neither shared, nor *known of,* by the other party. (If it was shared it would be a common mistake and if it were known of it would be unilateral in a sense already discussed.) For example, A buys a piece of land from B mistakenly thinking that the land is suitable for farming but B neither shares this mistake nor knows that A is labouring under this mistake. This type of mistake will never avail A. A can only have any relief if B had warranted that the land was fit for farming (in which case A is not really mistaken, at least as to the terms of the contract) or if B has made a misrepresentation that it is so suitable (in which case either the mistake is common or B is fraudulent). Again the real question is not helped by categorising the case as unilateral mistake but is really one of whether there are any relevant terms or representations. Where, as in *Riverlate Properties Ltd* v *Paul* [1975] Ch 133, the terms are clearly set out in a written document and there is no evidence of any oral statements contradicting that document, there is no room for any argument that there was a term or representation on which the mistaken party can claim relief. To say that this is 'merely a case of unilateral mistake' only expresses the conclusion that there is no ground for giving the mistaken lessor any relief. (Although until *Riverlate Properties Ltd* v *Paul* the misleading terminology had led to the position where it was thought, because of the decision in *Paget* v *Marshall* (1884) 28 ChD 255, that in this type of case the remedy of rectification might be available. *Paget* v *Marshall* itself was not really a case of *mere* unilateral mistake since the document didn't record the prior *common* intentions of the parties.) These cases show how the imprecise labelling of cases as mistake cases can lead to inappropriate relief being given.

Mutual Mistake

Here the parties mistake each other's intentions, e.g., as in *Scriven Brothers & Co.* v *Hindley & Co.* [1913] 3 KB 564 where one party intended to sell tow and the other to purchase hemp. Normally, the law would uphold the intention of the party whose intention was most reasonable on the facts in accordance with the general objective approach. Cases of mutual mistake are merely those where the objective test breaks down because the reasonable man would not be able to choose between the different interpretations put on the facts by the parties. Each party's view in *Scriven Brothers & Co.* v *Hindley & Co.* was equally reasonable and thus no contract had been formed. Similarly in *Raffles* v *Wichelhaus* (1864) 2 H & C 906 it was possibly unclear which ship called *Peerless* the parties were contracting about, although the case has acquired an unduly prominent position in view of the fact that no reasons were given for the judgment. The court didn't seem to understand the significance of the plaintiff's point that he didn't have any cotton on the other ship *Peerless* and that it surely did not matter to the defendant which ship was involved. Surely, objectively, the plaintiff was offering to sell cotton on board the particular *Peerless* which was carrying his cotton. In any case, the mistake was nothing like as material as the mistake in *Scriven Brothers & Co.* v *Hindley & Co.* Further discussion of the case can be found in Gilmore, *The Death of Contract*, pp. 35–9 and Smith (1979) 13 Law Teach 73, pp. 73–6.

Whatever view you take of *Raffles* v *Wichelhaus*, it is very rare for an apparent agreement to be so ambiguous that one party's interpretation is not objectively preferable to another's and the rare situations where this does happen hardly justify the creation of a separate category or doctrine of mutual mistake. It is perhaps not without significance that no cases after 1913 are mentioned in Cheshire and Fifoot's discussion of mutual mistake. The courts have become increasingly willing to select one meaning of the negotiations between the parties as the objectively reasonable one. (See, e.g., *Thake* v *Maurice* [1986] 1 All ER 497 (see Chapter 5) where the Thakes thought they were being guaranteed sterility whereas the surgeon thought he was merely undertaking to use his skill to try to achieve that result. The surgeon's view was upheld as objectively the more reasonable one on the facts and again the court had to choose one view or another because the contract had been executed.) Consider also the related problem of uncertainty of terms where the problem is not just choosing between the two meanings contended for by the parties but of selecting the sense of the contract from a whole range of possibilities. Even here, as is illustrated by *Hillas & Co. Ltd* v *Arcos Ltd* (1932) 147 LT 503, the courts will seek to give some effect to the agreement if at all possible and particularly where it has been acted upon. You are no doubt beginning to appreciate the artificiality of dividing the study of contract into separate components such as agreement, terms, mistake, certainty etc.

Common Mistake

This is the type of mistake which most justifies a separate category. The parties have reached an objective agreement which would be enforceable if the facts were as they both supposed them to be, but the facts are different and one of them wishes to use this as an excuse for not being bound by the contract. The analogy with frustration is at its closest and most obvious here since the difference between mistake and frustration is often merely one of timing. See for example *Amalgamated Investment & Property Co. Ltd* v *John Walker & Sons Ltd* [1976] 3 All ER 509 where the building was actually listed a short time after the formation of the contract so that the case had to be considered under the heading of frustration whereas if the list had been signed before the contract, the appropriate rules would have been those relating to mistake.

In this category too, the doctrine of mistake cannot of itself solve the problems without reference to questions of what are the terms of the agreement itself or what representations have induced it. In *McRae* v *Commonwealth Disposals Commission* (1950) 84 CLR 377, one had about as fundamental a common mistake as is possible in that the tanker which the parties thought they were contracting about simply did not exist. To apply the doctrine of mistake in isolation could automatically lead to the conclusion that there is no contract and this seems to be Cheshire and Fifoot's view (even though it leads to difficulties, e.g., in giving any relief at all under the Misrepresentation Act 1967, s. 2(1), which requires a contract to have been entered into.) In fact the High Court of Australia held that there was a contract and that the defendants had warranted the existence of the tanker. This was surely the appropriate inference on the facts of the case, although it would clearly have been different if the *plaintiffs* had approached the defendants and said 'We have reason to believe that there is a tanker lying on a certain reef, can we purchase it from you?' and an agreement had followed from that. There would clearly be no ground for implying any warranty by the defendants in this situation that the tanker exists and the appropriate result might well be that both parties are excused from their apparent obligations. (You might want to say that the contract is void but it is not clear that that takes matters any further.) Even here, this is not the inevitable solution, it might be that the proper construction of this situation is that the purchasers (not the sellers) bear the risk that the tanker might not exist, i.e., that they have promised to pay the agreed price whether or not the tanker exists. This might seem a curious interpretation at first sight but is not so curious if the tanker could potentially have a very great value in relation to the price paid and it is functionally not dissimilar to what happens when oil companies purchase the right to prospect for oil. This sort of analysis of *McRae* v *Commonwealth Disposals Commission* shows that you cannot really decide whether there is an operative common mistake without looking at all the circumstances of the contract and whether its terms properly construed put the risk on one or other of the parties. Since one of the functions of contract is to allocate risks, the inference normally drawn would be that the contract is still binding as in *Bell* v *Lever Brothers Ltd* [1932] AC 161, which can be seen as a case where Lever Brothers were impliedly taking the risk that Bell had previously been guilty of breaches of contract which would entitle them to dismiss him without compensation. The agreement was clearly not designed merely to settle Bell's rights under his service agreement since the £30,000 compensation paid was far in excess of what he was entitled to under those agreements. The inference from that is that the payment was substantially a gratuity which did not depend on Levers not having the right to terminate without compensation. (See also the comments of Steyn J in *Associated Japanese Bank International Ltd* v *Crédit du Nord SA* [1988] 3 All ER 902 and the case note by Treitel 104 (1988) LQR 501.)

In contrast with *Bell* v *Lever Brothers Ltd*, the Court of Appeal in *Magee* v *Pennine Insurance Co. Ltd* [1969] 2 QB 507 effectively took the view that the insurance company did not assume the risk that the insurance contract was voidable (i.e., like the service contract in *Bell* v *Lever Brothers Ltd*, could have been terminated without incurring liability to pay anything). It is customary to wonder how the two cases can be distinguished (Winn LJ, dissenting, found it impossible) except on the unconvincing ground that *Bell* v *Lever Brothers Ltd* deals with common law and *Magee's* case with the situation in equity, so you might like to consider the following explanation.

Levers were obviously not concerned with the validity of the service agreements because they paid more than was necessary under them. Pennine Insurance were concerned with the validity of the insurance policy because they paid out exactly what was due under the policy. Indeed the majority at one point canvassed the possibility that there never was a contract of settlement, merely a quantification of the amount due under the policy, before rejecting that interpretation. Nevertheless, given that the insurance company were not trying to settle for *less* than their true liability, it is quite reasonable to interpret the contract as not imposing the liability on them if the insurance policy turns out to be voidable. Conversely, if the insurance company *had* tried to get Magee to settle for less than the amount properly due under the policy it would be quite reasonable to construe the contract as one whereby in return they waive any defects there might be (not known by either party) in the policy, just as, for a different reason, in *Bell* v *Lever Brothers Ltd* it was reasonable to regard *Lever Brothers* as paying the money regardless of the validity of the service agreement.

Of course the above explanation does not make anything of Denning LJ's view, expressed in *Solle* v *Butcher* [1950] 1 KB 671, that mistake merely makes a contract voidable in equity. Faced with the very restrictive view of mistake apparently taken by *Bell* v *Lever Brothers Ltd* and the insistence in that case that if mistake is operative it makes the contract void (which for Denning LJ was too drastic a solution especially in view of the potential effect of voidness on third parties) his Lordship treated *Bell* v *Lever Brothers Ltd* as purely concerned with the common law and held that mistakes which would not be recognised by common law could be given relief in equity and cited *Cooper* v *Phibbs* (1867) LR 2 HL 149 in support. This was a particularly helpful case for Denning LJ because the setting aside of the lease appeared to be done only on terms, i.e., on certain conditions, which gave him the opportunity to say that in equity the setting aside of the contract could be on terms, a power which enables the court to do justice rather than be stuck simply with the power to set aside or not.

Unfortunately, *Cooper* v *Phibbs* was actually discussed in the House of Lords in *Bell* v *Lever Brothers Ltd* where it was approved subject to the qualification that the lease was not only voidable but void. Furthermore the terms imposed were not merely dependent on the fact that the contract was being set aside for mistake. The so-called terms were an order that the plaintiff reimbursed the supposed lessor for the expenses of improvement to the fishery. The supposed lessor was in fact the trustee of the property for the lessee and was entitled in any event to a lien for reimbursement of the expenses. It was a question of 'ascertaining' the 'rights and interests' of the parties, not of imposing terms lying in the court's discretion. Thus it is doubtful whether in *Solle* v *Butcher* the Court of Appeal had the power 'to set aside the lease on such terms as the court thinks fit' as Denning LJ put it and yet one has to agree that the case cried out for a remedy.

It is worth asking why this was so. A closer examination of the admittedly complex facts reveals that the tenant in *Solle* v *Butcher* (who was arguing for the validity of the lease) was a surveyor whom the lessor employed as a letting agent and on whom he relied 'in the matter of rents'. The tenant actually advised the lessor that the correct rent was £250 (this advice was accepted to be honest at the time it was given) and then having got the lease, turned round and tried to take advantage of his own mistake which he had induced the lessor to share. Relief (rescission at least) could therefore have been granted on the basis of innocent misrepresentation (a view for which Denning LJ himself said 'there was a good deal to be said'). One obstacle to that approach to the case was the supposed rule in *Angel* v *Jay* [1911] 1 KB 666 that an executed lease cannot be rescinded for innocent misrepresentation but Denning LJ expressly stated in *Solle* v *Butcher that Angel* v *Jay* was wrong in this respect and s. 1(b) of the Misrepresentation Act 1967 clearly removes that obstacle. (Jenkins LJ found not only *Angel* v *Jay* a problem but also treated the misrepresentation as one of law, but then he was dissenting and found that the mistake was inoperative also as being one of law.) Given the improved availability of rescission for misrepresentation there is less need today for the notion of contracts voidable for mistake.

Similarly, in *Oscar Chess Ltd* v *Williams* [1957] 1 WLR 370 Denning LJ said that the purchaser could have had the contract set aside in equity for mistake (that the car was a 1948 model) if he had sought relief earlier and Goff J relied on this case in *Grist* v *Bailey* [1967] Ch 532 as further support for following *Solle* v *Butcher*. Again though, the mistake was induced by a misrepresentation by the seller in *Oscar Chess Ltd* v *Williams* and the contract could have been set aside on that ground.

That leaves us with *Grist* v *Bailey* itself, where a house was agreed to be sold 'subject to the existing tenancy thereof' which both parties mistakenly believed to be a protected tenancy. Goff J thought that this mistake was sufficient (the property with vacant possession being worth £2,250) to make the contract voidable in equity and so ordered rescission of contract (on terms that the vendor offer it to the defendant for its true value of £2,250). Clearly there was no misrepresentation on which this case could be based but it might be regarded, partly for that reason, as rather generous to the vendor. The vendor after all was in the best position to know the status of her tenants. Again the facts are complex but need further examination. Unknown to the vendor, the two original tenants, Mr and Mrs Brewer, had already died and the person in possession at the time of the agreement was their son, Terry. It was never settled whether Terry was entitled to claim protection as this depended on whether Mr or Mrs Brewer was the original protected tenant, which was itself unclear. Goff J therefore dealt with the facts on the *assumption* that Terry was entitled to claim protection but noted that Terry subsequently did not claim protection anyway. Strictly speaking this last fact was irrelevant, it did not affect the question of the status of the tenant at the time of the agreement. Furthermore, suppose that Mr and Mrs Brewer had both been alive at the time of the contract (so that there was no question of mistake) but both had died shortly afterwards and their son still decided not to claim protection. The only issue then would have been frustration, and no court would have held the contract frustrated in such a situation. The risk of protected tenants dying or moving out is precisely the sort of risk that a vendor of tenanted property takes. Should it make any difference that these facts have already occurred, especially in view of the fact that the vendor could easily have checked up?

Suppose further that Terry had decided to stay on and claim protection so that the house was only worth the £850 agreed, and that the *purchaser* had found a better investment opportunity elsewhere and tried to get out of the agreement. The court would have been highly unlikely to upset the agreement in that situation and yet the mistake made (about who was the tenant) would have been precisely the same.

To sum up this admittedly incomplete survey of common-mistake cases, the labels 'void' and 'voidable' and the distinctions between various types of mistake do not seem to be helpful guides in deciding or explaining cases and the cases make much more sense if one looks at them in terms of who took the risk of this state of affairs and who was responsible for the mistake (a misrepresentation being the most obvious indication of this). Of course this does not solve all the problems or make the difficult cases go away but at least it exposes the real questions rather than dressing them up in an answerable form. This does not mean that you must not be aware of the reasons the courts actually give for their decisions, but you must also be able to point out the difficulties of reconciling all the different cases and you will be able to do this much more convincingly if you can put forward alternative explanations and solutions for them.

FRUSTRATION

In contrast to mistake, frustration is concerned with contracts which are clearly valid when formed but from which one party seeks to escape because subsequent events change the nature of what he is required to do or entitled to receive under the contract.

One of the questions which is frequently debated is what is the real basis of the doctrine of frustration? Is it based on an implied term, or on the disappearance of the foundation of the contract, or on the construction of the contract, or on the imposition by the court of a just solution? One can find support for all these propositions (and others) in the decided cases. The simple but ultimately unsatisfactory answer is that it does not matter but the clever answer is that these theories are not mutually inconsistent but are attempts to answer different versions of the question (see Atiyah, *An Introduction to the Law of Contract*). This is a useful technique, often adopted by philosophers, and which you yourself might use in answering examination questions, whereby apparently conflicting theories are reconciled by showing that they are merely attempts to answer a number of different questions rather than a single question as appears at first sight. Thus Atiyah distinguishes the questions:

(a)   Is frustration based on the will of the parties or not?
(b)   How do the courts actually reason about cases involving frustration?
(c)   In what situations are contracts actually found to be frustrated?

It has to be said that even when one splits up the question of the basis of frustration in this way, there isn't necessarily a single obvious answer to these questions (particularly question (b)) but the editor of *Anson's Law of Contract*, 26th ed., at least is quite clear on the answer to question (c) which is the one that probably matters most. He cites Lord Radcliffe in *Davis Contractors Ltd v Fareham Urban District Council* [1956] AC 696 for the proposition that frustration occurs when to require performance of the contract would be to require something 'radically different from that which was undertaken' and quotes Lord Simon of Glaisdale in *National Carriers Ltd v Panalpina (Northern) Ltd* [1981] AC 675 as supporting this test. This is all very well but the quotation from Lord Simon in fact merely goes to show that the different theories of frustration 'merge into one another' for Lord Simon not only talks about a significant change in the nature of the contractual rights but also refers to what 'the parties could reasonably have contemplated' and to it being 'unjust to hold them to the literal sense'. Thus his statement is not inconsistent with versions of the implied term, construction and just solution theories and these theories are not inconsistent with each other. It is clearly not just to hold someone to an agreement if the parties would have agreed not to be bound if they had thought about this situation or, putting the matter the other way around, if they never really agreed to be bound in this radically different situation.

The problem is that none of these theories is particularly helpful in deciding the difficult cases which you might find can most satisfactorily be resolved by asking who took the risk of this particular situation occurring. Of course, this itself is not a question to which there is an obvious answer in the absence of an express provision dealing with the matter (but at least it poses the question in a naked form without dressing it up with misleading, diverting frills). Furthermore, since the parties have not (usually at any rate) actually considered the matter, the question usually becomes: Who ought to bear the risk of this in the light of the benefits and burdens which the contract actually confers and imposes on each party? Only where it is not possible to say that either party can be taken to have assumed the risk of these circumstances arising, will the contract be properly frustrated. This theory of risk underlies the following discussion of some of the main situations in which frustration occurs.

Illegality

Neither party, normally, assumes the risk that the contract may become illegal and so subsequent illegality will normally automatically discharge a contract as where the outbreak of war means that the contract would mean trading with the enemy as in *Fibrosa SA* v *Fairbairn Lawson Combe Barbour Ltd* [1943] AC 32 or where a change in the law makes the performance of the contract illegal as in *Denny, Mott & Dickson Ltd* v *James B. Fraser & Co. Ltd* [1944] AC 265. Whilst this is the normal rule, there seems no reason, at least in cases of changes in the law, why the risk of the change should not be put on one party. Suppose, e.g., that A agrees to purchase a film to be made by B of a certain international yachting race, A having outbid a number of other eager purchasers. The price is agreed to be payable by the end of the month in which the race is scheduled even if the race is cancelled due to weather conditions (because B could easily have earned the same fee by filming some other sporting event if he didn't have to turn up with all his equipment at the yacht race). After the film has been made but before either the money is due or the film has been processed, the government makes it illegal for anyone other than the BBC to sell films of sporting events. (Governments have been known to do stranger things.) Given that A has expressly taken the risk under the contract of having to pay even though no film is actually made, it is not implausible to suggest that he impliedly also takes the risk that the film can't be delivered due to government action. On this view, the contract would not be frustrated and A would remain liable to pay the price. This would involve construing (note the relevance of the construction theory) B's obligation as merely one to attend and make a film if possible and deliver it if possible. The question could also be posed in the form of whether A's obligation to pay for a film which cannot be made because of adverse weather conditions is radically different from an obligation to pay for a film which can't be delivered due to government regulations.

It is of course equally plausible that having expressly assumed one risk, that of cancellation, A should not be regarded as assuming the risk of the contract becoming illegal, so that the contract would be frustrated. However, that would not necessarily be a satisfactory result since, as will be seen later in this chapter, even with the powers that the courts now have under the Law Reform (Frustrated Contracts) Act 1943, the effect would be that the whole risk falls on B, in that he receives nothing for all the work which he has done.

Where the contract is illegal as involving trading with the enemy it is said that the parties cannot ever expressly avoid frustration (see *Ertel Bieber & Co.* v *Rio Tinto Co. Ltd* [1918] AC 260) but this seems to be a special rule based on public policy rather than the normal principles of frustration.

Destruction of the Subject-matter

This is, at first sight, an obvious reason for holding the contract frustrated, as in *Taylor* v *Caldwell* (1863) 3 B & S 826, since normally neither party will have assumed this risk. Again, however, the inference is not automatic so that if A agrees to build a house for B which is destroyed by fire when 90 per cent completed, A is not discharged and has to start again for no extra money. This is a risk which builders are deemed to take (and against which they will therefore insure) along with such risks as the works turning out to be more expensive due to labour shortages etc. as in *Davis Contractors Ltd v Fareham Urban District Council* [1956] AC 696, just as the purchaser takes the risk that there might be a slump in property prices.

Death and Incapacity

If a contract requires performance by a specific individual and that person dies or becomes incapable of performing through illness as in *Notcutt v Universal Equipment Co. Ltd* [1986] 1 WLR 641, the contract would normally be frustrated. Whilst it is certainly possible for frustration to be excluded by one party expressly taking the risk of his own incapacity, e.g., if a celebrity agrees to attend the opening of a new supermarket and expressly agrees to pay damages if he is unable to attend through any cause including illness, it is difficult to imagine circumstances where, in the absence of an express provision, frustration would not apply (but see the discussion of self-induced frustration later).

Where the Contract Becomes Commercially Different

Most of the other cases where frustration has been argued can be brought under this heading. In contrast to the previous three categories, however, the normal inference here is that the contract is not sufficiently commercially different and is not frustrated, i.e., that one party took the risk of this change. Thus in *Tsakiroglou & Co. Ltd v Noblee Thorl GmbH* [1962] AC 93, the closure of the Suez Canal, through which both parties expected the goods to be shipped, was held not to frustrate the contract even though the alternative route was two and a half times as long. Similarly in *British Movietonews Ltd v London & District Cinemas Ltd* [1952] AC 166 the House of Lords held that an agreement made because of the special conditions applying during the war was not frustrated by the changed conditions which emerged after the war was ended. The House of Lords held that, contrary to Denning LJ in the Court of Appeal, 'an uncontemplated turn of events, was not sufficient to frustrate the contract.

The 'Coronation cases' of *Krell v Henry* [1903] 2 KB 740 and *Chandler v Webster* [1904] 1 KB 493 are notable exceptions to the general run of cases in this category denying that frustration has occurred and are explicable on the grounds that they were exceptional contracts. The high price being paid for the rooms and the fact that they were only to be available during the day made it implausible that the defendants assumed the risk of the procession being cancelled or, to put the same thing another way, agreed to pay whether or not the procession took place. Furthermore, in *Krell* v *Henry*, the plaintiff advertised 'windows to view the Coronation procession' which reinforced the inference that the contract was not about the hire of rooms but about the hire of a view. Indeed, if, as in *Chandler* v *Webster*, the contract specifically mentions the procession, it is as plausible (or implausible) to argue that the owner of the rooms should be liable in damages for the lack of a procession to view as it is to suggest that the hirer should be liable to pay for the rooms in the absence of a procession to view.

The real difficulty with *Krell* v *Henry* is the example that Vaughan Williams LJ gives of a contract to hire a cab to Epsom on Derby Day 'at a suitable enhanced price' and which he distinguishes on the grounds that any other cab would do so that the contract would not be frustrated by the running of the race becoming impossible. His Lordship added that in the case before him (*Krell* v *Henry*) it is the 'procession and the relative position of the rooms which is the basis of the contract as much for the lessor as the hirer' whereas the race, it is inferred, is only the purpose of the hirer not of the cabbie. The problem is that: (a) it might just as well be said of *Krell* v *Henry* that 'any other room overlooking the procession would do', and (b) that if the cabbie is charging a 'suitable enhanced price' he is only enabled to do that because of it being Derby Day and so the Derby is as much the basis of the contract for him as is the procession for the lessor in *Krell* v *Henry*. The fact that Vaughan Williams LJ's distinction is difficult to support does not invalidate the decision in *Krell* v *Henry* but does suggest that the example of the particular type of cab hire he gives could also be frustrated. It does not follow that wherever, e.g., someone hires a coach to go to a specific event the contract is frustrated if the event is cancelled. If the agreed charge is not out of line with the normal rate for coach hire and no premium was charged to take advantage of the special nature of the event, the contract may well still be binding. This will not normally inflict hardship on the hirers since the only damages will be the difference between the agreed charge and any receipts the coach operator can generate from alternative uses and if the charge is only the normal one, this is not likely to be a great deal. The need to excuse the hirer is only usually acute where he has agreed to pay over the normal rate and in this situation it is easier to show that the cancellation of the event removes 'the foundation of the contract'. A court will no doubt be influenced by the extent to which the coach operator has already turned down alternative hirers in order to perform his contract. If he has not lost other potential business because of this contract, the court would probably be more likely to hold the contract frustrated, whereas if he has lost other business in reliance on the contract, the court might want to compensate him for the loss and hold the contract to be binding. The courts do not normally expressly advert to these sorts of factors in their judgments but there can be little doubt that they are in fact influenced by them, so it is legitimate to mention them in your own discussion of problems in cases (cf. the similar sort of point made by Atiyah, *An Introduction to the Law of Contract*, 5th ed., p. 241 about *W. J. Tatem Ltd v Gamboa* [1939] 1 KB 132).

Of course any discussion of *Krell v Henry* is incomplete without contrasting it with *Herne Bay Steam Boat Co. v Hutton* [1903] 2 KB 683 which can easily be distinguished on the grounds that there were two purposes of the contract: (a) to see the review, and (b) to cruise around the fleet, only the former of which was defeated. One could also make the point that the price charged was not such a clearly inflated one (at least given that the fleet was still there) and that the effects of holding the relevant contract binding in the *Herne Bay* case were not as drastic as they would have been in *Krell v Henry* since the defendant in *Herne Bay* was able to deduct from his liability the profits made by the plaintiffs' alternative use of the ship on the two days in question.

Cases of Delay or Interruption

These cases can usually be brought under one of the four categories already discussed but they also form an identifiable group of their own about which it is worth saying a few words. An event or state of affairs that would frustrate a contract if it were permanent may not necessarily do so if it is only temporary or likely to be temporary. Thus in *Cricklewood Property & Investment Trust Ltd v Leighton's Investment Trust Ltd* [1945] AC 221 temporary restrictions imposed on building did not frustrate on the grounds of illegality a 99-year building lease and in *Nordman v Rayner & Sturgess* (1916) 33 TLR 87 a long-term contract of agency was not frustrated by the internment of the agent (who is rather drily described by Treitel as 'an Alsatian with anti-German sympathies') for just one month.

One way of looking at cases of delay or interruption is to ask whether, if it had been caused by a breach by one party, it would have justified the other party in terminating the contract. Thus the question of whether one party is deprived of 'substantially the whole benefit of the contract' is as relevant here as it was in *Hongkong Fir Shipping Co. Ltd v Kawasaki KK Ltd* [1962] 2 QB 26 (see chapter 5) even though the interruption there was due to a breach. Diplock LJ made it clear that, in his view, the issues of discharge by frustration and discharge by breach are governed by the same principles. Thus the proportion that the delay or interruption bears to the full period of the contract is relevant which is no doubt one reason why the lease in *National Carriers Ltd v Panalpina (Northern) Ltd* [1981] AC 675 was not frustrated since the interruption was only 18 months out of 10 years and there would still be three years left after the interruption ceased. By way of contrast, a Borstal sentence which turned out to be of 28 weeks' duration was held to frustrate a 4 year apprenticeship with more than 2 years left to run in *F. C. Shepherd Ltd* v *Jerrom* [1986] 3 WLR 801. The Court of Appeal justified this on the basis of the special nature of an apprenticeship but the case has been criticised on the grounds that it undermines the Employment Protection Legislation.

Self-induced Frustration

Mention of the relationship between frustration and breach leads on quite naturally to self-induced frustration which, despite the natural inference drawn from the expression by many students, is really not frustration at all, but breach of contract. The classic example is *Maritime National Fish Ltd* v *Ocean Trawlers Ltd* [1935] AC 524 where the appellants unsuccessfully claimed that a charter of a trawler was frustrated due to the refusal of the government to issue them with sufficient licences for the number of trawlers they wished to operate. The Privy Council held that it was the appellants' own decision to use the licences which they did receive on trawlers other than the chartered one which caused the contemplated use of the chartered trawler to become illegal and that the frustration was thus self-induced. In other words, their refusal to pay the hire was not excused by frustration but was on the contrary a breach.

The case is not as clear as is sometimes assumed and it is often questioned whether the same result would be reached if a charterer had entered a number of different charters and was bound to 'frustrate' one of them, whatever decision he made (this was not the case in the *Maritime Fish* case since the appellant allocated two licences to his own trawlers). It would seem harsh to say that the frustration is self-induced in such a case although another way of denying the excuse of frustration would be to say that the risk of gaining insufficient licences was one which the charterer assumed (indeed this was one of the grounds of the decision in the Nova Scotia Supreme Court in the *Maritime Fish* case but the Privy Council found it unnecessary to rely on this ground). However, in the *Super Servant Two* [1989] 1 Lloyd's Rep 148, Hobhouse J held that *Maritime Fish* should still apply to a case where in effect the defendants had to choose which contract to 'frustrate' and this decision was upheld by the Court of Appeal in [1990] 1 Lloyd's Rep 1.

Another issue is whether frustration due to mere negligence (as opposed to an intentional act) will be regarded as self-induced. It is not surprising that no clear answer has emerged since the question in effect is whether the contract imposes liability for negligence on one of the parties (to deprive someone of a defence of frustration because it was caused by negligence is the same thing as saying that that party is liable for negligence) and this will vary from case to case. The normal inference though would be that a person assumes the risk of events occurring due to his own negligence and will not be able to rely on frustration induced by negligence. On the other hand, it should be remembered that there is only room for an allegation of negligence where the frustrating event is a foreseeable result of the allegedly negligent conduct and that a person is not negligent if he has taken *reasonable* care. The prima donnas who, in the usual examples, catch cold or absent-mindedly step out in front of buses, would have to have disregarded very obvious risks before they could be regarded as negligently causing their own incapacity. In *Super Servant Two*, Hobhouse J thought that a more appropriate example would be 'an opera singer who carelessly overstrains her voice singing another role for a different impresario'. In any event, it is clear that the burden of showing that the frustration was due to one party's fault is on the other party to the contract — see *Joseph Constantine Steamship Line Ltd* v *Imperial Smelting Corporation Ltd* [1942] AC 154.

Frustration and Leases

The question of whether a lease can be frustrated is happily no longer controversial although the fact that there ever was any uncertainty is illuminating in itself. A lease creates an interest in land (if you have not yet studied land law it is probably easiest to visualise it as temporary ownership for the period of the lease) and thus, the argument ran, that interest in land still exists even though the buildings on the land might be destroyed by fire (there was no lease in *Taylor* v *Caldwell*, merely a licence) or the purpose for entering the lease wholly defeated. As long as the interest in land, 'the foundation of the contract', survived the contract was not frustrated.

Happily, it is now clear from *National Carriers Ltd* v *Panalpina (Northern) Ltd* [1981] AC 675 that, whilst a lease will only rarely be held to be frustrated, there is no rule that it cannot be. The sorts of cases which are most likely to lead to frustration are short-term leases for a highly specific purpose, such as holiday lettings, where, in any case, it is at times difficult to decide whether there is in law a lease or a licence. The longer the lease and the less specific the purpose dictating its terms, the stronger the inference that the parties each assume the risk of any change in the condition of the land or its value. Leases are rarely, if ever, frustrated because the whole point of a lease is to allocate such risks in advance but if there is strong enough evidence to rebut this assumption then the lease can be frustrated. Analysis in terms of risk is much more likely to lead to an appropriate result than talking about the 'foundation of the contract'.

Events Foreseen and Provided For

If an event is foreseen and no provision is made for it, then one would normally infer that the parties have assumed the risk of that event and the contract is not frustrated. Suppose that X, a film star, contracts to do filming over the next 12 months for Y, knowing full well that it is likely that he will be called up for National Service within that 12 months. A court would be unlikely to listen sympathetically to a plea of frustration if he is actually called up, particularly if the risk of call-up is unknown to the other party. Even if the risk was known to both parties, one would expect them to have expressly provided that the contract is terminated in such an event and in the absence of such a provision it might be difficult for either party to argue frustration. A factor that might be borne in mind in this context is the detail or lack of it in the contract. If the contract is informal with very few express terms, the absence of a provision dealing with a foreseen event should not be fatal to a plea of frustration, whereas if the contract is highly detailed the absence of a provision dealing with a foreseen event would be highly significant.

Where an event is actually provided for, then the inference that the contract is to continue if that event occurs is even stronger. However, even this rule is not absolute and the court may, as in *Bank Line Ltd* v *A. Capel & Co.* [1919] AC 435 find that the contractual provision is only intended to deal with events falling short of frustration. In that case the contract provided that the charterer could cancel, *inter alia*, if the ship was requisitioned by the government and said nothing about the effects of requisition on the *owner's* obligations. The House of Lords held that the contract merely gave the charterer a right to cancel where the delay caused by the requisition (e.g., one week) was not sufficiently long to frustrate the contract but that the actual delay of five months did amount to frustration.

Obviously this is another area where hard-and-fast rules cannot be laid down and it is a question of whether the parties appear, in the light of their actual agreement and circumstances, to have taken the risk of the particular events which have occurred. The fact that the events were foreseen or foreseeable or partly provided for is merely a factor, albeit a significant one, in answering that question.

Effects of Frustration

At common law the effects of frustration are fairly clear if somewhat inflexible. The contract is terminated as from the time of the frustrating event, i.e., each party is excused from his future obligations but obligations already accrued or due remain binding. Thus in *Chandler* v *Webster* [1904] 1 KB 493, the finding that the contract was frustrated did the plaintiff no good at all since the whole £141 15s was payable in advance and was therefore unaffected by a subsequent frustration. Not only did the plaintiff fail to obtain the return of the £100 already paid, he was also held liable to pay the balance of £41 15s not yet paid but already due.

By way of contrast, in *Krell* v *Henry* [1903] 2 KB 740, £50 of the £75 fee was not payable until *after* the cancellation of the procession and the defendant was therefore discharged from having to pay this sum by the frustrating event. The effect of frustration could therefore be something of a lottery depending on whether, or how much, money was payable in advance and was clearly inequitable in a case like *Chandler* v *Webster* where the whole amount was payable in advance and nothing had yet been received in return. Indeed the result of *Chandler* v *Webster* seems to be that the plaintiff was liable for the whole amount but could not have insisted on occupying the rooms for the agreed days! Such an absurd result would hardly be in accordance with sensible legal rules and the House of Lords so held in *Fibrosa SA* v *Fairbairn Lawson Combe Barbour Ltd* [1943] AC 32 where *Chandler* v *Webster* was overruled and it was held that a person can recover money paid in advance (and is no longer liable to pay if he has not yet paid) where the consideration for the payment has wholly failed, i.e., where no part of that which has been bargained for has been received. (Don't be confused by the expression 'total failure of consideration' — it doesn't mean there never was any consideration in the sense of a *promise* to perform — if it did there would be no contract in the first place — it merely means no part of the promised performance has been *received*.)

Even this decision didn't render the common law position much more satisfactory for two reasons:

(a)   Whilst one party may not have *received* anything under the contract and may thus be entitled to the return of any payments, the other party may have incurred considerable expense in performing or preparing to perform the contract, which expenditure may well be wasted and which therefore represents a loss falling solely on him, e.g., if the seller in *Fibrosa* had done a lot of work on the machines (as in fact it had) and if, further (which is not clear), the machines could not be sold elsewhere (they were in fact of a special kind) it would be just as harsh to make the seller return the prepayment as it would be to make the purchaser pay for something which he has not received.

(b)   The *Fibrosa* modification only applies where there has been a *total* failure of consideration — if *some* of the machinery had been delivered before the outbreak of war, even if it was only a few hundred pounds' worth, the purchasers would not be able to recover any part of their prepayment, no matter how large that prepayment might be.

Thus the common law rules were rather arbitrary in their application and effects. A just solution might be reached by accident if the amount prepaid happened to equal the benefit so far received by the purchaser which also happened to equal the amount of wasted expenditure by the seller but the facts would only rarely approximate to anything like this. What was needed was a more flexible, less arbitrary approach to the effects of frustration and this is to some extent what the Law Reform (Frustrated Contracts) Act 1943 provided.

The key provisions of the Act are subsections (2) and (3) of s. 1. I shall deal with them in turn.

Section 1(2)   Its meaning may not be immediately apparent to you but it can be broken down into two propositions as follows:

(a)   Any money *paid* by A to B before frustration can be recovered from B but ('provided that') if B, before frustration, has incurred expenses for the purpose of performing the contract, the court 'if it considers it just to do so' *may* allow B to retain an amount equal to or less than the expenses incurred.

Thus, applying the Act to the *Fibrosa* case, the purchasers had paid £1,000 in advance. Suppose the sellers had already incurred £800 worth of expenses for the purpose of performing the contract. The purchasers (A), are prima facie entitled to the return of their £1,000 but the court has a *discretion* to allow the sellers (B) to retain *up to* £800 of that £1,000 'if it considers it just to do so'. Obvious factors that will influence the court in exercising its discretion include how far the expenses could be recouped by selling to a third party — if the whole amount, then it would seem just to allow the sellers to retain nothing. It does not follow that if the work is totally wasted the seller can retain £800 since that would throw the whole loss on to the purchaser. The best solution might be to allow him to retain £400 as that would share the loss equally but on the facts of *Gamerco SA v ICM/Fair Warning (Agency) Ltd* [1995] 1 WLR 1226, the group Guns N' Roses were not allowed to retain any part of their ill-defined expenses of $50,000 out of a prepayment of $412,000, all of which had to be returned by them.

(b)   The second proposition inherent in s. 1(2) is that any money *payable* by A to B before frustration (but not yet paid) is no longer payable but, again, if B has incurred expenses etc. the court 'if it considers it just to do so' *may* allow B to recover an amount equal to or less than the expenses incurred.

In *Fibrosa* £1,600 was payable in advance although only £1,000 was actually paid. Suppose that nothing had been actually paid and that the sellers' expenses were £1,300. Under proposition (b) the purchaser (A) is prima facie liable to pay nothing (even though the contract required advance payment of £1,600) but the court has a *discretion* to allow the seller (B) to recover *up to* his £1,300 expenses. Similar factors will be relevant as mentioned in proposition (a) above.

If the sellers' expenses were £1,800, the maximum he could recover is still £1,600, the amount payable in advance. Consequently if nothing is paid or payable in advance, the seller (or other part performer) cannot recover anything for his expenses under s. 1(2) and must rely on s. 1(3) which as will be seen requires a valuable benefit to be conferred on the other party. The sellers in *Fibrosa* would not have been able to do this since nothing had been delivered to, and hence no valuable benefits obtained by, the purchaser. Similarly, if you turn back to the example earlier in this chapter of the contract to film the yachting race and assume that the contract is frustrated, since nothing was paid or payable before the frustrating events and no valuable benefit obtained by the purchaser, the seller would not be able to recover *anything* for the work he had already done. This appears to be both a defect in the Act and an additional factor suggesting that the contract ought not to have been frustrated in that example.

Section 1(3)   This subsection depends not on money being paid or payable in advance, but, as already noted, on one party 'obtaining a valuable benefit' before the time of frustration as a result of the other's part performance of the contract. If this occurs, then again the court has a *discretion* to award 'such sum (if any), not exceeding the value of the said benefit to the party obtaining it, as the court considers just'. In exercising its discretion, the court is to take account of all the circumstances of the case but the subsection specifically mentions two factors:

(a)   Any expenditure incurred by the benefited party, and
(b)   The effect on the benefit of the 'circumstances giving rise to the frustration'.

What all that means can be illustrated by further varying the facts of *Fibrosa*. Suppose that nothing was paid or payable in advance but that the sellers had delivered half of the machinery contracted for, worth £2,400 to the purchasers. The court would have power to award the sellers a 'just sum' up to £2,400 (the value of the benefit) and would probably award the full amount since the circumstances giving rise to frustration (the outbreak of war) wouldn't appear to reduce the value of the benefit under factor (b). However, if the purchaser had actually paid £1,000 in advance which the court had allowed the seller to retain under s. 1(2), the court would have to take account of that under factor (a) and would obviously reduce the award under s. 1(3) by £1,000. Alternatively the purchaser might not have paid anything to the seller but might have been required under the contract to pay, say, £500 to a third party for the carriage of the machines. Again that would be something to be taken into account under factor (a) although it is not clear that the whole £500 should be deducted from the amount awarded here (since the £500 has gone to a third party, not to the seller).

Thus under both s. 1(2) and s. 1(3) the court has a discretion, once certain conditions are fulfilled. Your task is to understand the necessary conditions and the factors which might influence the exercise of the discretion. You could summarise this as in Figure 8.1.

Figure 8. 1

Section 1(2)

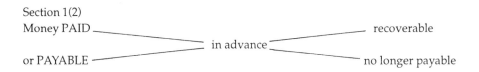

BUT   Expenses incurred in performance, can be compensated, but limited by amounts
paid or payable in advance.

DISCRETION — relevant factors likely to include whether expenditure
totally wasted or whether part performer is himself partially benefited by his
expenditure.

Section 1(3)
BENEFITS OBTAINED *may* have to be paid for.
DISCRETION to award 'just sum'.
Factors include (a) whether benefited party has incurred expenditure in order
to obtain benefit, (b) whether benefit has been reduced by frustrating event.

There is just one further complicating factor which needs to be added to
the above analysis, particularly of s. 1(3), and that is the decision in *BP
Exploration (Libya) Ltd* v *Hunt (No. 2)* [1979] 1 WLR 783. The facts are
somewhat complex to say the least and this is one case for which you might
be better off relying on textbook summaries, at least in order to familiarise
yourself with the central issues, before attempting to read the case itself, if at
all. Although the case Ultimately went to the House of Lords, the interpretation of s. 1(3) was only fully considered by Robert Goff J (as he then was) in
the High Court. It is easier to illustrate the learned judge's interpretation by
reference to *Appleby* v *Myers* (1867) LR 2 CP 651 where the plaintiff (P) had
agreed to erect machinery on the defendant's (D's) premises for a sum
payable on completion and the contract had been frustrated by a fire when a
large proportion of the work had been done. The obligation to pay not having
accrued at the time of frustration, P recovered nothing. The natural
interpretation of s. 1(3) as applied to such a case would involve that D had
obtained a valuable benefit (the part-completed machinery) before the time
of discharge and that the court has a discretion to award P a just sum, the
actual amount awarded no doubt influenced by 'the circumstances giving
rise to the frustration', i.e., the fact that the benefit was subsequently
destroyed by fire. In the absence of other relevant factors, a just sum might
be half the value of the work done which would effectively split the loss
caused by frustration equally.

Robert Goff J took a different view of s. 1(3) largely because he saw the Act as concerned with remedying unjust enrichment rather than apportioning losses and thought that in a situation like *Appleby* v *Myers* there would be no benefit and no award (there is no 'enrichment' to be remedied.) His Lordship partially supported his view by pointing to factor (b) 'the circumstances giving rise to the frustration' as showing that the benefit is nil in such a case. But that is where his Lordship, with respect, is most clearly wrong for the subsection clearly makes this a factor in deciding what is a just sum, rather than in assessing the value of the benefit obtained. Indeed factor (b) talks about 'the effect, *in relation to the said benefit,* of the circumstances giving rise to the frustration' so the benefit is clearly something which is ascertained *first* and then the effect of the fire is relevant in assessing a just sum. Furthermore, the Act says 'obtained the valuable benefit . . . *before* the time of discharge' so one has to look at the situation before, not after, the fire. The fire is merely a very good reason for not awarding the *whole* of the value of the benefit to the plaintiff. These points are helpfully discussed in Treitel, The Law of Contract, 8th ed., p. 813 and *BP Exploration (Libya) Ltd* v *Hunt (No. 2)* is convincingly criticised in more detail in an article by Haycroft and Waksman [1984] JBL 207. Robert Goff J's interpretation did not seem to do any harm on the actual facts of *BP Exploration (Libya) Ltd* v *Hunt* since the frustrating event (expropriation by Libya) did not destroy the benefits already received by Hunt so that his Lordship was able to award a just sum. In a case like *Appleby* v *Myers*, however, if the benefit is regarded as *nil* there is no discretion to award anything.

One problem that still remains in an *Appleby* v *Myers* type case (even if you reject Robert Goff J's interpretation) and which you can usefully point out to your examiner, is the issue of the extent to which half-completed work is a benefit at all (even before it is destroyed). In the Canadian case, *Parsons Brothers Ltd* v *Shea* (1966) 53 DLR 2d 36, a partially completed central heating system (subsequently destroyed by fire) was not regarded as a valuable benefit on the basis that, until completed, it was of no use to anyone. You might consider, as a useful counter-argument to this case, that partially completed work is valuable in the sense that it would cost less to complete than it would starting again from scratch and that if there is room for two interpretations of valuable benefit, the wider one should be preferred since at least that gives the court a discretion to make an award but doesn't actually *require* it to award anything.

THE EXAMINATION

Mistake

It is not easy to predict how this topic will be examined as examiners tend to have widely different views about the proper place of this topic in the syllabus and/or how it should be examined. It may not be separately examined at all, since in truth it represents boundaries of other topics which certainly will be examined such as offer and acceptance, terms and misrepresentation. If it is specifically examined the most likely areas are the unilateral mistake of identity cases and the problem in common mistake cases of the relationship between the common law position (whatever that is) and the supposed cases of mistakes voidable in equity, based on *Solle* v *Butcher* [1950] 1 KB 671. The important thing about this sort of issue is to have a view. The view that I have tried to express earlier in this chapter is that common mistakes of themselves are very rarely a ground for setting aside a contract (in the *Associated Japanese Bank* case [1988] 3 All ER 902, the judge was prepared to find common mistake but actually decided the case on the basis of an express or implied term) since the parties normally assume the risk that the facts are not as they suppose them to be. As Atiyah points out (*An Introduction to the Law of Contract*, 5th ed., p. 224) this inference that the parties have assumed the risk is even stronger in the case of mistake than frustration since it is usually easier to check present facts than to predict future events. Thus the narrow attitude taken in *Bell* v *Lever Brothers Ltd* [1932] AC 161 is a defensible one and most of the cases held voidable for mistake were really caused by the former inadequacies of the remedies for innocent misrepresentation. *Grist* v *Bailey* [1967] Ch 532 can be regarded as an over-generous decision and *Magee* v *Pennine Insurance Co. Ltd* [1969] 2 QB 507 was a case where the insurance company was clearly not assuming the risk that the policy was invalid. Alternatively the misrepresentation which induced the policy could be regarded as a continuing one which induced the settlement. You may not agree with this view (in which case it is a view on which you hold a view) but it might start you thinking so as to arrive at your own views!

Frustration

This topic is much more likely to have a question specifically devoted to it, perhaps also involving some issue as to mistake, and you need to be prepared to say something about the 'basis' of the doctrine (again, formulate your own views in advance) and to have a feel for the sorts of situations where the doctrine is invoked and understand at least s. 1(2) and (3) of the Law Reform (Frustrated Contracts) Act 1943. All these issues have already been discussed but remember that frustration is only one of the ways in which a contract can be discharged or terminated and note in this connection *Avery* v *Bowden* (1856) 6 E & B 953 where the plaintiff failed to exercise his option to terminate for anticipatory *breach* and the contract was subsequently frustrated by the outbreak of war which discharged the contract before any actual breach occurred so that not even damages could be claimed. This could itself be related to the case of *White & Carter (Councils) Ltd* v *McGregor* [1962] AC 413 which is discussed in the next chapter.

As always, you must pay careful attention to your own past papers but the following question, although rather longer than you might expect to have to face in the examination, covers a number of issues that could arise.

Angus lives in London and owns a large tract of Scottish moorland, ideal for grouse shooting, surrounding Loch Tavish. On 1 August he rents it 'with the benefit of its grouse' for £1,000 per month for the months of August and September to Sportshoot Ltd who intend to arrange grouse-shooting expeditions for American tourists. Unknown to either party, the previous day, a scientific expedition at the Loch had captured on film clear pictures of the supposedly mythical Loch Tavish Monster surfacing from the Loch. Two weeks later on the 14th, the film is publicised on television. Angus now claims that this agreement with Sportshoot is unenforceable due to mistake in order to cash in on the hordes of people wishing to visit the Loch.

Sportshoot, however, wish to exploit the interest in the Loch for themselves and in any case have already made agreements with a number of tourists, including Hiram N. Firem, to provide them with a week's grouse shooting for £1,000 each, £200 of which is payable in advance, the balance at the end of the week. The price is to include first-class rail travel and hotel accommodation near Loch Tavish and the contract states that since grouse are unpredictable 'no guarantee is given that there will be any grouse to shoot at'. When, on the 15th, Hiram has had just one day's shooting, a heath fire caused by visitors attracted by the monster, completely ruins the prospects of any grouse shooting. Hiram returns to London and demands his £200 back from Sportshoot and damages for his disappointment. Sportshoot who have already paid out £500 for Hiram's rail ticket and hotel accommodation claim the balance of £800. When, a few days later, the government declares the area around the Loch a protected area open only to visitors with a special permit, Sportshoot also claim that their agreement with Angus is now frustrated.

Discuss.

This problem is rather on the long and complicated side (a monster of a problem!) so it is imperative that you break it down into more digestible proportions. The obvious way to do this is to deal separately with the agreement between Angus and Sportshoot on the one hand and that between Sportshoot and Hiram on the other.

Angus and Sportshoot
Issues raised:

(a)   How can Angus escape from the agreement on the 14th:

(i)   On the grounds of mistake?

(ii)   On the grounds of frustration?

(b)   Can Sportshoot escape when the government bans visitors?

As far as (a)(i) is concerned, you need to identify the type and nature of the mistake made, if any. Both Angus and Sportshoot appear to make the same mistake, i.e., a common mistake, although precisely defining their mistake is not easy. Is their mistake (a) that no monster exists, or is the more relevant mistake (b) that no proof of the monster exists? (b) is probably the more relevant since whether or not the monster actually exists does not affect the value of the land, but *proof* of its existence will affect interest in the land and hence the value of the land.

Is this mistake sufficiently serious under the *Bell* v *Lever Brothers Ltd* test to make the land 'essentially different' from that contracted for? One would hardly think so since the only difference is that the contract has become one for a grouse moor surrounding a loch with a *proven* monster rather than a contract for a grouse moor surrounding a loch with an *unproven* monster. Angus may have a better chance under the *Solle* v *Butcher* line of cases holding mistakes voidable in equity. Goff J found that a mistake as to the type of tenant was sufficiently fundamental in *Grist* v *Bailey* because it significantly affected value, so it may be that a mistake as to the type of monster may have a similar effect! You could mention here any doubts you might have about the legitimacy or necessity of this line of cases but there is no denying their existence. You should also point out that under this line of cases, any relief can be given on terms so that if Angus did succeed in having the agreement set aside it might be on condition, e.g., that he allows any grouse shooting already arranged by Sportshoot to take place for a reasonable fee.

Perhaps more likely, Angus's claim could be based on frustration. The monster, after all, has always been there and it is not so much the making of the film which affects the contract as the publicising of the film which takes place *after* the contract has been formed. A discussion of *Amalgamated Investment & Property Co. Ltd* v *John Walker & Sons Ltd* [1976] 3 All ER 509 would not be out of place here since in that case too it was difficult to decide whether it was an event before contract (the preparation of a list by Miss Price) or after contract (the actual signing of the list by the Minister) which was the effective cause of the fall in value of the building and hence whether mistake or frustration was the applicable doctrine. One of the reasons for preferring frustration was that until the list was signed there was always the possibility that the property might be removed from the list. Equally, here, there was no certainty that the film would be publicised at least within the duration of the agreement, and hence the crucial date could be regarded as its actual publication.

Applying the rules of frustration would not make it any easier for Angus to get out of the contract and you could point out that there are very few decisions on frustration as generous as *Grist* v *Bailey* on mistake. The contract is for a grouse moor which is as yet unaffected, and Angus can be taken to have assumed the risk that the land would become more valuable during the period of the agreement. This would be further underlined if the agreement is a lease (which the question suggests, but does not make absolutely clear, by referring to rent) since even after *National Carriers Ltd* v *Panalpina (Northern) Ltd* [1981] AC 675, a lease will be rarely frustrated since the parties normally assume the risk of the land increasing or decreasing in value.

You should also point out that if, as is unlikely, the agreement is frustrated at this stage, the effect is slightly different from it being voidable for mistake (should it be any different?). Instead of rescinding on terms, the court would have to try to achieve a similar result under the provisions of the Law Reform (Frustrated Contracts) Act 1943. This would be rather difficult since the *most* the court could do for Sportshoot would be to allow them to recover back, under s, 1(2), the whole of any rent paid. Sportshoot would get nothing under s. 1(3) because they have not conferred any valuable benefits (other than money) on Angus and the court would seem unable to protect Sportshoot's contracts with tourists.

However, the likelihood is that Angus will not be able either to avoid the contract for mistake or to discharge it through frustration so that leads on to question (b): Can *Sportshoot* argue the contract is frustrated when the government bans visitors?

The question is complicated by three possible grounds for frustration:

(a)   The fire destroying the prospect of any grouse.
(b)   The government ban preventing visitors even for the purpose of grouse shooting.
(c)   The government ban preventing exploitation of the monster.

(a)   The fire could amount to frustration since the agreement expressly says 'with the benefit of its grouse', just as the rooms were advertised 'as windows to view the procession' in *Krell* v *Henry* [1903] 2 KB 740, but on the other hand the court might feel that the fire was a risk that Sportshoot assumed, especially if there is a lease. Furthermore, Sportshoot did not claim the contract was frustrated after the fire. They obviously wanted to continue to take advantage of the monster's attractions, so it might be arguable that they affirmed the contract by doing so. The problem with this argument is that frustration is normally regarded as something which operates automatically (see *Notcutt* v *Universal Equipment Co. Ltd* [1986] 1 WLR 641 where the contract was frustrated even though the employers subsequently purported to terminate it by notice), irrespective of the parties' wills, but the question of affirmation does not appear to have arisen in direct form (but see *Black Clawson International Ltd* v *Papierwerke Waldhof-Aschaffenburg AG* [1981] 2 Lloyd's Rep 446 at p. 457) so it is a point you could discuss.

(b)   The government ban in so far as it prevents grouse shooting. This would be a strong case for frustration if grouse shooting were still possible but Sportshoot are really using this ground as a smoke-screen, for their real reason is that they can no longer exploit the monster. The courts do take note of the parties' motives (although they do not always expressly admit this) — see *F. A. Tamplin Steamship Co. Ltd* v *Anglo-Mexican Petroleum Products Co. Ltd* [1916] 2 AC 397 where the House of Lords effectively prevented the shipowners from claiming frustration in order to make a profit.

(c)   The government ban as preventing exploitation of the monster is the real reason for Sportshoot's claim but this exploitation was not one of the original purposes of the contract anyway.

Overall, a court would probably be reluctant to hold the contract frustrated since Sportshoot resisted Angus's claim to avoid the contract earlier in the month and having been prepared to take the benefit of the monster's publicity they should be deemed to assume the risks that go with it.

The contract between Sportshoot and Hiram
The issues raised here are:

(a)   Is the fire capable of amounting to frustration?

(b)   Does the provision in the contract, about no grouse guaranteed, prevent it from being frustrated?

(c)   Are Sportshoot in any way responsible for the fire so as to render it self-induced?

(d)   If the contract is frustrated, what are the effects?

As to (a) one would think that there is a strong prima facie case of frustration. The basis of the contract is that there is at least a possibility of grouse to shoot at and a moor with no grouse is surely radically different, in the context of a contract for a grouse-shooting expedition, from a moor which is likely to support grouse.

However, Sportshoot might argue that the contract properly construed shows that Hiram took the risk of there being no grouse since it provides that no guarantee is given, etc. The event is provided for and cannot be frustration. This could be answered in two ways: (i) the provision is not intended to cover this extreme situation — see *Bank Line Ltd* v *A. Capel & Co.* [1919] AC 435 — but only to cover lack of grouse due to, e.g., weather conditions, (ii) the provision merely states that no guarantee is given, i.e., Sportshoot are not liable for breach if there are no grouse — it doesn't prevent the lack of grouse amounting to frustration — see *Jackson* v *Union Marine Insurance Co. Ltd* (1874) LR 10 CP 125 where the running aground of the ship was provided for and prevented from being a breach by an exemption clause but still amounted to frustration.

(c)   The question does not say why the visitor who starts the fire is there. If he has been invited (especially for a fee) by Sportshoot it is arguable that the frustration is self-induced — due to the act or election of Sportshoot in permitting visitors, other than grouse shooters. If that is the case (you can only pose the question) then Hiram will be justified in his claim for damages but not otherwise.

(d)   Assuming that the contract is frustrated (since it is at least a possibility), what are its effects? It is usually helpful to start off by summarising what the position would have been at common law (if only to show the examiners that you understand it), i.e., that Hiram would not be able to recover any of his £200 (there has been no *total* failure consideration) and that Sportshoot could not claim any part of the balance of £800 (due only after frustration). Then deal with s. 1(2) and s. 1(3) in turn. First, under s. 1(2), Hiram is prima facie entitled to the return of his £200 subject to the court's power to allow Sportshoot to retain something for their expenditure which in this case might account for the whole of the £200. Relevant factors might be whether Sportshoot can sell the hotel accommodation already paid for to someone else or whether they can get any sort of refund from the hotel. You can't be expected to come up with any hard-and-fast solution here since the court has a discretion but you ought to point out that the *most* the court can do under s. 1(2) is to allow them to retain the £200. The £300 balance of the expenditure can only be recouped, if at all, under s. 1(3).

Under this latter subsection, the issue is one of valuable benefit received by Hiram. He has had the benefit of travel from London to Scotland, presumably one night's accommodation and one day's shooting. The test is value to him ('end product' in Robert Goff J's terminology) not the cost to Sportshoot, so a rough-and-ready valuation might be on the basis that he was willing to pay £1,000 for a week and he has got one-seventh of that which would put the benefit at about £160. In assessing the just sum (not exceeding £160) to be awarded the court has to take account of the frustrating event (this probably has no effect on the benefit in this case) and expenses incurred (s. 1(3)(a)) by Hiram, including especially any part of his deposit which Sportshoot have been allowed to retain under s. 1(2). The net result might well be that a court looking at both subsections together would allow Sportshoot to keep £200 as expenditure under s. 1(2) but that Sportshoot would recover nothing in addition under s. 1(3). This would lead to the ironic result that the Act would in this case make no difference to the common law position! If, on the other hand, the benefit already received by Hiram was valued at more than £200, the court could award the excess if it considered it just under s. 1(3).

You will have noted that, as usual, the above analysis leaves many issues in the balance and that such conclusions as are offered are generally only tentative ones. Your own answer could perfectly correctly reach different conclusions on many of these issues provided that you identify the possible arguments on both sides and demonstrate your awareness of the way similar issues have been handled in the decided cases. Particularly under the 1943 Act, which confers discretions on the courts, it would be a mistake to become frustrated in the search for definitive answers!

9 PRIVITY AND REMEDIES

As in the previous chapter, this chapter deals with two topics that are often treated separately but which in fact are closely interrelated. The doctrine of privity is largely concerned with the question of *who* is entitled to the various remedies whilst the law on remedies is concerned with the substance of those remedies but a number of relatively recent cases have been concerned with the interrelationship between the privity rule and the principles under which various remedies will be awarded and on which damages will be assessed. This chapter will look at both areas in turn before considering a question which raises issues relevant to both.

REMEDIES

Damages

This is the primary remedy for breach of contract and is always available though this will be of little comfort if the amount awarded is nominal. The principles on which damages are or should be assessed would merit a separate course of their own but contractual damages have to be dealt with in a relatively small corner of your contract course so it is necessary to select the key issues which are most likely to be of use to you in the examination, as follows:

(a) The aim of contractual damages.
(b) Remoteness.
(c) Non-pecuniary losses.
(d) Mitigation.
(e) Contributory negligence.
(f) Penalties and agreed damages.

The aim of contractual damages

This is not something to which the English courts have always paid too much conscious attention but the cases are now beginning to confront the issue directly and so it is something which you can expect to begin to feature more prominently in examination papers. It was noted in chapter 4 that remedies can aim, *inter alia*, to protect the reliance interest or the expectation interest, i.e., can seek to put the plaintiff in the position as though he had not relied on the contract or can seek to put the plaintiff in the position as though the contract had been performed as expected. The classic discussion of this distinction is by Fuller and Perdue (1936) 46 Yale LJ 52 and it would certainly do no harm at all to read that article before proceeding any further. You may not understand everything said in it on first reading (indeed it would be extremely surprising if you did) but it will undoubtedly expose you to some illuminating and stimulating ways of looking at not only the law on damages, but the purpose of legal rules in general.

The normal approach to contract damages is to give the plaintiff the value of his expectancy — to try to put him in the position he would have been in if the contract had been performed. This will be preferable from the plaintiff's point of view provided he has made a good bargain. For example, if P has bought for £1,000 goods which would have been worth £1,200 if they had been in accordance with the contractual specification, but which are defective and only worth £900, then the expectation measure gives damages of £300 — i.e., the £1,200 value he should have got less the £900 he has actually received — and this is the prima facie rule enshrined in s. 53 of the Sale of Goods Act 1979. The reliance measure is not as favourable to the plaintiff because that would only produce damages of £100 — in reliance on the contract P has paid out £1,000 and only received £900 worth of goods in return.

Note that the contract in the above example turns out to be a *bad* bargain because of the defendant's breach but the point is that it would have been a good bargain if the defendant had performed in accordance with the contract and it is in this latter sense that one talks about good bargains. A 'bad bargain' properly refers to the situation where the bargain would be bad even if the defendant performs as promised, e.g., if P has paid £1,400 for the goods (in the example given above) which would only have been worth £1,200 even if in accordance with the contract specification. In this type of situation the normal expectancy measure will still only give him £300 (the bargain might have been bad anyway, but the defendant's breach means that it is £300 worse than it should have been) whereas the reliance measure will produce £500. This example raises in simple but troublesome form the thorny question of whether P is entitled to prefer the reliance measure of damages to the more usual expectation measure.

The basic answer to this question is that the plaintiff can claim the reliance measure instead of the expectation measure *except* in the situation outlined in the above example where to do so would be to shift a loss which he would have suffered even if the contract had been performed to the defendant. (In the example P would have lost £200 anyway and he would be shifting this loss by claiming £500 reliance damages — £200 more than he would be entitled to under the expectation measure.) This was made clear (if clear is the right word) in English law by a pair of decisions: *C & P Haulage* v *Middleton* [1983] 3 All ER 94 and *CCC Films (London) Ltd* v *Impact Quadrant Films Ltd* [1985] QB 16 — see further (1984) 18 Law Teach 217.

You might wonder what is the point of having the separate reliance measure of damages if the plaintiff can't use it where it gives him a larger award. Part of the answer is that sometimes it may be very difficult to prove the expectation measure, e.g., it may be impossible to say what profits would have been made if the contract had been performed and so the plaintiff may choose to claim the money he has thrown away in reliance on the contract instead. This is what happened in the Australian case of *McRae* v *Commonwealth Disposals Commission* (1950) 84 CLR 377 (discussed in the previous chapter under 'Mistake') where it was impossible to show what the tanker would have been worth since it didn't exist so the plaintiffs had to be content with compensation for their wasted expenditure. (Another interpretation of the case would be that, had the category of negligent misrepresentation been recognised at the time, the court would have based the Commission's liability on that so that there would have been no question of expectancy damages anyway.) *Anglia Television Ltd* v *Reed* [1972] 1 QB 60 is an English case where the plaintiffs had difficulty in proving their lost profits and so recovered instead their wasted expenditure (with the added complication that the expenditure was pre-contractual). These reliance claims would only be barred to the extent that it is shown (the burden is on the defendant, see *CCC Films (London) Ltd* v *Impact Quadrant Films Ltd* [1985] QB 16) that the expenditure would not have been recouped (i.e., would still have been wasted) had the contract been performed.

This is clearly an area of law which is constantly developing and indeed I was caused to modify my own views by an article by Marc Owen (1984) 4 OJLS 393 which you might find worth reading. The important point that emerges from it is that despite the impressive analysis of Fuller and Perdue, there is little justification for the reliance interest as an *independent* measure of damages for breach of contract aimed at putting the plaintiff in 'as good a position as he was in before the promise was made', as Fuller and Perdue put it. The defendant's breach of contract has not caused the plaintiff to enter into or rely on the contract (unlike misrepresentation, so this argument in no way invalidates reliance as the basis for damages for misrepresentation), it has caused him not to receive the expected performance, so the lost expectancy is the proper *basis* for damages. Reliance damages are merely *part* of the expectancy — contracting parties normally expect to recover their reliance expenditures *plus* an element of profit. If the full profit cannot be proved, the reliance measure can be allowed as a substitute prima facie measure, since it is assumed that the contract would have been sufficiently profitable to at least recoup the expenditure but if the defendant proves otherwise (cf. *CCC Films (London) Ltd* v *Impact Quadrant Films Ltd*) the reliance expenditure will not be awarded.

The virtue of this modified analysis (which you can therefore point out to your examiner if you get the chance) is that it resolves any doubts about whether the plaintiff can choose the reliance measure where the expectation measure would be less. He clearly cannot if the so-called reliance measure is merely a limited portion of the expectancy. Neither is this analysis out of line with *all* that Fuller and Perdue said. One of the roles which they assign to the reliance measure is as a limiting factor where one has a 'not quite' contract or where there are other reasons for denying full protection of the expectation interest.

To sum up, the expectation measure can really be seen as the maximum measure of damages — the full measure of damages actually caused by the failure to perform. None the less, the reliance interest is a possible subsidiary measure, contained within the expectancy, which can be utilised, *inter alia*, as a prima facie measure where the full expectancy is difficult to prove or perhaps as a compromise measure where it is not 'wise to make the defaulting promisor pay for all the damages which follow as a consequence of his breach'. This last principle is more traditionally and more commonly recognised as the 'rule in *Hadley* v *Baxendale*' which is the subject of the next section.

Remoteness If any system of compensation imposed liability for all the consequences of a given act it would be safest to stay in bed in the morning and avoid the risk of being found liable for anything. Thus the award of contractual damages, like damages in tort, is subject to rules of remoteness which limit the types of loss which are recoverable.

The basic rule, of course, stated in *Hadley* v *Baxendale* (1854) 9 Exch 341, is that a contracting party is liable for losses either:

(a) arising naturally, i.e., according to the usual course of things, or

(b) such as may reasonably be supposed to have been in the contemplation of both parties, at the time they made the contract, as the probable result of the breach of it.

This was transmuted to the test of 'reasonably foreseeable as liable to result' in *Victoria Laundry (Windsor) Ltd* v *Newman Industries Ltd* [1949] 2 KB 528 which itself has two subdivisions corresponding to the two limbs of the rule in *Hadley* v *Baxendale*, one dealing with losses that anyone, 'as a reasonable person', could foresee and the second dealing with losses that are foreseeable given the special knowledge of the defendant. Thus the late delivery of the boiler in the *Victoria Laundry* case caused foreseeable (and hence recoverable) loss of profits since the defendants knew the boiler was required for immediate use but the loss of the 'highly lucrative' dyeing contracts was not foreseeable since the defendants had no knowledge of these contracts.

Although the actual decision in this case has not been doubted, in *The Heron II* [1969] 1 AC 350 Lord Reid thought that the language used in *Victoria Laundry* was 'likely to be misunderstood' as confusing the test of remoteness in contract with that in tort where it is more generous and includes damage foreseeable as a mere possibility whereas in contract it has to be foreseeable as 'not unlikely' or as a 'serious possibility' etc. The House of Lords had difficulty in formulating a single test but all their Lordships were agreed that a higher degree of foreseeability is required in contract than in tort. (The justification for the difference is that if a contracting party wants greater protection against the possible consequences of breach he can provide for this in the contract and/or notify the other party of factors rendering a particular risk more likely. The other party will calculate his price and terms and arrange his insurance on the basis of the quantifiable risks which he knows about and not on the basis of possible but unlikely risks.)

The problem with the distinction between remoteness in tort and in contract (which you should therefore be prepared to discuss) is that often the same act can be both a breach of contract and a tort (usually negligence). This concurrent liability is most likely to arise where physical damage is caused (purely economic loss is subject to its own limitations in negligence) and this led Lord Denning MR to suggest in *H. Parsons (Livestock) Ltd* v *Uttley Ingham & Co. Ltd* [1978] QB 791 that the tort test is applicable also to damages in contract where the loss is physical damage. Thus the plaintiffs in that case recovered for the physical damage (diseased and deceased pigs!) but not for loss of profits on future sales. However, Lord Scarman disagreed on this distinction between loss of profit and physical damage and yet agreed in result because some physical damage to the pigs was a serious possibility and once that type of damage is within the contemplation of the parties it does not matter that actual damage is much more serious in degree.

Whilst Lord Scarman used the language adopted by the House of Lords in *The Heron II* ('serious possibility') he also said: 'notwithstanding the interpretation put on some dicta in *The Heron II* the law is not so absurd as to differentiate between contract and tort save in situations where the agreement or the factual relationship of the parties with each other requires it in the interests of justice'.

It is difficult in the light of comments like this to resist the conclusion that the courts will adopt the particular test of remoteness which seems most likely to achieve what is considered to be a just result, the knowledge of the parties and their respective opportunities to specify in the contract the risks for which they would or would not be liable being important factors to be taken into account. What you must be aware of are the different formulations that the courts have come up with and how these have been applied in the cases together with an appreciation of how to manipulate the tests to achieve a reasonable result on the facts of any problems you may be given.

A key concept in any discussion of remoteness is a notion of the 'type' of loss. The principle is that if a given 'type' of loss is foreseeable (in the relevant sense) the whole amount of that type of loss is recoverable. We have already seen that this was applied by Lord Scarman so as to regard the illness of pigs as a type and that the same approach was taken to an increase in house prices in *Wroth* v *Tyler* [1974] Ch 30 so as to make the defendant liable for an unforeseeably large rise. This is again a concept that can be easily manipulated as is shown by the *Victoria Laundry* case itself where normal loss of profits was regarded as a different 'type' of loss from the profits on the highly lucrative contracts. No doubt, if the court had wished to allow for recovery for these second type of lost profits they could have categorised 'lost profits' as all of one 'type'.

Non-pecuniary losses   Contractual damages have been traditionally concerned with economic and physical losses readily quantifiable in financial terms (although it has always been the case that if a financial loss has been suffered, the courts will, if at all possible, find a way round the difficulties of assessing the amount — see, e.g., *Chaplin* v *Hicks* [1911] 2 KB 786). The refusal of damages for injured feelings caused by the humiliating and wrongful dismissal in *Addis* v *Gramophone Co. Ltd* [1909] AC 488 is the classic authority. However, there have always been exceptions for pain and suffering consequent upon personal injury and for actual physical inconvenience as in *Bailey* v *Bullock* [1950] 2 All ER 1167 where a breach of contract caused the plaintiff to have to live with his in-laws (some might think this is more properly regarded as pain and suffering rather than mere physical inconvenience!). In more recent years the courts have also begun to award damages for disappointment and mental distress, the breakthrough in English law having being made in *Jarvis* v *Swans Tours Ltd* [1973] QB 233 where the plaintiff was promised a 'great time' on a holiday costing £63 and was awarded £125 when he didn't get it.

The question which you need to be prepared to discuss is how far will this principle extend? There were some dicta suggesting that such damages may be recovered wherever the remoteness test is satisfied, i.e., where it is in the parties' contemplation that a breach will result in mental distress or disappointment (see Lawson J in *Cox* v *Philips Industries Ltd* [1976] 3 All ER 161) but this has been generally thought to be too generous and imprecise a test (see Dawson (1983) 10 NZULR 232). Indeed in *Bliss* v *S. E. Thames Regional*

Health Authority [1985] IRLR 308, the Court of Appeal disapproved *Cox v Philips Industries Ltd* and treated the cases awarding damages for mental distress as exceptions which can be explained as contracts to provide pleasure or to prevent distress (*Heywood* v *Wellers* [1976] 1 All ER 300 being a good example of the latter, where solicitors were employed to obtain an injunction to prevent molestation. Contrast *Hayes* v *Dodd* [1990] 2 All ER 815 where the Court of Appeal followed *Bliss* in disallowing the trial judge's award of £3,000 for negligent advice about a right of way). Similarly in *Watts* v *Morrow* [1991] 4 All ER 937, the Court of Appeal overturned awards of £4,000 for damages for distress resulting from breach 'of an ordinary surveyor's contract'. A similar approach to that in *Bliss* has now been adopted by the High Court of Australia in *Baltic Shipping Co.* v *Dillon* (1993) 176 CLR 344 (passenger's disappointment recoverable when cruise ship sank on tenth day of fourteen day cruise holiday!). A slightly less obvious case for recovery is that in *McLeish* v *Amoo-Gottfried & Co., The Times*, 13 October 1993, where solicitors were liable for mental distress caused to a client whom they represented negligently in criminal proceedings (his conviction was later quashed on appeal). The contract was classified as one 'to ensure his peace of mind by taking all reasonable steps to secure his acquittal'. More typical of the increasingly narrow approach towards the category of contracts in which mental distress is recoverable is the decision in *Branchett* v *Beaney* [1992] 3 All ER 910 where the Court of Appeal expressed the view that a covenant for quiet enjoyment in a lease is not within the exceptional category of contracts to provide peace of mind or freedom from distress since 'quiet enjoyment' has a technical meaning relating to exercising and using rights over property rather than deriving pleasure from it.

A further point about the mental distress cases is that they were to some extent inevitable given the increasing recognition of 'consumer contracts' as opposed to the traditional concept of contract as a commercial exchange. Loss of profits is the typical loss in the latter context but a consumer isn't looking so much for a profit as for some more intangible benefit out of the contract. This has been dubbed the 'consumer surplus' (a term well-known to economists) in an article by Harris, Ogus and Phillips (1979) 95 LQR 581 which is well worth reading. Too rigid a limit on non-pecuniary losses would be particularly inappropriate in the context of such consumer contracts, something now recognised by the House of Lords in *Ruxley Electronics* v *Forsyth* [1996] AC 344.

Mitigation This is a serious qualification to the rule that damages are designed to put the plaintiff in as good a position as if the contract had been performed. The plaintiff is expected to take *reasonable* steps to put *himself* into that position and if he is able to do this he can only claim the extra costs incurred in doing so. Suppose A agrees to purchase goods in advance from

B for £100 and has contracted to resell them for £130 and B fails to deliver and the market price is £120 at the date set for delivery. A cannot sit back and claim £30 loss of profit on his sale to B. He is expected to buy substitute goods in the market with which to supply C and is thus limited to the extra cost of doing so (£20 plus any expenses of buying in the market).

The corollary of this rule is that if A *reasonably* tries to mitigate his losses, but this in fact turns out to increase them, he can claim this increased loss. See for example *Hoffberger* v *Ascot International Bloodstock Bureau Ltd* (1976) 120 SJ 130, where the plaintiff had agreed to sell a horse for £6,000 to the defendant who refused, in breach of contract, to accept the horse. The plaintiff kept the horse at considerable expense in the hope of finding a buyer but was unsuccessful in doing so and the horse was sold in the December sales, a year later, for only £1,085. Keeping the horse over the year had in fact made matters worse but the Court of Appeal held that the expenses of so keeping it could be recovered in addition to the loss of profit since the plaintiff had acted reasonably.

Difficult questions arise where, although the plaintiff is not actually required to mitigate, he does take steps which do actually improve his position — see *British Westinghouse Electric & Manufacturing Co. Ltd* v *Underground Electric Railways Co. of London Ltd* [1912] AC 673. Can the defendant claim the benefits of the plaintiff's initiative in order to reduce his liability? Suppose, in the example given earlier of B failing to deliver goods which he has contracted to sell for £100 when the market price has risen to £120, that A manages to buy goods for £110 instead. A's initiative has reduced his loss from the extra £20 which he would have had to pay for substitute goods in the market to the extra £10 he has actually paid. Should his damages be £10 or £20? The answer seems to depend on whether the profitable purchase is a 'collateral benefit' in which case the answer is £20 or whether it is a consequence of the breach, in which case it will reduce the damages to £10. The answer in this particular example might turn on whether A would have bought the substitute goods for £110 in any case even if B had not broken his contract. It is not always easy to decide whether something is a collateral benefit or not (cf. the case of *C & P Haulage* v *Middleton* [1983] 3 All ER 94 where the opportunity of being able to work rent-free from his own garage would probably never have arisen if it had not been for the other party's breach) but it is a point which you ought to be prepared to discuss.

Contributory negligence   Another potential way in which damages may be reduced is through the contributory fault of the plaintiff. If the plaintiff's negligence is the overriding cause of the damage, then indeed it will remove liability completely as in *Quinn* v *Burch Brothers (Builders) Ltd* [1966] 2 QB 370 where the accident would not have occurred if the defendants had not failed, in breach of contract, to provide a ladder but the plaintiff's decision to use a trestle instead was the substantial cause.

The more difficult issue is where the plaintiff's negligence is regarded as making a less substantial contribution. Can it be a reason for merely reducing the damages under the Law Reform (Contributory Negligence) Act 1945, which applies where the plaintiff 'suffers damage as the result partly of his own fault and partly of the fault of any other person'? The answer turns on the meaning of 'fault' in the 1945 Act and whether a breach of contract amounts to fault. If the breach is merely of a strict duty under the contract then the answer is clearly no and the Act doesn't apply (and the defendant is liable in full). See *Barclays Bank* v *Fairclough Building* [1995] 1 All ER 289. If on the other hand the breach of contract consists of a failure to take reasonable care then the Act can apply even if the action is brought in contract. This latter point has only recently been settled by the Court of Appeal in *Forsikrings Vesta* v *Butcher* [1988] 2 All ER 43 after a number of inconclusive first instance decisions. However, it would seem that a person who breaches a contractual term to take reasonable care cannot plead contributory negligence if there would be no liability in tort independently of the contract. It is perhaps unfortunate that in order to determine whether the Act is applicable to a claim for negligent breach of contract one has to investigate the hypothetical and, at least in some cases, potentially difficult question of whether there would be independent liability in tort. In its Report No. 219 (1993) the Law Commission has recommended that contributory negligence should be available to a contractual duty to take reasonable care or exercise reasonable skill whether or not there is a concurrent duty in tort.

Penalties and agreed damages   Because the assessment of damages can itself give rise to difficult and controversial questions of law and because disputes about damages, like any other sort of dispute, can cause a continuing relationship to deteriorate and perhaps even terminate unnecessarily, a contract will often provide in advance what damages should be payable for particular types of breach. This sort of clause not only avoids the expense of legal proceedings to determine the amount of damages but also makes it more likely that the innocent party will feel able to claim his damages for breach without the fear of upsetting his future relationships with the party in breach.

Although businessmen often refer to such clauses indiscriminately as 'penalty clauses' the law draws a sharp distinction between agreed (or 'liquidated') damages clauses on the one hand (which are a genuine pre-estimate of the loss and which are enforceable) and penalty clauses on the other hand (which do not genuinely attempt to estimate the real loss but which are merely designed to provide a strong incentive to one party to perform and to penalise him if he doesn't). As with exclusion clauses — which Diplock LJ has described as 'penalty clauses in reverse' — the courts have developed rules of construction for determining whether a particular clause is a penalty or an agreed-damages clause. These rules are set out in the leading case of *Dunlop Pneumatic Tyre Co. Ltd* v *New Garage & Motor Co. Ltd* [1915] AC 79 and are summarised and discussed in the standard textbooks and were the subject matter of a Privy Council decision in *Philips Hong Kong* v *A-G of Hong Kong* (1993) 61 BLR 41. Clearly you should be familiar with these rules and be able to apply them but there are three other issues which you should additionally be aware of:

(a)   The relationship between exemption, liquidated damages and penalty clauses.
(b)   The distinction between penalties for breach and sums payable on other events.
(c)   The relationship between penalties and forfeiture clauses.

Exemption, liquidated damages and penalty clauses
This issue can arise where the actual loss caused by the breach turns out to be greater than the amount provided for in the relevant clause. If a clause is on its true construction a penalty clause, then paradoxically the victim of the breach, who will normally be the person who has insisted on the penalty clause in the first place, will be able to ignore the penalty clause and recover his actual loss exceeding the amount provided for in the penalty clause! This was what the respondent tried to do in *Cellulose Acetate Silk Co.* v *Widnes Foundry (1925) Ltd* [1933] AC 20 but the House of Lords held that the clause providing for a 'penalty' of £20 per week for late delivery was not a penalty clause since 'it must have been obvious to both parties that the actual damage would be much *more* than £20 per week' (emphasis added). As a result the respondent's damages were limited to the amount specified in the clause but whilst the clause was not a penalty it does not seem to have been a 'genuine pre-estimate of the loss' either and was in reality a limitation clause which may well nowadays be required to be reasonable under the Unfair Contract Terms Act 1977.

Penalties for breach and sums payable on other events
In *Alder* v *Moore* [1961] 2 QB 57 a professional footballer was paid £500 insurance money because of total disablement but signed a declaration that he would not play professional football again and that in 'the event of infringement of this condition, will be subject to a penalty of £500'. The Court of Appeal interpreted this (Devlin LJ dissenting) as a promise to repay the £500 if he played football again rather than as a promise not to play with a penalty of £500 for breach of that promise. The rule against penalties only applied to sums payable on breach and since the footballer was not, in playing again, guilty of any breach of any promise, he had to repay the money. (This was no doubt the most expensive missed penalty of his career but Devlin LJ

was not apparently booked for his dissent!) On a more serious note, the case illustrates the difficulty of distinguishing between sums payable on breach and sums payable on other events, a distinction which can in any case lead to the 'absurd paradox', as Lord Denning put it in *Bridge v Campbell Discount Co. Ltd* [1962] AC 600, that a party in breach is given more protection than one who is not. None the less in *Export Credits Guarantee Department v Universal Oil Products Co.* [1983] 2 All ER 205, the House of Lords confirmed that the penalty rule only applied to sums payable on breach.

Penalties and forfeiture clauses

A forfeiture clause in this context means one whereby a person who has *already* paid a sum of money under the contract forfeits (i.e., cannot recover) the money when it is terminated because of his own breach. Rather surprisingly, the law here is that there is no general right to recover a deposit (which has to be distinguished from a mere part payment) even though it clearly exceeds the other party's loss and is intended as an incentive to perform. If such a sum was to *become* payable on breach it would undoubtedly be unenforceable as a penalty and it is rather inconsistent for the law not to allow it to be recovered where it has already been paid. Equity will give *some* relief against forfeiture but the traditional view espoused by Romer LJ in *Stockloser v Johnson* [1954] 1 QB 476 is that in the absence of sharp practice or fraud the only relief available is to give the party in breach *further time* in which to perform his obligations under the contract and that equity will not actually order the repayment of the money to a party in breach. On the other hand, Denning and Somervell LLJ in the same case thought that equity could order repayment if it was unconscionable for the other party to keep the payment (it was not unconscionable on the facts) but it was the view of Romer LJ that was followed in *Galbraith v Mitchenall Estates Ltd* [1965] 2 QB 473 where the plaintiff failed to recover £550 paid in advance hire for a caravan (even though this clearly exceeded the defendant's loss). The plaintiff mistakenly thought it was a contract for hire-purchase (i.e., that the caravan would become his at the end of the five-year hire period) and the contract was terminated after only four months because of his failure to pay the monthly rental. It is difficult to see why the rule as to forfeited deposits should be different from those applicable to penalties but you ought to be aware of the distinction and the dissatisfaction with it (although Atiyah suggests that the distinction is perhaps explicable on the grounds that in both cases the law is merely favouring the status quo). In any case, the precise position is not finally settled at the highest level since Lord Diplock in *Scandinavian Trading Tanker Co. AB v Flota Petrolera Ecuatoriana* [1983] 2 AC 694 appeared to look not unfavourably on the Denning and Somervell LLJ line in *Stockloser v Johnson* although it was not applicable to the facts before the House since the payments already made merely covered the benefits already received under the contract.

Action for the Price or Other Agreed Sum

This is an extremely important remedy in practice but gives rise to relatively few difficulties as there is no question of quantification, the plaintiff is merely claiming the remuneration specified in the contract. The difficulties that can arise are of two main sorts.

Has the right to the price yet accrued?   This right generally only arises when the contract has been fully performed, cf. *Cutter* v *Powell* (1795) 6 TR 320, but if the contract is severable there will be a right to the appropriate portion of the price as each stage of the contract is completed. Furthermore, full performance, particularly in the context of contracts for services, is not an absolute concept. As long as the contract (or the severable part of it) has been *substantially* performed the price is still payable as in *Hoenig* v *Isaacs* [1952] 2 All ER 176 where the plaintiff was employed to decorate and furnish a flat for £750 and did so but not without defects. The Court of Appeal held that since the defects would only cost £55 to remedy, the work was finished in the ordinary sense (although the court thought the case was near the borderline on this point) and the plaintiff was entitled to the price subject to the defendant's set-off for the £55. *Bolton* v *Mahadeva* [1972] 1 WLR 1009 is a case on the other side of the line where the contract price for installing central heating was £564 and the defects would have cost £174 to put right and the plaintiff was entitled to nothing. (The defendant thus received a considerable benefit free of charge because of the plaintiff's breach and failure to render even substantial performance. The Law Commission have *recommended* (Report No. 121, 1983) that the plaintiff should be able to recover the value of what he *has* done in this situation but this would not be an action for the price.) The distinction between *Hoenig* v *Isaacs* and *Bolton* v *Mahadeva* is essentially the same as the distinction between breach of warranty and breach of condition — only in the latter case is the innocent party entitled to reject the other party's performance and terminate his own obligations, i.e., in this case, to pay the price. If the breach is merely a breach of warranty and doesn't justify termination, he must perform his own obligations, i.e., pay the price, and merely claim damages for the breach as in *Hoenig* v *Isaacs*.

Can the plaintiff insist on performing and thereby earning the price even if the other party repudiates the contract in advance of performance?   This is the problem of *White & Carter (Councils) Ltd* v *McGregor* [1962] AC 413 where the pursuers (this was a Scottish case) insisted on their right to perform their contract to advertise the defender's business on litter-bins for three years and to claim the contract price of £196 4s even though the defender repudiated the contract on the same day it was made. The House of Lords, rather controversially by three to two, upheld the pursuers' claim for this amount.

The points to note about this case are:

(a)   The reasons why the decision has been questioned such as:

(i)   The pursuers could have claimed damages, i.e., their loss of net profit, and avoided the waste of the expenses of performance which was unwanted by the other party. This leads on to:

(ii)   The case is inconsistent with the policy underlying the duty to mitigate damages (even though it was not itself a damages claim).

(b)   The limitations inherent in the case which answer some of these criticisms, i.e.:

(i)   The plaintiff can only insist on performing if he can do so without the other party's cooperation (and he cannot do so if performance involves doing work to *property* of the defendant — see Megarry J in *Hounslow London Borough Council* v *Twickenham Garden Developments Ltd* [1971] Ch 233 and also *Telephone Rentals* v *Burgess Salmon, The Independent*, (1987) 22 April).

(ii)   The right to perform is defeated if it is shown that the plaintiff has no legitimate interest in performing the contract rather than claiming damages (see Lord Reid in *White & Carter (Councils) Ltd* v *McGregor*) or, what amounts to the same thing, where damages would be an adequate remedy (note the link with specific performance) — see Lord Denning MR in *Attica Sea Carriers Corporation* v *Ferrostaal Poseidon Bulk Reederei GmbH* [1976] 1 Lloyd's Rep 250.

The result of all that is that only rarely will a plaintiff be allowed to do what the pursuers did in *White & Carter (Councils) Ltd* v *McGregor*, e.g., as in *The Odenfeld* [1978] 2 Lloyd's Rep 357 where the plaintiffs had obligations to third parties which would be adversely affected by terminating the contract. By way of contrast, in *Clea Shipping Corporation* v *Bulk Oil International Ltd* [1984] 1 All ER 129 Lord Reid's dicta about legitimate interest were applied so as to deny a plaintiff the right to perform and claim the agreed sum. The view of Lloyd J that this sort of limitation might only be applicable in exceptional cases should be contrasted with Lord Denning's view in the *Attica Sea Carriers Corporation* case that *White & Carter (Councils) Ltd* v *McGregor* should only be followed in cases which are 'precisely on all fours with it'.

Equitable Remedies: Specific Performance and Injunction

Because of their equitable origins these remedies are, unlike the common law remedy of damages, not available as of right and the basic attitude is that they will not be granted if damages would be an adequate remedy. Thus a plaintiff will *normally* only be entitied to damages for non-delivery in a contract for the sale of goods as he can usually purchase similar goods elsewhere whereas land is regarded as unique so specific performance is regularly ordered of contracts for the sale of land. Damages can also be inadequate in the sense that the true loss cannot be recovered because it is not legally recoverable or is suffered by a third party as in *Beswick* v *Beswick* [1968] AC 58.

Again, one could fill a whole book discussing the equitable remedies but the following points crop up more than most.

Contracts of personal service These are not normally specifically performable since to do so would be an undue restriction on personal liberty. Furthermore the courts will not enforce by way of injunction an express promise not to work for others if the practical effect is to compel the defendant to continue to work with or for the plaintiff. Thus in *Page One Records Ltd* v *Britton* [1967] 3 All ER 822 the court refused to grant an injunction restraining the Troggs from recording for anyone other than their present manager, the plaintiff, since to do so would in effect be to compel them to continue to work for the plaintiff and amount to specific performance of a personal service contract. This is generally regarded as a more realistic approach than the one taken in *Warner Brothers Pictures Inc.* v *Nelson* [1937] 1 KB 209 where an injunction to restrain the defendant, Bette Davis, from appearing in 'any motion picture or stage production for anyone other than the plaintiffs' was granted since she could still be employed in other activities and would 'not be driven, though she may be tempted, to perform the contract'. On the other hand, it should be said that the purpose of the injunction was not to force the defendant to continue to work for the plaintiffs but to prevent her from reducing the value of the films already made for the plaintiffs by appearing, in breach of contract, in others. This is evident from the fact that Branson J limited the injunction, to a maximum of 3 years 'to give reasonable protection and no more to the plaintiffs against the ill effects to them of the defendant's breach of contract.' Similarly in *Evening Standard Company Ltd* v *Henderson* [1987] IRLR 64 the Court of Appeal granted an interlocutory injunction to restrain the defendant from working for a rival during his 12-month notice period. The case was peculiar in that there was no danger of the defendant being forced to perform or else starve since the plaintiffs were prepared to continue to pay him etc., provided he did not work for their bitter rival. Contrast *Provident Financial Group* v *Hayward* [1989] IRLR 84 where an employer was left to his remedy in damages.

None of the rules about equitable remedies is absolute and in the context of personal services this is further illustrated by the exceptional case of *Hill* v *C. A. Parsons & Co. Ltd* [1972] Ch 305 where an injunction was granted to restrain a dismissal in breach of contract and thus, in effect, specific performance was ordered of a personal service contract. The reason for the exception was that the employer did not really wish to dismiss the employee but was only doing so under pressure from a union and thus upholding the contract did not violate any personal liberty of the parties to the contract which is the main objection to specific enforcement of personal service contracts.

For an amusing case about personal service contracts see the extracts from *De Rivafinoli* v *Corsetti* (1833) 4 Paige Ch 264 in Swan and Reiter's Case Book pp. 1-82 where the defendant was an opera singer who had contracted to 'sing, gesticulate and recite' exclusively for the plaintiffs. The judge having ruled that 'a bird that can sing and will not sing must be made to sing' went on to acknowledge that it would be 'very difficult for the master [not possessing the necessary exquisite sensitivity in the auricular nerve] to determine what effect coercion might produce upon the defendant's singing especially in the livelier airs: although the fear of imprisonment would unquestionably deepen his seriousness in the graver parts of the drama'. The case was, and could only have been, decided in New York. Its interest for present purposes is in the court's awareness of the difficulty of supervising effectively a contract for personal service, a difficulty which is sometimes given as the reason for refusing specific performance of other types of contracts which require constant supervision — see *Ryan* v *Mutual Tontine Westminster Chambers Association* [1893] 1 Ch 116. This particular difficulty is not today regarded as so great and in *Tito* v *Waddell (No. 2)* [1977] Ch 106 at p. 322 Megarry V-C said that the real issue is whether it is possible to state with precision what has to be done in order to perform the contract and comply with the order of the court. In fact the increasingly flexible approach to specific performance can be seen in the recent case of *Posner* v *Scott-Lewis* [1986] 3 WLR 531, where *Ryan* v *Mutual Tontine* was distinguished and specific performance ordered of a covenant in a lease to employ a resident porter. The court emphasised the distinction between a contract of personal service and one merely procuring the execution of an agreement 'which contains a provision for such services or acts'. Nevertheless, in *Co-operative Insurance Society* v *Argyll Stores* [1997] 2 WLR 898, the House of Lords reiterated the significance of the difficulties of constant supervision in reversing the Court of Appeal and confirming the previous settled practice of not ordering specific performance of a contract to carry on a business.

Mutuality   It is only fair that if one party is able to obtain the actual performance of the contract then the other party should be able to do so and equity being particularly concerned with fairness reflects this through the doctrine of mutuality. The history of the doctrine involves, amongst others, Fry and Spry but has nothing to do with a certain brand of cooking oil! Fry on *Specific Performance*, 6th ed., expresses the doctrine as requiring that the remedy of specific performance should be potentially available to either party at the time the contract is made, which would mean that, e.g., an agreement by D to grant a lease of a house to P if P subsequently renovates the house in return could not be specifically enforced against D since D would not be able to get specific performance of P's obligation to renovate. Furthermore, according to Fry, the objection of lack of mutality would still persist even if P had already done the renovation because the mutuality had to exist at the time of formation of the contract.

This formulation of the mutuality rule (in the 3rd ed. of Fry's work) was criticised initially by Ames (1903) 3 Colum L Rev 1 who put forward an alternative formulation whereby mutuality only requires that the party who is ordered to specifically perform should have *either* received or be *assured* of performance in return. In other words the defendant doesn't himself have to be able to obtain *an order* of specific performance if the performance of the contract is otherwise assured, the most obvious example of which being where it has already been carried out. On this view, in the example given above, P would be able to obtain specific performance if he has *already* carried out the renovations since there is no danger of D being ordered to specifically perform and then being left without any effective remedy of his own should P himself default. This view is much easier to reconcile with even the older cases (see, e.g., *Wilkinson* v *Clements* (1872) LR 8 Ch App 96) and Fry's formulation has been criticised in many textbooks since Ames's article including Spry, *The Principles of Equitable Remedies*, where the proper rule is succinctly expressed as requiring merely that mutuality 'be looked at only as at the time of the making of the proposed order', so that the fact that the contract involves, e.g., personal services by the plaintiff which cannot be the subject of an order of specific performance is no objection if those services have already been carried out. This view has now been confirmed by the Court of Appeal in *Price* v *Strange* [1977] 3 All ER 371 where the decision of the trial judge, that specific performance of an agreement to grant an underlease of a flat could not be ordered against the defendant because it could not have been ordered against the plaintiff who had contracted to repair and decorate the flat, was reversed since the repairs and decoration had all been done. (Not all of these were done by the plaintiff but that was only because he was prevented from doing so by the defendant who had them done herself and the court granted her an allowance in respect of these.)

Discretion The issues discussed above in relation to the adequacy of damages, personal service contracts, constant supervision and mutuality are merely illustrations of the fact that equitable remedies are discretionary (which is why none of the above rules can be regarded as absolute). Other factors can obviously affect the exercise of the discretion including public policy which can be a factor in favour of specific performance, as in *Verrall* v *Great Yarmouth Borough Council* [1981] QB 202 where it would tend to promote political liberties, or against, as in *Wroth* v *Tyler* [1974] Ch 30 where specific performance, of a contract for the sale of land, subject to the wife's right of occupation was refused as that might mean splitting up a family. *Shell UK Ltd* v *Lostock Garage Ltd* [1977] 1 All ER 481 is a striking example of the discretionary nature of equitable remedies where Ormrod LJ considered the covenant in restraint of trade to be reasonable and thus binding but refused an injunction restraining its breach since Shell were unfairly subsidising neighbouring garages and inflicting hardship on the defendants.

At the end of the day, all that you can really be expected to do with equitable remedies is to be aware of the major factors which govern their availability and have a feeling for the direction in which the courts' attitudes towards particular issues seem to be moving. The general drift seems to be a relaxation of the traditional restrictions by reference to particular categories towards a more general approach whereby 'the court will decree specific performance only if this will do more perfect and complete justice than an award of damages' per Megarry V-C in *Tito* v *Waddell (No. 2)* [1977] Ch 106. A question which you might usefully consider is whether there should be a much greater relaxation of the restrictions on specific performance and if not, why not?

Restitution

The remedies considered so far in this chapter are remedies which attempt in one way or another to enforce the contract (reliance damages may be an exception to this in so far as they are properly designed to put the plaintiff in the position as though he hadn't entered the contract in the first place). However, there is another set of important remedies which make no pretence of trying to enforce the contract as such but which seek to *restore* benefits transferred under a contract which is discharged by breach. There are two main possible benefits that the plaintiff might have transferred to the defendant before his breach discharges the contract:

(a) Money
(b) Services, property and other benefits.

Money   The basic rule is that money can only be recovered where there has been a total failure of consideration, i.e., where no part of that which has been bargained for is received in return for the money. For example, A agrees to hire a car from B for one week commencing on the first day of the next month and a fee of £100 has been paid in advance. Come the first of the month, B is unable to supply the car and A can recover his £100. Note that this is true even if A has made a bad bargain, e.g., if similar cars can be hired elsewhere for only £70 a week. A can hire an alternative and is thus saved £30 by B's breach. (If, instead, alternatives would cost £130, A would claim damages for breach at £130 rather than merely the restitution of his £100.)

However, if the failure of consideration is not *total* A cannot recover his £100 in restitution but must claim damages for breach. Thus if B supplies a car for one day only, A cannot claim back six-sevenths of his £100 (£85 approximately) but must claim damages, which are prima facie the cost of hiring a substitute for the remaining six days. If alternatives are available for only £70 per week he is still stuck with his bad bargain, since he will still have paid a net £100 for the week. Conversely, if alternatives cost more than £100, he still gets the benefit of his good bargain.

At one point (Working Paper No. 65, 1975) the Law Commission was in favour of allowing recovery of money even where the failure of consideration was not total but in its final report on the matter (No. 121, 1983) it has recanted on the grounds that this would often involve putting the plaintiff in a better position than if the contract had been performed. The fact remains that this can happen where the failure is total.

Another point to note is that a total failure of consideration can sometimes be found in unexpected circumstances such as those in *Rowland* v *Divall* [1923] 2 KB 500 where the plaintiff motor dealer bought a car from the defendant for £334 and four months later discovered that the defendant had no title since the car had been stolen previously. Despite his interim possession of the car he was successful, at least in the Court of Appeal, in his claim for the return of the £334 on the grounds that he had not received any part of what he bargained for — a car with a good title. This was fair enough on the facts since the plaintiff bought not to use but to resell (and had in fact resold and had to refund his own customer) so that title was all he was really interested in but the case has been followed in cases where the plaintiff is not buying to resell and has had the benefit of the use of the car for a substantial period as in *Butterworth* v *Kingsway Motors Ltd* [1954] 1 WLR 1286. In such a case the purchaser gets the benefit of the free *use* (for 11 months in *Butterworth*) at the expense of the seller who was himself the innocent victim of the original thief. To avoid this apparent injustice, the Law Commission recommended in Working Paper No. 65 that the purchaser's right to claim back the price from an innocent seller should be made subject to an allowance to the seller for the use that the purchaser has already had. Even this solution would not be problem-free since the purchaser might additionally be liable to the true owner in tort for his use. Having canvassed various complex solutions in Working Paper No 85 the Law Commission has now decided in its Report No 160 (1987) that the complexities are such that the law is best left as it stands!

Services or property   An innocent party who renders services or transfers property under a contract which is discharged by breach before he can complete and earn the full contract price can recover their reasonable value under a *quantum meruit* ('how much it is worth'). Thus in *Planché* v *Colburn* (1831) 8 Bing 14 the plaintiff was engaged by the defendants to write a volume for £100 which they were to publish in a periodical series called *The Juvenile Library*. When the plaintiff had done a considerable amount of work (but nothing had been handed over) the periodical was abandoned which amounted to a breach entitling the plaintiff to terminate the contract. The plaintiff was awarded £50 on a *quantum meruit* for the work he had already done. Note that in this context requested services are regarded as a benefit to the person requesting them even though no *actual* benefit is received.

The question here is whether there is any need for this type of *quantum meruit* claim and whether any such claim should be limited by reference to the contract price. In *Planché* v *Colburn* there is no suggestion that Planché had agreed to do the work for too low a price so the issue did not arise. But suppose that the jury had decided that the work already done was worth £125, not £50, could they have awarded him £125 given that he would only have got £100 if he had been allowed to complete the work, thus putting him in a better position than if the contract had been performed? Such a result was allowed in the notorious American case of *Boomer* v *Muir* (1933) 24 P2d 570 where the plaintiff recovered $250,000 even though he would only have been entitled to a further $20,000 if he had been allowed to complete the contract. On the other hand in *Kehoe* v *Borough of Rutherford* (1893) 27 A 912 the plaintiff had done about three-fifths of the work required by the contract and this work was worth $3,153 on a *quantum meruit* basis. However, the contract price was only $2,743 and so his claim was limited to three-fifths of that figure (approx $1,600). This looks like a fairer result than that in *Boomer* v *Muir* at first sight but is not itself without problems, e.g., because it might be more costly to perform the early stages of a contract than the later stages and a strict pro rata limit as in *Kehoe* v *Rutherford* takes no account of this. If these issues interest you they are discussed further by Palmer (1959) 20 Ohio St LJ 264.

These questions are certainly not settled in English law but are related to the issue of whether reliance damages can be claimed where that would put the plaintiff in a better position than if the contract had been performed. As was said earlier in this chapter, the answer to this question now seems to be pretty clearly no. This might suggest that a similar rule ought to apply to a *quantum meruit* claim, i.e., that *Kehoe* v *Rutherford* would apply in English law. On the other hand, if this is so it is difficult to see the point in recognising a separate right to a *quantum meruit* claim in these circumstances since the plaintiff can obtain exactly the same result by claiming damages on a reliance basis for breach of contract (this would perhaps be a more obvious way to put the plaintiff's claim today in a case like *Planché* v *Colburn*). Again, the American literature has explored these sorts of issues more fully than has been the case in England. See, e.g., Childres and Garamella (1969) 64 Nw UL Rev 433.

Note that the above discussion only relates to restitutionary claims where the defendant is in breach. Such claims can arise in other circumstances including cases where the *plaintiff* is in breach where quite different considerations apply. In particular, a part performer who is in *breach* cannot recover the value of his part performance unless the other party freely accepts the part performance and this normally involves that he is in a position to return the benefit — see *Sumpter v Hedges* [1898] 1 QB 673 where the plaintiff could not recover the value of the work he had done on the defendant's land since the defendant had no choice whether or not to accept the partly completed work but he could recover the value of the material left on the land which the defendant chose to use to complete the work. The Law Commission have now recommended (Report No. 121) that a claimant in such a case should be able to recover the value of the work done but this will be limited to a proportionate part of the contract price and would of course be subject to any claim by the defendant for damages for breach of contract.

As can be seen from this brief survey, the place of restitutionary claims in the scheme of contractual remedies is rich with perplexities, uncertainties and proposals for reform but as always, if you can develop an awareness of the central themes and issues, it will increase your understanding of the whole area and will be suitably rewarded in the examination.

PRIVITY

Most students are reasonably clear on what the privity doctrine is — that only the parties to a contract can sue or be liable on it — and after all the basic idea is simple enough. The difficulties arise in determining who is a party and in understanding the myriad exceptions to, and ways around, the doctrine. Contract courses tend to be most concerned with the problem on the benefit side — who can sue on, or take the benefit of, a contract — so we will concentrate on that at the expense of the question of when can a contract exceptionally impose a burden on a third party since the most important of these exceptions belong to contracts concerning land which are normally dealt with in land law courses.

Who is a Party?

One view here is that only persons who supply consideration are parties (whatever the contract might say) which would mean that the privity rule is the same as the rule that consideration must move from the promisee. Atiyah

(*Consideration in Contracts,* p. 384) has argued against this and tried to show that a person to whom a promise is made (a promisee) counts as a party to the contract (and therefore can enforce a promise) even if the real consideration is supplied by someone else. It is very difficult to prove or disprove this sort of theory because of the vagueness of the doctrine of consideration itself and, as is shown by Treitel's response (1976) 50 ALJ 444–6, if the courts want to allow a promisee to enforce a promise, they can usually find some sort of consideration moving from him. See, eg., *Charnock* v *Liverpool Corporation* [1968] 1 WLR 1498 where a garage impliedly promised P (the promisee) to execute the repairs to his car with reasonable speed. The bill was to be paid by the insurance company who were hence supplying the obvious consideration but P was able to enforce the promise. For Atiyah this is really an example of the courts allowing a promisee (a party) to enforce a promise even though he provided no consideration whereas for Treitel, consideration can be found moving from P (thus making him not merely a promisee but a party) in that his choosing of the garage conferred a benefit on the garage by enabling it to earn the remuneration from the insurance company.

In this context, it is worth recalling that consideration may be either executed or executory. Suppose that A and B go to a restaurant and at the end of the evening, A pays the bill. Subsequently they are ill as a result of drinking contaminated wine. Can B sue the restaurant for breach of contract? Even if one insists that a person is only party to a contract if he or she provides consideration (i.e., that consideration must move from the promisee) B may still be a party even though A *actually* pays the bill. The normal inference would be that when ordering this meal both A and B undertake to pay their own share, so that A and B both provide executory consideration by promising to pay. The fact that their obligations are later discharged by merely *one* of them paying (and thus actually executing or performing consideration) doesn't alter this fact. See the facts that arose in *Lockett* v *A. & M. Charles Ltd* [1938] 4 All ER 170. One way of testing whether executory consideration is provided in this way is to ask whether the restaurant would have regarded themselves as entitled to sue either party if they had left without paying? If the answer is yes, it must be on the basis that each had promised to pay and thereby provided consideration. The only situation where this would not be the natural inference is where it is made clear in advance that only one party is to be liable, which is essentially what happened when Mr Jackson booked a holiday for himself and his family in *Jackson* v *Horizon Holidays Ltd* [1975] 1 WLR 1468. In this situation, one is directly confronted with the privity rule, the family are clearly third parties who have given no consideration and the question is how can their position under the contract which is undoubtedly made for their benefit be protected?

Third-party Beneficiaries

There are of course a number of ways around the privity rule including agency and the device of the contracting party declaring himself a trustee of his rights under the contract for the benefit of the third-party beneficiary. One problem with agency is that this really only gets round the problem of privity and still leaves the problem of the third party's consideration. In *Dunlop Pneumatic Tyre Co. Ltd* v *Selfridge & Co. Ltd* [1915] AC 847 itself, Lord Dunedin at least was prepared to accept that A. J. Dew & Co. made their agreement as agent for Dunlop but that was of no avail to Dunlop since they provided no consideration. On top of that, in a case like *Jackson* v *Horizon Holidays Ltd* [1975] 1 WLR 1468 it is just unrealistic (or 'absurd' as Lord Denning MR put it) to say that the father contracted as agent on behalf of his three-year-old children (and unrealistic to say any consideration is provided on their behalf).

At one time, the device of finding a trust was regularly adopted in order to evade the privity rule. One advantage of a trust is that there is no need at all for the third-party beneficiary to provide consideration and in 1930 Corbin showed in 46 LQR 12 that the courts were able to avoid the privity rule wherever it suited them to do so.

In response to that, the Privy Council in *Vandepitte* v *Preferred Accident Insurance Corporation of New York* [1933] AC 70 refused to apply the trust device and so reasserted the doctrine of privity in a car insurance contract which purported to cover third-party drivers (which in the case happened to be the contracting party's daughter). The Privy Council refused to find that the father intended to create a trust for his daughter (or others driving with his consent) and Swan and Reiter somewhat pointedly comment 'one wonders what the father thought he was doing if he was not intending to provide protection for his daughter!' This is perhaps a little hard on the Privy Council since in British Columbia, where the facts arose, the father could himself be personally liable for his daughter's torts so the policy did make some sense as protecting him *personally* from liability and as not covering his daughter. Although this consideration is not applicable in England, where parents are not vicariously liable for their children, the position is now made clear by a statute (Road Traffic Act 1972, s. 148(4)) that third parties can take the benefit of motor insurance policies in order to avoid the difficulties of proving that the car owner contracted as trustee for them.

The difficulties of deciding whether there was an *intention* to create a trust were not the only problems with the trust device. In one sense, the trust provides *too good* a right for the third party since it deprives the contracting parties of the right to vary the agreement, a right which they will normally wish to preserve. For these reasons, the use of the trust device has now declined (although some of the cases in which the courts have refused to recognise a trust have been cases where it is in the interest of the third party (because of the law on bankruptcy or taxation) for there to be no *enforceable* rights in their favour. See *Re Schebsman* [1944] Ch 83 and *Re Miller's agreement* [1947] Ch 615 — the promisors being quite willing to *actually perform* the promise and pay the third parties).

The significance of the trust cases is that they show that the absolute removal of the privity rule may not necessarily be in the interests of either the contracting parties or the beneficiaries. You should bear this in mind if you have to discuss the question of whether the privity rule should be abolished. Abolition alone is insufficient, something else has to be put in its place. Otherwise you could have the situation whereby, e.g., two boxers who have cancelled their agreement to take part in a title fight are sued by a disappointed boxing fan! The American solution is to give the right to sue only to intended beneficiaries and not to incidental beneficiaries (like the boxing fan) and to provide that the parties can still vary their agreement before an intended beneficiary has relied on the promise etc. In England, the Law Revision Committee in 1937 similarly proposed modifications to, rather than outright abolition of, the rule that a third party cannot enforce a contract by providing a right to sue 'where a contract *by its express terms* purports to confer a benefit on a third party' and subject to the contracting party's rights to vary the contract until the third party has 'adopted it either expressly or by conduct'.

As is well known, Parliament has still not acted on that recommendation (the House of Lords pointedly remarked in *Woodar Investment Development Ltd* v *Wimpey Construction UK Ltd* [1980] 1 All ER 571 that if Parliament didn't act soon, it would) but the Law Commission published its final report (Cm 3329) in 1996 and legislation is expected in the next couple of years. In the meantime, the courts are still faced with the problem, following the demise of the trust concept, of how to protect the interests of third parties where the promisor is refusing to perform in their favour or has performed defectively. In recent years the attention in the courts has switched from trying to give third parties their own right to sue towards manipulating the remedies which the promisee has so as to enable the promisee to ensure that the third party gets the benefit. This approach is of course dependent on the promisee being prepared to sue on the third party's behalf but that is merely the price of failing to have a thorough reform of the privity rule. Having said that, judicial impatience with the effects of the privity rule in certain particular situations, such as a solicitor failing to draw up a will for a testator which would have benefited third party beneficiaries, has led to the courts giving a *tortious* right to sue directly to the third party. See *White* v *Jones* [1995] 1 All ER 691, HL where as Lord Keith (dissenting) pointed out, the decision of the majority gave the beneficiaries 'in substance ... the benefit of a contract to which they were not parties'.

The most obvious contractual remedy by means of which the *contracting party* can provide the third party the promised benefit is specific performance and this of course is the way in which the worst effects of the privity rule were avoided in *Beswick* v *Beswick* [1968] AC 58. However, it has to be remembered that there were a number of features in that case which will not always be present:

(a)   The promisee (old Mr Beswick) had performed all his side of the contract (transferring the business), thus there was no problem about mutuality.

(b)   The third party (his widow) was able to stand in his shoes in her other capacity as administratrix (thus there was no problem about whether the promisee chooses to sue).

(c)   Damages could be said to be inadequate *either* because the promisee (as opposed to the third party) had suffered no loss *or*, even if the promisee had suffered loss, damages as a lump sum were inappropriate given that the contract was to pay a weekly sum.

Specific performance is a splendid remedy for the third party where it is available because it orders the benefit to be conferred on the third party as promised in the contract but, as stated earlier, it is subject to various limitations. Furthermore, specific performance is not much use when the contract *has* been carried out but in a defective manner, as in *Jackson* v *Horizon Holidays Ltd*. In a case like that (of a ruined holiday) the only appropriate remedy is damages but then the problem arises that if the contracting party sues (the husband in that case) he may only be able to claim in respect of his own loss. Lord Denning MR of course relied on a dictum of Lush J to the effect that a contracting party may recover damages covering a third party's loss as well but the House of Lords strongly disapproved that aspect of Lord Denning's speech a few years later in *Woodar Investment Development Ltd* v *Wimpey Construction UK Ltd* pointing out that Lush J was talking about a case where the promisee was an agent for the alleged third party (who is thus actually a principal and hence a party to the contract). The actual decision in *Jackson* was not disapproved. Lord Wilberforce said the damages could be justified (as James LJ in *Jackson* itself based them) on Mr Jackson's *own* disappointment or 'as an example of a type of contract ... calling for special treatment'. Just what distinguishes this special category isn't made clear but the examples given by Lord Wilberforce of contracts for family holidays, meals in restaurants, hiring taxis for a group suggest perhaps contracts where the contract is made only by one person, rather than the whole group, largely for reasons for convenience. At any rate, it is clear that a fair result can still be reached on facts like those in *Jackson*.

It should not be assumed though, that, as a result of the disapproval of Lord Denning's approach, the contracting party's damages will not reflect the third party's loss in cases falling outside the special category of family holidays and the like. In *Woodar Investment Development Ltd* v *Wimpey Construction UK Ltd* itself, Wimpey had agreed to pay £1 million for land, £150,000 of which was payable to a third party. The House of Lords didn't actually have to decide whether Woodar's damages would include the £150,000 payable to the third party since they decided Wimpey had not repudiated the contract anyway and were thus not in breach. Certainly they could not recover it *on behalf of* the third party as Lord Denning's view would involve but there are indications, especially in Lord Scarman's judgment, that they might have been able to recover it as representing their *own* loss. The most likely reason why payment was to be made to a third party was that Woodar owed money to that third party and if Wimpey didn't pay it, Woodar would have to find the money from somewhere else. Thus the contracting party may be able to obtain substantial damages in his own right out of which he can then directly provide to the third party the benefit intended to be conferred by the contract. As can be seen, there is more than one way to skin a rabbit!

THE EXAMINATION

The issue of remedies can crop up as part of virtually any other topic since, as we saw particularly in the chapter on consideration, there is or should be an interrelationship between the type of remedy which the law is prepared to give for breach of contract and the conditions under which contractual liability will be regarded as established. None the less, you can also be sure that a specific question devoted to one or more of the major remedies will also be asked. Essay questions are most likely to focus on the remedy of damages or possibly also on equitable remedies whilst restitutionary remedies and to some extent equitable remedies are more likely to crop up as one of the issues in a problem question. Again though, you cannot do better than to look at past papers, to analyse the sorts of questions that you find there and prepare your own views about the scope and proper role of the various remedies.

Privity is slightly more limited in the contexts in which it can arise. The most obvious include an essay linking consideration and privity and asking, e.g., how far they are two sides of the same coin and, of course, the effect of exemption clauses on third parties. Since privity and remedies have been considered together in this chapter it makes sense now to analyse a question which involves these two issues.

Tom is a painter and decorator. His daughter is about to get married and her house needs rewiring and Tom has agreed to have this done as a wedding present for her. He agrees to decorate the outside of Dennis's house in return for Dennis (an electrician) doing the rewiring on his daughter's house. He also agrees to redecorate the inside of Paul's house in return for Paul giving Tom's mother £200. Tom performs his side of both these agreements but Dennis refuses to do the rewiring and Paul refuses to pay Tom's mother the £200. Discuss.

The first step with any problem is to break it down into smaller sections and sketch out a plan of the issues that can be discussed in relation to each section. An obvious division in this problem is between the two contracts, one involving Dennis, the other Paul, and within these contracts the division between the rights of the third party and the rights of Tom. Thus a plan for this question might look something like the following:

Tom, Dennis and his daughter:

(a) Can the daughter sue? No consideration and not a promisee. Exceptions? Agency? Trust?
(b) Can Tom get an effective remedy?

  (i) Specific performance? Personal service?
  (ii) Damages:

  (1) On behalf of daughter: *Jackson* v *Horizon Holiday Ltd* (Denning); *Woodar Investment Development Ltd* v *Wimpey Construction UK Ltd*; special category?
  (2) Tom's own loss? Moral obligation to daughter?
  (3) Need to pay for substitute present? (*Woodar Investment Development Ltd* v *Wimpey Construction UK Ltd*)
  (4) Personal satisfaction in seeing rewiring done? (*Radford* v *De Froberville*)
  (5) Alternative reliance basis — wasted work — but if own expectancy loss nil can he claim this?
  (6) Restitution — *quantum meruit* — lack of loss irrelevant — stronger case than *Planché* v *Colburn* since clear benefit — but *quantum meruit* usually where *partial* performance.

Tom, Paul and the mother:

(a) Can the mother sue? As above (a).
(b) Can Tom obtain an effective remedy?

Specific performance? Mutuality? Damages inadequate? Compare *Beswick* v *Beswick*.

As to the first issue, Can the daughter sue? It is pretty clear that she is neither a promisee nor does she provide any form of consideration so she has no right to sue whether or not the doctrine of privity which was confirmed in *Dunlop Pneumatic Tyre Co. Ltd* v *Selfridge & Co. Ltd* [1915] AC 847 is distinguishable from the rule in *Tweddle* v *Atkinson* (1861) 1 B & S 393 that consideration must move from the promisee. (It is useful to put the matter that way in your answer, rather than merely saying 'The daughter is a third party and cannot sue' since it shows that you not only know the relevant cases but are aware of the controversy over whether the privity and consideration rules are distinguishable.)

As for exceptions to the privity rule, Tom is clearly not contracting as agent for his daughter and whilst the trust device is not impossible to apply here, as noted earlier, it has rather gone out of fashion and to say that Tom created a trust of the benefit of Dennis's promise would mean that he would have no right to vary the contract, e.g., to agree that Dennis should pay cash if Tom gets into financial difficulties before the contract has been performed. Again it is worth mentioning the trust device even if you ultimately reject it, in order to show that you understand it and the reasons why it is inappropriate here.

That leads on to the second issue, the remedies available to Tom. Specific performance would, of course, be ideal from the daughter's point of view but there is the major difficulty that this is a personal service contract which, you can point out, apart from exceptional circumstances such as those in *Hill* v *C. A. Parsons & Co. Ltd* [1972] Ch 305, the courts will not specifically enforce. As a result, an award of damages looks the likeliest form of sanction against the recalcitrant Dennis, but this remedy itself is not straightforward on these facts. If Dennis had agreed to rewire Tom's house, there would of course be no problem — the damages would be the cost of getting someone else to do the work. However, it may be that it is the daughter who will incur this expense and thus the loss will be hers, not Tom's. You should mention here Lord Denning's view in *Jackson* v *Horizon Holidays Ltd* [1975] 1 WLR 1468 that the plaintiff can obtain damages on behalf of the third party's loss in order to show your awareness of the disapproval of that view as a general rule by the House of Lords in *Woodar Investment Development Ltd* v *Wimpey Construction UK Ltd* [1980] 1 All ER 571. You could also briefly discuss whether the facts of this problem could be regarded as one of the special situations where Lord Denning's view would be applicable, of which there is little evidence on the facts.

Having rejected the notion of damages *on behalf of the daughter, there* remains the issue of damages for Tom's own loss. This could be put in a number of ways, e.g., that Tom may feel morally obliged to pay someone else to do the rewiring for his daughter and thus will suffer a loss himself as a result of the breach (see Lord Scarman in *Woodar Investment Development Ltd* v *Wimpey Construction UK Ltd* and *Anson's Law of Contract*). Alternatively it could be that, rather than paying for someone else to rewire, Tom will provide an alternative wedding present (in which case the quantum of damages may be different — the cost of the alternative rather than the cost of rewiring). It could also be put on the basis that Tom has contracted for the satisfaction of seeing his daughter's house rewired and is entitled to damages which will enable that result to be achieved. See *Radford* v *De Froberville* [1978] 1 All ER 33 (cf. Briggs (1981) 131 New LJ 343) where the plaintiff was held to be entitled to the costs of building a boundary wall even though he would not suffer any loss in the sense of diminution in value of his property if the wall was not built. Oliver J emphasised that the plaintiff did genuinely intend to have the wall built with the damages and so it would be helpful if Tom similarly intended to have the rewiring done if he wished to succeed on this basis. Although in *Dean* v *Ainley* [1987] 3 All ER 749 Kerr LJ at least thought it was irrelevant what the plaintiff intended to do with his damages, the House of Lords in *Ruxley Electronics* v *Forsyth* [1996] AC 344 considered that this was a relevant factor in holding that the full cost of reconstructing a pool in accordance with the contractual specifications was not recoverable.

An alternative course for Tom might be to claim damages on a reliance basis — the time and money he has wasted in performing his own side of the contract when Dennis has refused to carry out the work agreed in exchange. This of course would be a quite different measure. The cost of rewiring would be irrelevant. The reasonable cost of the decorating would be the relevant amount and that might be more or less than the cost of rewiring depending on whether Tom has made a good or bad bargain. This raises the further issue of whether Tom can claim *more* than the cost of rewiring in this way — and the answer given by *C & P Haulage* v *Middleton* [1983] 3 All ER 94 is that no, he can't (although it is up to Dennis to show this — see *CCC Films (London) Ltd* v *Impact Quadrant Films Ltd* [1985] QB 16). There is the further problem that there is only a point in claiming reliance damages here if the loss to Tom on the normal expectancy basis is nil (the loss being his daughter's). Dennis *could* argue (but the argument is so unmeritorious it is unlikely to succeed) that reliance damages should not be awarded since that would put *Tom* (though not his daughter) in a better position than if the contract had been performed. The answer to that might be that Tom is not in a better position since he contracted for the satisfaction of seeing his daughter benefited which really comes back again to saying that Tom has suffered a loss anyway on the expectancy basis.

Another way of providing Tom with a substantial remedy might lie in restitution, i.e., a *quantum meruit* for the work done by Tom under the contract as in *Planché* v *Colburn* (1831) 8 Bing 14. As noted earlier in this chapter, this would be very similar to allowing a reliance damages claim. The problem of putting it on this basis is that this sort of *quantum meruit* is normally only appropriate where the plaintiff has been prevented from *completing* performance and thus claiming the contract price. Here, Tom has completed performance but can't claim the contractual 'price' since it is, in effect, payable to a third party. However, there is no doubt that Tom could have claimed in restitution if Tom had done only part of the work before Dennis repudiated the contract and it would be rather odd if Tom was regarded as being in a *worse* position where he has already completed performance. A second point which you could make in this context is that in *Planché* v *Colburn* a *quantum meruit* was allowed even though the defendant publishers had not actually received any real benefit from the plaintiff's services. Here by contrast, Dennis has *received* the full benefit of Tom's performance and so the case for a restitutionary claim is all the stronger.

Thus in conclusion on the contract with Dennis, there are a number of different ways in which the courts can give Tom a substantial remedy and avoid reaching the conclusion that Dennis can refuse to perform with impunity. Your task is to try to identify as many possibilities as you can give reasonable grounds for and to identify the possible counter-arguments for each one. Don't be downhearted if you don't think you would have thought of all the ones discussed here (and please don't feel superior if you've thought of more!). Examiners usually have a range of potential arguments which they are looking for and will normally be satisfied if you identify a reasonable number, even though not all, of these.

The contract with Paul can be dealt with relatively briefly since many of the relevant points have already been made in dealing with the contract with Dennis. The mother is equally clearly a third party and cannot sue in her own right and damages could not be obtained on her behalf by Tom. It is less easy to argue that Tom can claim damages for his own loss since there does not appear to be any obligation on him to find £200 from elsewhere for his mother because of Paul's breach but he could still argue that, if he does genuinely intend to do this, he will have suffered a real loss as in *Radford* v *De Froberville*. However, the major difference as far as this contract is concerned is that to enforce it would not involve enforcing a personal service contract so specific performance could be the most appropriate remedy as in *Beswick* v *Beswick* [1968] AC 58. You should point out that at one time there might have been a problem with the requirement of mutuality since Paul would not have been likely to be able to obtain specific performance against Tom if Tom had failed to perform, but, following *Price* v *Strange* [1977] 3 All ER 371, that is now irrelevant since Tom has already performed. There is thus no danger that if Paul is ordered to perform he will have no guarantee that Tom will perform. Whilst this aspect of the case is similar to *Beswick* v *Beswick* where specific performance was granted, you should take the opportunity to show you can see possibly relevant distinctions from that case. Some of their Lordships in *Beswick* thought that damages might only be nominal which in the view of Lord Upjohn meant that 'the court ought to grant a specific performance order all the more'. In the problem, as I have said, it is possible to argue that damages are substantial which might therefore militate against an order of specific performance although Lord Pearce in *Beswick* thought that damages would have been substantial and yet still thought specific performance was the more appropriate remedy. However, that was partly because the contract was to pay an annuity whereas damages are a lump sum and that ground is inapplicable here since the promise is merely to pay a lump sum. As so often, the correct answer is not obvious, nor even desperately important in an examination context, but the issues are there to be discussed. Although the major part of any answer to this type of problem will be rightly concerned with the question of who can sue and for what, it would not be out of place, if you can find the time, to offer a comment about the state of the law portrayed in your answer. You could show your awareness of the Law Commission's recommendation that third parties should themselves be able to sue in this sort of situation and, e.g., remark that this would help to remove the necessity for the courts to manipulate the remedies available to the contracting party in order to do justice.

CONCLUSION

The law of remedies (and the doctrine of privity to the extent that it determines to whom the remedies should be available) is a topic which should help you to put many other areas of the syllabus in perspective. It is only after seeing what the law does where the contract is broken that you can fully understand the nature of an obligation undertaken in a contract. It is thus an essential topic for careful study and one in which, because of the practical nature of the issues raised, it is relatively easy to acquire an interest.

10   *ILLEGALITY AND INEQUALITY*

This final chapter will look at two issues which, although they are quite commonly looked at separately, have acquired a habit of arising together in the litigated cases. Again, there are also aspects of both areas which are largely unrelated to one another and so I will deal with each in turn, pointing out the common themes where applicable before investigating how these areas might be dealt with in the examination.

ILLEGALITY

The topic of illegality in fact covers a wide variety of problems and appropriate solutions. Because there is little agreement about how best the different types of illegality should be classified, the law is rather complex and difficult to state. Trying to learn all the possible types of illegality and attempting to discern the effects attributable to each separate type will only drive you silly and is not likely to be required by any sensible contracts course. Instead, a broader two-fold division is more manageable which involves dividing illegal contracts into those which are truly *illegal* on the one hand and those which are merely *void or* unenforceable on the other. This is a distinction which is used by Smith and Thomas, and Cheshire and Fifoot, for example, but which Treitel considers to be likely to lead to over-simplification. As long as you are aware of the pitfalls, the danger of over-simplification is probably preferable to the risk of being completely baffled by the complexity of the subject so the distinction between illegal and void contracts will be adopted here. The essence of the distinction is that illegal contracts are regarded by the courts as more tainted than merely void contracts with the result that the effects of a contract being treated as illegal can be more drastic than the effect of the contract merely being regarded as void. It should also be pointed out at the start that, as in so many areas, the courts do not use the terminology at all consistently, the adjectives 'illegal', 'void' and 'unenforceable' being bandied about as though they were interchangeable.

Illegal Contracts

The archetypal case here is of a contract which involves the commission of a criminal offence. Put as simply as that, one would not be surprised to find that the civil courts will not enforce the contract nor indeed want to be tainted by having anything to do with it by coming to the assistance of either of the parties. However, the criminal law comprehends a great variety of offences, some serious, others much less so and an attitude that may be defensible towards a contract involving a serious offence may not be appropriate where the offence is of a more technical nature. Where one has a merely regulatory offence created by statute as in *St John Shipping Corporation* v *Joseph Rank Ltd* [1957] 1 QB 267 and it is not proved that the parties intended to infringe the statute from the outset (in which case there would be a criminal conspiracy) the question has to be asked whether the statute was intended to prohibit just the offence or the contract as well. In *St John Shipping* the answer was no. The statutory offence was to load a ship so that her load line was submerged. Whilst this may have prohibited a contract to overload a ship it did not make illegal a contract to carry goods which then happened to be performed by means of an overloaded ship.

The category of illegal contracts also includes other types of agreements not necessarily involving the commission of a specific offence but being contrary to public policy in other ways such as involving sexual immorality. Cf. *Pearce* v *Brooks* (1866) LR 1 Ex 213 where the plaintiff could not sue on a contract for the hire-purchase of a miniature brougham (not a broom!) rented to a prostitute for use as part of her profession. Because of the variety of ways and degrees in which a contract can have an illegal purpose or be carried out in an illegal way the courts have a variety of responses at their disposal. The cases can be divided into two main categories:

(a)   those where an attempt is being made to enforce the contract or to claim damages for its breach,
(b)   those where a restitutionary remedy is being sought.

Under (a) a plaintiff who is aware of the illegality (which in this context means knows the *facts* even though he does not realise they render the contract illegal *in law*) will not succeed: see *Ashmore, Benson, Pease & Co. Ltd* v *A. V. Dawson Ltd* [1973] 2 All ER 856. But where as in *Archbolds (Freightage) Ltd* v *S. Spanglett Ltd* [1961] 1 QB 374 the plaintiff was unaware of the fact that the defendants lacked the appropriate licence for their van, the court may allow the plaintiff to recover damages. This, however, is not applicable where the contract is to do precisely what the statute prohibits. (In *Archbolds (Freightage) Ltd v S. Spanglett Ltd* the contract was one of carriage whereas the statute prohibited the *use* of the vehicle, cf. *St John Shipping Corporation v Joseph Rank Ltd* where the contract was not illegal at all for this reason — the contract was illegal in *Archbolds (Freightage) Ltd v S. Spanglett Ltd* because the defendants (but not the plaintiffs) intended to perform it illegally from the outset.) In *Re Mahmoud and Ispahani* [1921] 2 KB 716 the innocent seller couldn't sue on a contract for the sale of linseed oil since the contract was one of sale and such contracts of sale were prohibited unless *both* parties had a licence (the seller had one and mistakenly believed that the purchaser had one due to the purchaser's misrepresentation). *Strongman (1945) Ltd v Sincock* [1955] 2 QB 525 is a case, at first sight similar, where the innocent plaintiff was unable to sue on the contract to build which was illegal due to the lack of a licence but justice was done by awarding damages for breach of a collateral contract by the defendant to obtain a licence. Be wary of concluding that *Re Mahmoud and Ispahani* could be, or ought to be, similarly resolved today. There was a strong incentive to give a remedy in *Strongman (1945) Ltd v Sincock* since the work had been done and otherwise the defendant, who was responsible for the illegality, would have been unjustly enriched. In *Re Mahmoud and Ispahani* the purchaser had not received the linseed oil (he had refused to accept delivery) and thus was not unjustly enriched.

The plaintiff in *Re Mahmoud and Ispahani* could perhaps have claimed damages for misrepresentation by the purchaser (cf. damages for fraud awarded in *Shelley v Paddock* [1980] QB 348) but this would only provide reliance damages which would probably be nil on the facts. (Note by way of contrast that the damages in *Strongman (1945) Ltd v Sincock* could probably be justified on the reliance basis as much as on the expectancy — in reliance on the defendant's promise to obtain a licence, the plaintiff did what he would not otherwise have done.) Giving reliance damages to an innocent party does not cut across the policy of the statutory prohibition of the contract in the way that awarding the expectancy would — in fact it promotes the purpose of the prohibition by providing the defendant with an incentive not to mislead the plaintiff into innocently performing or preparing to perform an illegal contract. The claim in *Re Mahmoud and Ispahani* was essentially one for expectation damages.

Restitutionary claims: The basic position   A party to an illegal contract may well find that he has already transferred money or property for which he is unable to obtain the performance promised in return because the courts refuse to enforce the illegal contract. For example, in *Bigos v Bousted* [1951] 1 All ER 92, the defendant agreed to supply £150 of lire to the plaintiff in contravention of the Exchange Control Act 1947 and the plaintiff deposited a share certificate as security with the defendant. The defendant failed to supply the lire and the courts would obviously not help the plaintiff to enforce the illegal object of the contract directly so the plaintiff instead claimed back his share certificate. The court rejected this claim too and followed the normal rule in illegal contracts of refusing to come to the help of either party. The rationale for this approach is that the court does not sully itself by assisting either party to an illegal agreement and, more importantly, that this will discourage people from making illegal contracts in the first place since they know that if something goes wrong the courts will not come to their assistance. This basic 'do nothing' approach is often summed up in the maxim *'in pari delicto, potior est conditio defendentis'* which you will of course effortlessly translate as, 'where both parties are equally in the wrong, the defendant is in the stronger position', i.e., the court will not interfere with the status quo.

Whilst this is the starting-point, the law recognises a number of exceptions where it will intervene and allow restitution because doing nothing would not further the policy behind making the contract illegal in the first place.

Not in pari delicto
One group of exceptions can be explained as resting on the fact that the parties ,are not *in pari delicto,* i.e., not equally in the wrong. Thus in *Kiriri Cotton Co. Ltd* v *Dewani* [1960] AC 192, a flat was leased for an illegal premium. Neither party realised the premium was illegal since they made the 'easy mistake' of thinking that the lease of the flat for more than seven years was exempted by the proviso to s. 3 of the Uganda Rent Restriction Ordinance 1949 which, in fact, due to the definition of 'premises' in s. 2, only exempted long leases of *business* premises. None the less, Lord Denning (giving the judgment of the Privy Council) held that since the Ordinance was passed to protect tenants and put the burden of observing it on the landlord (the Ordinance imposed a fine on the landlord but not on the tenant) the parties were not *in pari delicto* and the tenant could recover. The decision makes sense in that it encourages the party who can most realistically discover the true legal position (the landlord) to do just that and is thus likely to promote the purpose of the statute. Not all statutes are interpreted as protecting one party rather than the other in this way — see *Green v Portsmouth Stadium Ltd* [1953] 2 QB 190 (statute not for the protection of bookmakers who could not recover illegal entrance fees) and *Harse* v *Pearl Life Assurance Co.* [1904] 1 KB 558 which seems a little harsh today. The plaintiff took out an insurance policy on his mother's life which was illegal since, contrary to what the insurance agent told him, there is no insurable interest in one's mother's life. The plaintiff failed to recover the premiums, even though the policy was unenforceable, because the parties were *in pari delicto.* Romer LJ said: 'I do not think agents of an insurance company must be treated as under a greater obligation to

know the law than the persons whom they approach'. Such sentiments hardly seem appropriate today when the courts would appear to be much more ready to recognise the onus of observing the statute as falling on one party, as in *Kiriri Cotton*.

It should be noted that the insurance agent was not fraudulent in *Harse* because if he had been, and had fraudulently misled the plaintiff into the illegal contract, the plaintiff would not have been *in pari delicto* with him and could have recovered as happened in *Hughes* v *Liverpool Victoria Legal Friendly Society* [1916] 2 KB 482. Similarly recovery will be allowed where the plaintiff has only entered the illegal contract under improper pressure from the defendant as in *Atkinson* v *Denby* (1862) 7 H & N 934.

Withdrawal from illegal purpose

The law not only wishes to discourage persons from entering illegal contracts in the first place, but also wishes to discourage them from performing them once they have been entered into. For this reason, the law provides an incentive to the parties to withdraw from an illegal contract by allowing restitution if the withdrawal is made voluntarily before the illegal purpose is achieved. Since the whole point is to provide an incentive to withdraw, the rule will not permit recovery if the withdrawal is not voluntary and is really due to some other reason as in *Bigos* v *Bousted* [1951] 1 All ER 92 where the only reason the plaintiff withdrew was because the defendant was refusing to perform. There is no need to provide an incentive to withdraw if the illegal purpose is going to be defeated anyway. By way of contrast recovery was allowed in *Taylor* v *Bowers* (1876) 1 QBD 291 since the plaintiff did voluntarily withdraw from the scheme to defraud his creditors before it could be successfully completed. However, in *Kearley* v *Thomson* (1890) 24 QBD 742, recovery was not allowed even though the plaintiff withdrew before the contract was completed because *part* of the illegal purpose had been carried out. It is sometimes thought to be difficult to reconcile these latter two cases since it is possible to say that the illegal purpose was partly carried out in *Taylor* v *Bowers*. An interesting and quite satisfying suggestion is made in a short note by Beatson (1975) 91 LQR 313 where he points out that both cases are consistent with the basic rationale for allowing recovery, i.e., to prevent the illegal purpose being consummated. If the plaintiff had been unable to recover his property in *Taylor* v *Bowers* there would have been nothing to distribute amongst the creditors and so if the law refused restitution it would have achieved the same result as was contemplated by the illegal contract. By contrast, in *Kearley* v *Thomson* allowing recovery would not have provided anything for the bankrupt's creditors so there was no incentive to intervene on that score and, furthermore, the plaintiff had not really resiled voluntarily but only because his fraudulent scheme had been discovered.

Rights independent of the contract or its illegality

A plaintiff can recover property transferred under an illegal contract if he can show that he has a right to it without relying either on the terms of the illegal contract or on its illegality. This rule does not make much sense unless one also accepts that ownership can be transferred when an illegal contract of sale is executed and that a more limited special property can be transferred when an illegal hire-purchase agreement or pledge or similar agreement is executed. Thus, in *Taylor v Chester* (1869) LR 4 QB 309 the plaintiff could not recover the half £50 note which he had pledged to the defendant for food and wine in a brothel. Although it was originally his own property he could not invalidate the special property which the pledgee appeared to have acquired except by relying on the illegal nature of the contract.

A key case here is *Bowmakers Ltd v Barnet Instruments Ltd* [1945] KB 65 where the plaintiffs let machine tools on hire-purchase to the defendants who sold some of them to third parties before all the instalments had been paid. The Court of Appeal held that even if the hire-purchase agreements were illegal (which was not clear) the plaintiffs could succeed in conversion against the defendants by relying on their original title. They did not have to claim under the illegal hire-purchase contract or plead its illegality. One problem with the case is that the plaintiffs themselves only obtained the tools under a contract of sale which was just as illegal as the hire-purchase agreement. If the plaintiffs obtained their title under this illegal contract, why could not the defendants assert that they acquired a limited property under the hire-purchase contract just as the defendant in *Taylor v Chester* could assert her apparently valid lien on the £50 which the defendant had pledged with her. A partial answer could be that the pledge in *Taylor v Chester* could only be shown to be invalid by pointing to its illegality whereas the special property which normally passes under a hire-purchase agreement could be shown to have been invalidated by the act of selling the tools to a third party. In other words, the plaintiff in *Taylor v Chester* had to rely on the illegal nature of the transaction whereas the plaintiff in *Bowmakers Ltd v Barnet Instruments Ltd* merely had to rely on the fact that the defendant had committed a serious breach (there was no breach in *Taylor v Chester*). That still doesn't explain, though, why the plaintiffs in *Bowmakers* also succeeded in respect of the tools which had not been sold to third parties. Why couldn't the defendants rely on their special property in respect of these tools? Treitel suggests that the contract in *Bowmakers* must have provided that the special property automatically terminated once the defendants defaulted on any instalments and that therefore there was no longer any special property which the defendants could assert against the plaintiffs. These issues are certainly difficult ones and if you wish to appreciate them fully you need to read the articles in (1949) 10 CLJ 249 and (1972) 35 MLR 78 by Hamson and Coote respectively. See also Enonchong, 'Title Claims and Illegal Transactions' (1995) 111 LQR 135.

'Void' Contracts

Whilst it is convenient to distinguish these from the 'illegal' contracts in the previous section it ought to be said at once that the label 'void contract' is an unhappy one because the contract is not totally void for all purposes and also one is not talking here of the whole contract but rather of a particular provision within it. The rest of the contract is normally perfectly valid.

The most important type of contract (or provision) in this class are contracts in restraint of trade so this discussion will concentrate on these. A contract in restraint of trade is prima facie void (i.e., unenforceable, see *O'Sullivan* v *Management Agency & Music Ltd* [1985] QB 428) but it may still be valid if the restraint is reasonable in the interests of the parties and in the interests of the public. There are three main issues which need to be addressed in this area:

(a)   What contracts fall within the doctrine of restraint of trade and thus require justification as being reasonable?

(b)   How do the courts decide the question of reasonableness when it arises?

(c)   What is the effect of a contract being found to be an unreasonable restraint of trade?

What contracts are in restraint of trade?   Contracts in restraint of trade include:

(a)   Contracts whereby an employer seeks to restrain an employee from competing with him *after* leaving the employment.

(b)   Contracts whereby a vendor of a business agrees not to compete with the purchaser.

(c)   Exclusive dealing agreements such as solus agreements whereby a garage agrees to purchase all its petrol from a particular oil company.

(d)   Exclusive service agreements which are designed to sterilise rather than to utilise an individual's talents (as in *A. Schroeder Music Publishing Co. Ltd* v *Macaulay* [1974] 1 WLR 1308).

(e)   Agreements between employers and other bodies which restrain the liberty of employees to earn their living (see, e.g., *Eastham* v *Newcastle United Football Club Ltd* [1964] Ch 413 and *Greig* v *Insole* [1978] 3 All ER 449).

The important point to note is that whilst the above categories are amongst those which have been recognised, the courts can recognise new types of contracts in restraint of trade if they should develop. Indeed categories (c) and (d) are relatively novel in that they are not restraints which apply *after* the period of the contract but during it and solus agreements are also novel in that they restrain an individual only in his use of a particular piece of land. Category (e) is distinctive in that the restraint affects persons other than parties to the contract. The flexibility of the restraint-of-trade doctrine and its capacity to apply to new types of contract was stressed by the House of Lords both in *Esso Petroleum Co. Ltd v Harper's Garage (Stourport) Ltd* [1968] AC 269 and also in *A. Schroeder Music Publishing Co. Ltd v Macaulay* (see *Dawnay Day & Co. v D'Alphen, The Times*, 24 June 1997 for a recent example applying the doctrine to a joint venture agreement). On the other hand, it appears that some contracts that *in fact* appear to restrain trade may be outside the doctrine. For example, the decision in *Cleveland Petroleum Ltd v Dartstone Ltd* [1969] 1 WLR 116 seems to mean that a solus agreement is outside the doctrine if the person restrained only obtained the right to trade from the garage as a result of the contract containing the solus agreement. The theory is that the agreement does not take away any freedom to trade which the covenantor previously had. The difficulty with this theory is that it largely ignores the question of the public interest on which the restraint-of-trade doctrine is supposedly based. A long-term solus agreement may be just as contrary to the public interest where the trader had no previous right to trade from the site as where he previously had an unrestricted right. However, it may be that the *Cleveland* decision is an exceptional one which will not be liberally applied: see *Alec Lobb (Garages) Ltd v Total Oil GB Ltd* [1985] 1 All ER 303 where premises were leased back to a company which had no previous right to trade but the restraint doctrine still applied since the company was wholly owned by the Lobbs who did have a previous right to trade. The lease-back was a 'palpable device' to try to evade the doctrine, which the court would not allow to succeed.

Once the contract is found to be in restraint of trade, that is not the end of the matter, it might still be perfectly valid. It merely becomes subject to special rules not applicable to contracts in general, requiring it to be reasonable in the interests of the parties and of the public.

The assessment of reasonableness This is largely a question of comparing the extent and width of the restraint with the justification (if any) for it and of enquiring whether the restrictions agreed to are fair or 'commensurate with the benefits secured to the promisor' as Lord Diplock put it in *A. Schroeder Music Publishing Co. Ltd v Macaulay* [1974] 1 WLR 1308. There is also the question of whether the restraint is justified 'in the interest of the public' but all these issues tend to merge into one another since the interest of the public has been explained as meaning merely the public interest in 'men being able to trade freely subject to reasonable limitations' and as not involving 'balancing a mass of conflicting economic, social and other interests' (see Ungoed-Thomas J in *Texaco Ltd v Mulberry Filling Station Ltd* [1972] 1 WLR 814 at p. 827). More recently in *Bridge v Deacons* [1984] AC 705 the Privy Council rejected the argument that a restraint on a solicitor was invalidated by the alleged public policy that solicitors should be free to take any client. The issue of reasonableness will tend to be raised in terms of fairness where there is an apparent disparity between the parties in terms of their respective bargaining power (as the House of Lords assumed in *A. Schroeder Music Publishing Co. Ltd* v *Macaulay* — for criticism of this assumption see Trebilcock (1976) 26 UTLJ 359) and in terms of the 'legitimate interest' being protected in other cases. The public interest only rarely arises directly since neither party is likely to challenge the contract if it is reasonable as between them. *Wyatt* v *Kreglinger & Fernau* [1933] 1 KB 793 is one of those rare cases where the public interest was crucial.

As in all areas where the issue is one of reasonableness there is not much more that you can do other than to be aware of the sorts of factors which have influenced the courts and be able to refer to illustrative cases. That each case turns on its own facts was vividly illustrated recently in *Alec Lobb (Garages) Ltd* v *Total Oil GB Ltd* [1985] 1 All ER 303. Until that decision, there seemed to be a rule of thumb based on *Esso Petroleum Co. Ltd* v *Harper's Garage (Stourport) Ltd* [1968] AC 269 that five years was a reasonable period for a solus agreement but anything substantially in excess of that would not be. Because of the special factors in *Alec Lobb*, such as the transaction being a rescue operation without which the plaintiffs would have gone out of business anyway, a 21-year tie was held to be reasonable by the Court of Appeal. The tic was also reasonable because ample consideration was given for it which underlines once again the fact that the restraint doctrine is concerned as much with fairness between the parties as with the public interest.

In employer-employee contracts, the law recognises the employer's 'proprietary interest' in his own trade secrets and other confidential information and in his existing customer relationships so that a covenant designed to protect these will normally be reasonable, provided it goes no further than is necessary. Thus the restraints can only possibly be valid where the employee has had access to confidential information or has been in a position to acquire the loyalty of customers and can only last as long as that influence over customers is likely to persevere. The employer is not entitled to protect himself merely against competition by former employees nor can he restrain the exercise after the employment of skills acquired by employees during the period of employment. A covenant restraining the active solicitation of customers is much more likely to be reasonable than one which puts a blanket restriction on working in a certain area.

Restraints in contracts on the sale of a business are looked at rather more favourably since there is less likely to be inequality of bargaining power (at least the courts assume this) and the 'goodwill' of the business is after all something that the purchaser has actually paid for. None the less, the restraint can only validly protect the business sold and will be unreasonable if it seeks also to prevent competition with other businesses that the purchaser might already own or subsequently acquire.

In the other categories of contracts in restraint of trade, there are no obvious proprietary interests such as trade secrets or goodwill that can be protected and the courts tend to talk here about the 'legitimate interests' of the covenantee. In solus agreements this seems to be the petrol company's interests in having a stable system of outlets for petrol (which itself is in the public interest since otherwise no one would be prepared to invest the vast sums of money necessary for entering the petrol distribution industry). In *Eastham* v *Newcastle United Football Club Ltd* [1964] Ch 413 the health of the football industry and the enjoyment of the football-watching public was recognised as an interest. It is noticeable how in the more recent categories of restraint of trade, legitimate interests seem to owe rather a lot to the public interest which supports the idea that reasonableness in the interest of the public is not really an issue which can be separated from reasonableness in the interest of the parties.

The effect of a restraint being found to be unreasonable   The restraint itself is clearly unenforceable but the rest of the contract would normally be valid. So even though an employee's covenant in restraint of trade is 'void' in this sense, he is still entitled to his wages and other benefits under the contract (such as a pension) since he has provided plenty of other considerations for his employer's obligations. In other words, the void covenant can be severed from the rest of the consideration which he supplies. This will not always be true, if the covenant is the *only* consideration it obviously cannot be severed and the invalidity of the covenant may rebound on the employee as in *Wyatt* v *Kreglinger & Fernau* [1933] 1 KB 793 where the former employee lost his right to a pension. Furthermore, if the restraint is not the only but is substantially the main consideration for the contract, the whole agreement will be unenforceable as in *Amoco Australia Pty Ltd* v *Rocco Brothers Motor Engineering Pty Ltd* [1975] 1 All ER 968 where, apart from the restraints, the covenantor's only obligation was to pay a nominal rent. Contrast *Alec Lobb (Garages) Ltd* v *Total Oil GB Ltd* [1985] 1 All ER 303 where there were ample other considerations and thus the covenants would have been severed had they been unreasonable. The question of severing does not appear to have been discussed in *A. Schroeder Music Publishing Co. Ltd* v *Macaulay* [1974] 1 WLR 1308 but that seems to have been a case where the restraints permeated the contract to such an extent that the whole contract rather than any particular provision within it was an unreasonable restraint so that the contract as a whole was unenforceable. Similarly, the whole boxer-manager contract in *Watson* v *Prager* [1991] 1 WLR 726 was held to be unenforceable against the boxer Michael Watson who, tragically, suffered serious brain damage in a fight a few months later.

Quite apart from the question of severing a restraint clause from the rest of the contract, there is the issue of severing *within* the clause itself. For example, in the aptly named *Goldsoll* v *Goldman* [1915] 1 Ch 292 a covenant on the sale of an imitation jewellery business restrained the vendor from being engaged in the sale of 'real or imitation jewellery' in the United Kingdom or in France, USA, Russia etc. The covenant as it stood was too wide in geographical area and in referring to real jewellery as well as to imitation jewellery (because the business sold did not deal in real jewellery) but the court held it could be saved by severing the words 'real or' and the reference to foreign countries. Thus cut down, the covenant was enforceable against the defendant who had become involved in selling imitation jewellery in the very same street as the business sold!

There are, however, two limitations on this principle of severance. Firstly, the courts will only sever where the 'blue pencil' test is satisfied. The colour of the pencil is not particularly material but the point is that you can only use it to strike out offending words not to rewrite or substitute new ones. In *Goldsoll* v *Goldman* the covenant could be rendered reasonable just by striking out but that is not possible if, e.g., a covenant is expressed for too long a period as in *M & S Drapers* v *Reynolds* [1956] 3 All ER 814 where five years was 'wholly unwarranted'. The courts will not strike out the figure five and substitute what they consider a reasonable figure and of course if they merely strike out the reference to five years that would make the covenant perpetual and hence even more unreasonable. Secondly, severance will only be allowed where it does not alter the nature of the original contract, so it was not allowed in *Attwood* v *Lamont* [1920] 3 KB 571 where the original covenant was said to be for the protection of the employer's whole business and to restrict it to merely protecting the tailors' department where the covenantor worked would have altered its nature. This limitation is rather vague, perhaps deliberately so, and in effect gives the courts the power to veto severance where they think it is inappropriate. Severance is less likely to be allowed in employer-employee contracts where the courts assume the covenant is more likely to have been imposed on one party by the other, than in other contexts. Similar factors are relevant here to those which were discussed in chapter 6 relating to the partial validity of exclusion clauses. Unscrupulous parties might be tempted to draft extremely wide covenants hoping that the other party would be cowed into adhering to them and knowing that if the clause is challenged, the courts would enforce it in so far as it is reasonable. The limitations on severance can be seen as attempts to provide an incentive to draft reasonable clauses in the first place. A complete ban on severance would, however, produce injustice in cases like *Goldsoll* v *Goldman*. The sort of question you ought to be thinking about is whether the rather mechanistic 'blue pencil' test and the *Attwood* v *Lamont* limitations are the most appropriate restrictions or whether they in fact owe more to the rhetoric of 'not making a contract for the parties'.

A final point which you ought to be aware of in relation to restraint of trade is a rather obvious one that the doctrine is largely dependent on one of the parties not wishing to be bound by the restraint. (This is another reason why the cases tend to focus on reasonableness between the parties rather than on the interest of the public.) There are exceptions to this such as *Eastham v Newcastle United Football Club Ltd* [1964] Ch 413 but even here the plaintiff himself had been in a contractual relationship with one of the parties to the illegal arrangement. Cartel agreements between suppliers of goods or services whereby markets are carved up and prices fixed may be highly prejudicial to the public interest, but the agreement is likely to be carried out because it suits the actual parties and the common law restraint-of-trade doctrine in such circumstances can do little about it. That is one reason why the Restrictive Trade Practices Act 1976 (the scheme originated in 1956) requires such agreements to be registered and validated by the Restrictive Practices Court where the public interest can be fully considered. Third parties have a right to damages for any loss suffered if an unregistered or invalidated agreement is given effect to by the parties. Few, if any contract courses will require you to study this legislation in detail but you should be aware of the contrasting approach enshrined in it as compared with the restraint-of-trade doctrine and it should help you to see the latter doctrine in a more realistic light as one concerned with fairness between the parties as much as the protection of the public interest. That leads on nicely to the other subject of this chapter.

INEQUALITY OF BARGAINING POWER

The law of contract has traditionally not been overtly concerned with the fairness of the bargain between the parties, an attitude which is summed up by the maxim 'consideration must be sufficient but need not be adequate'. Whilst this may be formally true of the doctrine of consideration, the law is not, and never has been, indifferent to the fairness of a contract where the parties are not contracting on equal terms. What is true is that the courts are not prepared to intervene *purely* on the grounds of unfairness in contracts generally. The contract must either be one of a special type such as one in restraint of trade (above), or, especially following the Unfair Contract Terms Act 1977, involving a particular type of exemption clause *or* there must appear to be something in the conduct of the advantaged party which would justify the courts in intervening. Since I have already looked at restraint of trade and exemption clauses it is the second category of cases involving actual or presumed misconduct which will be discussed now. This category can be dealt with under three main headings:

(a) Duress (common law).
(b) Undue influence (equity).
(c) Unconscionable bargains (equity).

Duress

The common law notion of duress was very limited, requiring threats of death or physical violence (see *Barton* v *Armstrong* [1975] 2 All ER 465 for an example) before it could be sufficient to avoid a contract. However, rather anomalously, the courts did allow a person to recover money *actually paid* as a result of lesser threats, namely duress of goods, i.e., where the defendant threatens wrongfully to detain the plaintiff's property — see *Astley* v *Reynolds* (1731) 2 Barn KB 40. This made the rule that lesser threats were not sufficient to avoid an *agreement* to pay look rather nonsensical and in the past decade or so the courts have recognised a wider concept of duress known as 'economic duress' applicable to agreements as well. See especially *North Ocean Shipping Co. Ltd* v *Hyundai Construction Co. Ltd* [1979] QB 705 where the threat to break the contract unless the plaintiffs paid an extra 10 per cent was held to be sufficient duress to entitle the purchasers to avoid the contract to pay (but the plaintiffs failed because they were also held to have later affirmed the contract). The problem now is in identifying what types of threat would be sufficient to amount to economic duress. It seems that the fact that a breach of contract is threatened is not of itself sufficient and that the threats must be beyond ordinary commercial pressure and be 'a coercion of the will that vitiates consent' (per Lord Scarman in *Pao On* v *Lau Yiu Long* [1980] AC 614). This sort of language is not, you might think, terribly helpful in trying to apply the doctrine except as an indication that economic duress will be kept within limits (see Atiyah (1982) 98 LQR 197). The formula was, however, repeated in *Hennessy* v *Craigmyle* [1986] IRLR 304, where the Court of Appeal refused to upset a settlement of a potential claim for unfair dismissal. Other factors mentioned by Lord Scarman, such as whether the plaintiff had any alternative open to him, may seem more helpful at first sight, but there is always an alternative — the problem is that the very nature of a threat means that this alternative will be unpleasant. The question is really whether this second alternative is sufficiently dire to excuse the plaintiff from the agreement which he has entered.

Another factor that is worth discussing in economic duress is the legitimacy or illegitimacy of the threat. A threat may have very serious consequences and yet not constitute duress because it is legitimate — see *Alec Lobb (Garages) Ltd* v *Total Oil GB Ltd* at first instance [1983] 1 WLR 87 where insisting on existing contractual *rights* was held not to be duress even though it may have resulted in the bankruptcy of the other party. In *Universe Tankships Inc. of Monrovia* v *International Transport Workers Federation* [1983] 1 AC 366 the duress was a threat by a union to continue to black a ship and the House of Lords linked the question of whether the threat was legitimate with the question of whether the union would have been protected from tort liability as acting in contemplation of a trade dispute. The House didn't require the duress actually to be a tort or positively unlawful in any particular way. This is clearly another area in which the law is developing — see *B & S Contracts & Design Ltd* v *Victor Green Publications Ltd* [1984] ICR 419 and *Atlas Express Ltd* v *Kafco Ltd* [1989] 1 All ER 641 for two cases where economic duress was applied (where the threat was to break a contract) and compare *CTN Cash and Carry Ltd* v *Gallaher Ltd* [1994] 4 All ER 714 where the fact that the threat was not unlawful was a powerful factor in reaching the conclusion that it did not amount to duress. Your task is to be aware of the factors that seem to be relevant and preferably to have a view which you can stress. For example, it might be that the legitimacy of the threat and the seriousness of the consequences to the other party if the threat is carried out are twin requirements that are directly proportional to one another — the more serious the consequences, the better the justification required to legitimate the threat.

Undue Influence

The strictness of the common law on duress was mitigated to some extent by equity through the doctrine of undue influence. This itself can be divided into two types. The first type is actual undue influence as in *Williams* v *Bayley* (1866) LR 1 HL 200 where a father was pressured into giving security for his son's debts by implicit threats that otherwise his son would be prosecuted. This sort of case could now probably be dealt with under the wider modern notion of duress. (Note also, in the context of this chapter, that another possible ground for the decision discussed in the judgments was that the agreement was illegal as being to suppress a prosecution and that the father was not *in pari delicto* with the defendants.)

The second, and more common, type of undue influence is 'relational' undue influence where the law presumes from the relationship of the parties, without any evidence of *actual* undue influence, that the contract is the result of improper pressure from one party. This second type can itself be subdivided into:

(a) Relationships where undue influence is automatically presumed, such as trustee and beneficiary or solicitor and client.

(b) Other cases where the actual relationship between the parties is such that undue influence can be presumed as in *Lloyds Bank Ltd* v *Bundy* [1975] QB 326 where old Mr Bundy totally relied on the bank's advice in guaranteeing his son's debts and in charging his house to the bank. Apart from such a special situation, the relationship of banker and customer would not normally or automatically give rise to a presumption of undue influence as is graphically illustrated by the House of Lords decision in *National Westminster Bank plc* v *Morgan* [1985] 1 All ER 821 where the House rejected the plea of undue influence even though the bank visited Mrs Morgan at her home and the charge was signed there. It should be noted that, despite some of the language used by Lord Scarman, a 'dominating influence' is not necessary. See *Goldsworthy* v *Brickell* [1987] 1 All ER 853. The principle is one of *undue* influence not *total* domination.

In addition to the relevant type of relationship, the agreement itself must actually confer an unfair advantage on the party in a position to exercise undue influence. This was made clear in *National Westminster Bank plc* v *Morgan* in the House of Lords where the view of the Court of Appeal, that relational undue influence could apply to an agreement which was not actually disadvantageous, was overruled. (The Court of Appeal subsequently decided that the requirement of manifest disadvantage also applies to cases of *actual* undue influence in *Bank of Credit & Commerce International* v *Aboody* [1989] 2 WLR 759 but the House of Lords has now decided in *CIBC Mortgages* v *Pitt* [1993] 4 All ER 433 that manifest disadvantage is not required in cases of *actual* as opposed to *relational* (presumed) undue influence.) Mrs Morgan's charge of the matrimonial home to the bank was not disadvantageous because it relieved her from the prospect of eviction by a building society to whom the house was already mortgaged. She was also misled (innocently) by the bank into thinking the charge only covered the existing debt and could not be used to cover her husband's business liability but she was not disadvantaged by that either since the bank only ever sought to enforce the charge to cover the existing debt. She may have had a better claim on the ground of misrepresentation but that would have been little use to her:

(a)   Because it would have been a condition of rescission that she repaid the bank the money advanced, and

(b)   Any damages (in lieu of rescission) would be nominal as the misrepresentation caused her no loss.

Don't lose sight of the fact that where the presumption of undue influence does apply, it is only a presumption. It can be rebutted by proof that no actual advantage was taken of the relationship but of course this will not be easy since it will involve finding an alternative explanation for the unbalanced nature of the transaction. The most likely manner of rebutting the presumption is to show that the disadvantaged party had independent advice. If that independent advice is rejected then the contract is normally regarded as being a result of the person's own folly rather than of the undue influence of the other party and so no relief will be given (see *Banco Exterior Internacional* v *Thomas* [1997] 1 All ER 46). Lack of independent advice may be crucial even though, as in *Allcard* v *Skinner* (1887) 36 ChD 145, the plaintiff (a nun at the time of her gifts to her own superior) would have undoubtedly rejected any such advice (as coming from the devil). In *Barclays Bank* v *O'Brien* [1993] 4 All

ER 417, the bank's failure to warn the wife of the risks involved in standing surety for her husband's debt and to advise her of the need to take independent advice was again a crucial factor in rendering the transaction unenforceable against the wife. The Bank's failure to do this fixed it with constructive notice of any undue influence or, in this case, the misrepresentation made by the husband to the wife. In contrast, in *CIBC Mortgages v Pitt* [1993] 4 All ER 433, the creditor was not fixed with such notice since the loan was one jointly to the husband and wife ostensibly for their joint purposes as opposed to a guarantee of the husband's debt with no obvious benefit to the wife. There was nothing to indicate that there was a special risk of undue influence in the case of a normal loan to a husband and wife for their joint purposes.

Unconscionable Bargains

This group of cases seems to differ from undue influence mainly in the potential means of obtaining the advantage — which is not so much a matter of being in a position to abuse one's *influence* as being able to exploit the *weakness* of the other party. The sort of cases where relief has been given include loans at a penal rate of interest to a young heir to a large fortune as in *Earl of Aylesford v Morris* (1873) LR 8 Ch App 484 and one-sided bargains with poor and ignorant persons, which in modern conditions in the context of conveyancing documents, seems to include telephonists! — see *Cresswell v Potter* [1978] 1 WLR 255 n. Although the limits of the category of unconscionable bargains are not very precisely set, the courts only interfere in exceptional cases where the unfairness of the bargain suggests that a position of strength has been *abused*. The Court of Appeal was not prepared to intervene in *Alec Lobb (Garages) Ltd v Total Oil GB Ltd* [1985] 1 All ER 303 where, it was said, there was no evidence of oppressive or unconscionable conduct on the part of Total. The plaintiffs were in a very difficult and weak position but Total didn't put any unfair pressure on them and indeed Total were the more reluctant of the two parties to enter the contract. Furthermore, the plaintiffs received independent advice which they chose to ignore (cf. 'Undue influence' above). In contrast, in *Watkin v Watson-Smith, The Times*, 3 July 1986, a frail old man of 80 had agreed to sell his bungalow worth £29,000 for £2,950. His age and diminished capacity brought him within the category of poor and ignorant persons and he had not received independent advice largely because of the defendant's anxiety to speedily conclude the contract. See also *Boustany v Pigott* (1993) 109 LQR 530.

A General Doctrine of Inequality of Bargaining Power?

The existing bases on which the courts would interfere with unfair contracts were all very well but were rather piecemeal in their operation and were capable of leaving gaps where a harsh bargain would be enforceable. Not surprisingly then, Lord Denning MR in *Lloyds Bank Ltd v Bundy* [1975] QB 326 suggested that the various separate heads of relief were all examples of one unifying principle of inequality of bargaining power which could be a ground of relief where a person 'without independent advice, enters into a contract in terms which are very unfair or transferred property for a consideration which is grossly inadequate, when his bargaining power is grievously impaired by reason of his own needs or desires, or by his own ignorance or infirmity, coupled with undue influences or pressure brought to bear on him by or for the benefit of the other'.

Quite apart from the fact that this was *obiter* even in Lord Denning's judgment (his decision being based on traditional undue influence as an alternative) there has been little support for this general principle from other judges (but see Waddams (1976) 39 MLR 364 for sympathy from an academic quarter). The major criticism that is made of Lord Denning's principle is that it could introduce uncertainty but it is not altogether clear that the motley collection of existing heads of relief is itself productive of certainty. However, given Lord Denning's retirement there seems little chance of the principle being vigorously applied and indeed it was given short shrift by the House of Lords in *National Westminster Bank plc v Morgan* [1985] 1 All ER 821 where Lord Scarman thought it was for Parliament to continue to determine such restrictions on freedom of contract as it deemed necessary and his Lordship doubted whether 'the courts should assume the burden of formulating further restrictions'.

For what it's worth, my own personal view (and you would do well to formulate your own view on this) is that Lord Denning's principle has received an unduly critical reception, partly by being associated with a more loosely stated American doctrine of unconscionability. The catch-phrase 'inequality of bargaining power' is no doubt too vague and potentially wide-ranging but the details of the principle (quoted above) are more restrictive and seem to require both substantive unfairness (the terms must be unfair or the consideration grossly inadequate) and procedural impropriety ('coupled with undue influences or pressure'). The principle, therefore, given a cautious interpretation (perhaps more cautious than Lord Denning himself would have been prepared to give it) would not have upset a freely negotiated bargain *merely* on the grounds of its contents being one-sided but only if it was also secured in an unfair way. Neither would it have dictated a different decision than that reached by the House of Lords in *National Westminster Bank plc v Morgan* since the fact that the bargain was not disadvantageous would equally have precluded the operation of Lord Denning's principle.

Whatever the merits or otherwise of Lord Denning's unifying principle, English law seems now likely to stick to its separate categories but, given their flexibility (as Lord Scarman put it in *National Westminster Bank plc* v *Morgan* 'this is the world of doctrine not of neat and tidy rules'), the results may not be all that different.

A final point to note concerns the distinction drawn above between procedural and substantive unfairness. The distinction had been emphasised on the other side of the Atlantic (see especially Leff (1967) 115 UPaLR 485) and may be beginning to gain a foothold even with the judiciary in this country. In a recent Privy Council decision, *Hart* v *O'Connor* [1985] 3 WLR 214 Lord Brightman recognised a distinction between two types of unfairness:

(a)   Contractual imbalance (substantive unfairness) and
(b)   Procedural unfairness.

The Privy Council disapproved an earlier New Zealand case, *Archer* v *Cutler* [1980] 1 NZLR 386 where the court had refused to enforce a contract for the sale of land basically on the grounds of contractual imbalance alone. (The defendant was of unsound mind but the plaintiff was unaware of this and acted quite properly.) Some sort of procedural unfairness was also required (or knowledge of the other person's disability), said the Privy Council, before the court could legitimately intervene. The converse of this rule may be that procedural unfairness alone will not normally be enough unless there is also some contractual imbalance (substantive unfairness). This certainly seems to be true of the *presumption* of undue influence — see *National Westminster Bank plc* v *Morgan* — but this may be because without the evidence of substantive unfairness there is insufficient evidence to raise the presumption of procedural unfairness (the actual exercise of undue influence) in the first place. Some other types of procedural unfairness (e.g., duress, misrepresentation and actual undue influence) may be sufficient in themselves without any evidence of resultant contractual imbalance, perhaps on the basis that the exercise of duress, misrepresentation or undue influence ought to be discouraged. At any rate, it will be interesting to see if the English courts start to discuss the distinction between substantive and procedural unfairness in the wake of *Hart* v *O'Connor* and if you can present the examiner with your views on the matter you will probably gain both his interest and a few extra, possibly vital, marks.

THE EXAMINATION

Because public policy considerations underlie both the areas of illegality and inequality these are both areas where an essay question might require you to evaluate the relevant law, but before considering a couple of essays it might be useful to look at the following problem question which might help to clarify some of the more technical issues which can arise.

A Problem

In January, Richard agreed with Leftee Books to prepare for publication by the end of the year the private diaries of his late brother (a former Cabinet Minister). The agreed fee is £10,000, £2,000 being paid in advance. In February, Leftee Books sell the serial rights to a newspaper, the *Sunday Slab*, for £100,000 and on hearing of this Richard demands an increase in his fee which Leftee refuse. In May, Richard discovers that under the contract with the *Sunday Slab* Leftee must have the first extracts ready for publication on New Year's Day (otherwise the contract is terminated) since the *Sunday Slab* wish to combat the planned launch of a new competitor on that day. Richard tells Leftee that he will not submit his manuscript until five to midnight on New Year's Eve (so making the publication of an extract on New Year's day impossible) unless both his advance and his fee are doubled. Leftee agree to double the fee and advance the extra £2,000 on condition that at least half the manuscript is delivered by 1 December. In November when Richard has done all the work and has the manuscript ready for delivery, Leftee discover that under government regulations made the previous year, the publication of *any* private papers of Cabinet Ministers within 30 years of them being a member of the Cabinet is made a criminal offence, unless the consent of the Prime Minister of the day is obtained. Leftee are unable to obtain this consent and realise that they cannot now publish the diaries and seek the return of the £4,000 advanced whilst Richard tenders his manuscript and claims the balance of the £16,000.

Discuss.

A simple plan of how to answer this question would involve distinguishing the question of the effect of the illegality from the issue of Richard's threat to delay handing over the manuscript (possible duress) and within those two issues the question of whether Richard can sue for the promised fee and whether he has to repay all or part of what he has received.

Duress
Modern expansion — *North Ocean Shipping Co. Ltd* v *Hyundai Construction Co. Ltd*:

(a)   Cogency of threat — serious loss to Leftee.
(b)   Legitimacy - *Universe Tankships Inc. of Monrovia* v *International Transport Workers Federation* — *Alec Lobb (Garages) Ltd* v *Total Oil GB Ltd* — no breach?
(c)   Effect — if any at all, only on second £10,000 and extra advance. (NB: consideration.)

Illegality

(a)   Is contract illegal — to prepare as distinct from to publish?

(b)   If illegal — can R sue? — *Re Mahmoud and Ispahani,* unlikely unless implied obligation on Leftee to obtain any necessary consent - *Strongman (1945) Ltd v Sincock.*

(c)   Can Leftee reclaim £4,000 advance?

(d)   Class protecting? — Hardly.

(e)   *Pari delicto?* — Nothing to suggest either party responsible for illegality — relevance of duress here?

(f)   Withdrawal by publishers? Incentive to prevent illegality.

Fleshing out that plan a little, under 'duress' you would need to show your appreciation of the way in which the ambit of duress has been widened to go beyond threats of violence. The cogency of the threat depends on the loss of the £100,000 for the serial rights — is this mere commercial pressure or is it a coercion of the will? (You should comment on the utility (or otherwise) of this test.) The threat may be a legitimate one anyway — it would not appear to be a breach of contract to delay delivery of the manuscript to the last moment — but actual unlawfulness may not be necessary. In *Universe Tankships Inc. of Monrovia* v *International Transport Workers Federation* [1983] 1 AC 366, Lord Scarman referred to the fact that threats of things not in themselves unlawful can still amount to blackmail in the criminal law. For the offence of blackmail, the test is whether:

(a)   the accused believed he had reasonable grounds for making the demands, and

(b)   whether he believed the threats were a proper way of enforcing the demands.

Could this test or a variant be applied here? Richard may feel he is justified in making the demand because of the excess profits Leftee seemed to be making from the serialisation etc.

Even if you think duress is not made out here or that the threat is a legitimate one, it would still be wise to discuss what the effect of duress, if proved, would be. Clearly it would not affect the first £2,000 advance or the £10,000 original fee. It would merely give Leftee the right to avoid the agreement to increase the fee and the right to recover the extra money paid in advance. Note also the relevance of consideration here (as in *North Ocean Shipping Co. Ltd* v *Hyundai Construction Co. Ltd* [1979] QB 705 itself). Even if there is no duress, is there any consideration for the agreement to increase the fee? The answer seems to be yes since Richard is going beyond his existing duty by agreeing to submit at least half the manuscript by 1 December.

Turning to the issue of illegality, performance of the contract pretty clearly involves the commission of a criminal offence (even though neither party was aware of this originally) and is thus illegal. One might argue that Richard has only contracted to *prepare* for publication and that this in itself, as opposed to actual publication, is not illegal but the only purpose of preparing is in order to facilitate the illegal purpose of publishing and there can be little doubt that this contract would be treated as illegal.

Can then Richard, who has done all the work, claim under the contract? The basic answer is of course no, although Richard could possibly base a claim on *Strongman (1945) Ltd* v *Sincock* [1955] 2 QB 525 by arguing that Leftee had impliedly promised they would obtain any necessary consent for publishing, but this seems to have no real basis in the facts. Furthermore, to allow Richard to sue on the contract might encourage Leftee to go ahead and publish in order to try to recoup their expenditure, the very thing which the law wishes to prevent.

The starting-point in answering the question of whether Leftee can obtain the return of the advance is the basic 'do nothing' approach of the courts towards restitution in illegal contracts. The issue then becomes whether any of the exceptions, where the courts will allow recovery, are applicable. The statute does not appear to be a class-protecting one — it is certainly not for the protection of publishers — though Leftee could not rely on cases like *Kiriri Cotton Co. Ltd* v *Dewani* [1960] AC 192. Could Leftee show themselves not to be *in pari delicto* in some other way? Should Richard, as the brother of an ex Cabinet Minister, have known about the regulations and thus be regarded as primarily responsible for the illegality? It could probably be argued equally strongly that it is part of the business of publishers to know about these things.

Could the alleged duress by Richard mean that the publishers are not *in pari delicto* — cf. *Williams* v *Bayley* (1866) LR 1 HL 200? If so, would this entitle Leftee to recover the whole £4,000 or just the £2,000 paid after the duress? Another view might be that, given that duress is given wider recognition in its own right today, it should be proved as an independent ground of relief or should be irrelevant, i.e., if Leftee failed to establish that the contract should be avoided because of duress, they should not be able to reintroduce it in the context of illegality. Obviously, there is room for differences of opinion here but your task is to canvass the possibilities.

Finally, there is the possibility of recovery despite the illegality, on the grounds of withdrawal by Leftee as in *Taylor* v *Bowers* (1876) 1 QBD 291. No part of the illegal purpose seems yet to have been carried out (unless you count the preparation of the manuscript as such) and in any case the policy of the regulations seems to be better served by allowing recovery and thus giving Leftee an incentive to abandon the scheme rather than denying the restitution here. Leftee have sought to withdraw as soon as they discovered that publication would be illegal and it is not a case like *Bigos* v *Bousted* [1951] 1 All ER 92 of withdrawing because the other side is refusing to perform.

In conclusion, it would seem to be at least open to a court to allow Leftee to recover despite the illegality but this might seem rather harsh on Richard who has, quite unaware of the illegality, done a lot of work for no reward. The desire to reach a compromise between two innocent parties might tempt a court to find that the second £2,000 can be recovered (either on the grounds of duress alone or perhaps, more likely, on the grounds that the parties were not *in pari delicto* at this point) but that Richard can keep the £2,000 paid under the original agreement. The rules in this area are sufficiently vague and unspecific to allow a court considerable discretion in reaching whatever it considers to be the just solution. This thought brings us on quite nicely to the theme of what could be a possible essay question in this area:

An Essay

> 'The rules governing illegal contracts are unnecessarily complex and unpredictable.'
> Discuss.

It is quite easy for an examiner to ask a very similar sort of question on inequality of bargaining power etc., thus:

> 'The law's response to inequality and unfairness in contracts is regrettably fragmented and unpredictable.'
> Discuss.

Both of these questions could be answered in a similar *manner* (though the actual content would obviously differ) and enough has probably been said about essay questions in earlier chapters for you to know how to deal with these. The main point, of course, is to answer the question, so in the first essay you should illustrate in what ways the rules on illegality are complex. Complex in what ways? Different sorts of rules for different sorts of illegality — refer to the lack of consensus on how different types of illegality should be classified. The difficulties of knowing when a contract is illegal (cf. *St John Shipping Corporation* v *Joseph Rank Ltd* [1957] 1 QB 267) and the multifarious exceptions to the basic rule that the courts will not give any relief to either party to an illegal contract could also be discussed. Having demonstrated the complexity (which is not difficult) you should ask is it *unnecessary* complexity or is it on the other hand inevitable in such a field given the great variety of possible modes and degrees of illegality? Having discussed complexity and whether it is necessary you should then do the same for unpredictability, again by referring to illustrative case law. A view that you could take here is that unpredictability is not necessarily a bad thing. Some overseas jurisdictions confer an overt discretion on the court. The unpredictable English rules perhaps achieve the same effect more covertly. Predictability is important when you wish people to be able to arrange their affairs in reliance on the law of contract and to use the law of contract as a facilitating medium (e.g., where the parties deliberately designate a term as a condition so that their respective rights will be clear in the event of a breach). By way of contrast, where the law is trying to discourage illegal contracts or contracts that conflict with public policy, too much certainty may encourage people to sail as close as possible to the wind and to manipulate the precise rules to their own advantage.

A similar sort of point can be made in answering the second question (once you have discussed the many different ways in which the law takes account of unfairness and Lord Denning's attempt to synthesise them in *Lloyds Bank Ltd* v *Bundy* [1975] QB 326). The lack of precision in doctrines such as undue influence and unconscionable bargains (and indeed in the test of reasonableness in the Unfair Contract Terms Act 1977 or in restraint cases) is sometimes seen as a desirable characteristic which will encourage parties in a position to abuse their bargaining position to act scrupulously fairly to avoid the risk of being caught by an uncertain discretion. Lord Scarman seemed to have this sort of point in mind when he warned in *National Westminster Bank plc* v *Morgan* [1985] 1 All ER 821 that 'there is no precisely defined law setting limits to the equitable jurisdiction of a court to relieve against undue influence' (having, rather ironically, refused relief on the particular facts).

Of course, as usual, there is the other side of the argument to consider. Uncertainty might have advantages in some contexts in terms of the way it might modify the behaviour of otherwise unscrupulous or strongly placed parties but it also has disadvantages — not the least that when disputes do arise, it makes it more difficult for them to be settled out of court. Each party may feel he or she has a reasonable prospect of success, which is not unreasonable given, e.g., the differences between the Court of Appeal and the House of Lords in *National Westminster Bank plc* v *Morgan* or the different views of the reasonableness of the 21-year solus tie between the judge at first instance and the Court of Appeal in *Alec Lobb (Garages) Ltd* v *Total Oil GB Ltd* [1985] 1 All ER 303.

You can perhaps console yourself with the thought that unpredictability is not really a problem for the student since you do not have to make actual decisions but are only expected to discuss the relevant factors on either side. You can now also console yourself with the certainty that you have at least reached the end of this book! It only remains for me to wish you well in any examinations which you may be taking and to remind you that most examiners will share these sentiments and be looking for the positive rather than the negative aspect of your answers.

BIBLIOGRAPHY

Sir W. R. Anson, *Anson's Law of Contract,* 26th ed. by A. G. Guest (Oxford: Clarendon Press, 1984).

P. S. Atiyah, *An Introduction to the Law of Contract,* 5th ed. (Oxford: Clarendon Press, 1995).

P. S. Atiyah, *Consideration in Contracts: A Fundamental Restatement* (Canberra: Australian National University Press, 1971).

P. S. Atiyah, *Essays on Contract* (Oxford: Clarendon Press, 1986).

P. S. Atiyah, *The Rise and Fall of Freedom of Contract* (Oxford: Clarendon Press, 1979).

V. Aubert (ed.), *Sociology of Law* (Harmondsworth: Penguin Books, 1969).

H. G. Beale, W. D. Bishop & M. P. Furmston, *Contract Cases and Materials,* 3rd ed. (London: Butterworths, 1995).

A. Burrows, *The Law of Restitution* (London: Butterworths, 1993).

P. Burrows & C. G. Veljanovski (ed.), *The Economic Approach to Law* (London: Butterworths, 1981).

G. C. Cheshire, C. H. S. Fifoot & M. P. Furmston, *Cheshire & Fifoot's Law of Contract,* 13th ed. by M. P. Furmston (London: Butterworths, 1996).

J. Chitty, *Chitty on Contracts,* 26th ed. (general editor A. G. Guest) (London: Sweet & Maxwell, 1989).

H. Collins, *The Law of Contract* 3rd ed. (London: Butterworths, 1997).

B. Coote, *Exception Clauses* (London: Sweet & Maxwell, 1964).

T. A. Downes, *Textbook on Contract,* 5th ed. (London: Blackstone Press, 1997).

C. Fried, *Contract as Promise* (Cambridge, Mass: Harvard University Press, 1981).

Sir E. Fry, *A Treatise on the Specific Performance of Contracts,* 6th ed. (London: Stevens, 1921).

G. Gilmore, *The Death of Contract* (Columbus, Ohio: Ohio State University Press, 1974).

K. N. Llewellyn, *The Bramble Bush* (New York: Oceana, 1951).

E. McKendrick, *Contract Law* 3rd ed. (London: Macmillan, 1997).

G. J. Miller & B. W. Harvey, *Consumer and Trading Law Cases and Materials* (London: Butterworths, 1985).

J. Poole, *Casebook on Contract*, 3rd ed. (London: Blackstone Press, 1997).

B. J. Reiter & J. Swan (ed.), *Studies in Contract Law* (Toronto: Butterworths, 1980).

J. C. Smith & J. A. C. Thomas, A *Casebook on Contract,* 10th ed. (London: Sweet & Maxwell, 1996).

I. C. F. Spry, *The Principles of Equitable Remedies,* 5th ed. (London: Sweet & Maxwell, 1997).

J. Swan & B. J. Reiter, *Contracts Cases, Notes and Materials* (Toronto: Butterworths, 1978).

G. H. Treitel, The *Law of Contract,* 9th ed. (London: Sweet & Maxwell, 1995).

W. Twining & D. Miers, *How to Do Things with Rules,* 3rd ed. (London: Butterworths, 1991).

S. M. Waddams, *The Law of Contracts,* 2nd ed. (Toronto: Canada Law Book, 1984).

S. Wheeler & J. Shaw, *Contract Law, Cases, Materials and Commentary* (Oxford: Clarendon Press, 1994).

D. Yates, *Exclusion Clauses in Contracts,* 2nd ed. (London: Sweet & Maxwell, 1982).

INDEX

Acceptance 44–5, 50–1
  by Telex 45
  postal rule 45–6
  silence as 45, 52–3
Action for price *see* Price, action for
Actual loss 189
Advertisements 46, 47
Affirmation 135, 145, 176–7
Agency 201
  agent of offeree 50
Agreed damages 188–9
Agreement
  acceptance of 50–1
    silence as 45, 52–3
  counter-offers 51–2
  objective test of 42–4
  offer and acceptance 44–5
  questions 53–7
  revocation 48, 49–50
  unilateral contracts 46–50
Apprenticeships 165
Articles 15–17

'Back-up' rule 88
Bargaining power
  inequality *see* Inequality of bargaining
    power
  relative strengths of 114, 118
Bargains 75–7
  unconscionable 221, 225
Benefit 59, 60
Blind plaintiff 107
Blue-pencil test 220
Breach of contract
  deliberate 81, 94, 95
  fundamental 102, 104, 112
  penalties 189–90

Breach of contract — *continued*
  protection of interests 61–2
  remedies *see* Remedies
'But for' test 132

Cartel agreements 221
Cases
  casebooks 13–14
  citing in examinations 39
  notetaking 12
  in revision 32–3
Causation 132
Collateral
  contract 82, 212
  warranties 82–4
Common mistake 150–1, 155–9
Compensation *see* Damages
Conditions 84–9
Conformity with specifications 119
Consensus ad idem 42
Consideration
  bargained for 60–1, 62–3, 75–7
  benefit and detriment 59, 60
  definition 58–63
    Currie v Misa 59–60
  executed or executory 52, 63, 200
  existing duties *see* Existing duties
  implied promise 64
  part payment of debt 71–4, 76
  past 61, 63–5, 76–7, 78
  performed or return promise 61
  protection of interest 62–3
  questions 74–9
  total failure of 197
Constant supervision 193–4
Consumer, dealing as 114, 115, 121–2
Contra proferentem rule 102, 103

Contracts
  bilateral   47, 48, 49
  breach *see* Breach of contract
  collateral   82, 212
  executed and executory   52
  freedom of   100–1
  illegal   210–15
  personal service   193–4, 208
  repudiation   92–3, 94
  termination *see* Termination of contract
  terms *see* Terms of contract
  unilateral   46–50
  void and voidable   151, 152, 156–7, 158,
    216–21
Contractual damages *see* Damages
Contractual duties
  owed to promisor   65–8
  owed to third-party   65–8
  Stilk v *Myrick* rule   65–6, 68, 70, 76
Contractual warranty   83–4
Contributory negligence   187–8
'Coronation' cases   162–4
Counter-offers   51–2
Course of dealing, incorporation by
    107–8, 121–2
Currie v *Misa* definition   59–60

Damages
  agreed   188–9
  contractual   180, 181–3
  contributory negligence   187–8
  depreciation   141–2
  disappointment   186
  exemplary   138
  exemption   189
  fraudulent misrepresentation   137–8
  injured feelings   138, 185
  instead of rescission   136–7, 145, 147–8
  liquidated   189
  lost profits   185
  mitigation   186–7
  negligent misrepresentation   138–42, 145
  non-pecuniary losses   185–6
  penalties *see* Penalties
  reliance   83, 212
  remoteness   180, 183–5
Dealing
  as a consumer   114, 115, 121–2
  incorporation by course or   107–8, 121–2
Death   162
  exemption clauses and causing   114
Delay   164–5
Deliberate breaches   81, 94, 95
Depreciation damages   141–2
Destruction of subject-matter   161–2
Detrimental interest   59, 60, 62
Disappointment, damages for   186

Discretion   195–6
Dismissal, wrongful   185
Distress, mental   185–6
Duress   221, 222–3, 229–30
Duties *see* Existing duties

Equitable remedies   192–6
  discretion   195–6
  mutuality   194–5
  personal service contracts   193–4, 208
Essays   18–19
Estoppel
  extinctive   73, 79
  promissory   60, 72–4, 76, 78–9
  suspensory   73, 79
Events foreseen and provided for   166–7
Examinations   21–41
  final check   40
  past papers   22–4
  questions *see* Questions
  revision   24–35
  sitting the exam   35–40
Exclusion clauses *see* Exemption clauses
Exclusive agreements *see* Restraint of trade
Executed consideration   52, 63
Exemplary damages   138
Exemption clauses   100–26, 189
  contra proferentum rule   102, 103
  death or personal injury caused by
      negligence   114
  disallowing reliance   103, 125
  examination questions   119–26
  fundamental breach   102, 112
  historical development   100–4
  incorporation
    by course of dealing   107–8
    by notice   105–7
    by signature   105, 122
  interpretation of   108–10
  limitation clauses   109–10, 112–13, 123
  negligence and   102, 104, 108–10
  reasonableness test   114–15, 116–19, 124–5
  Unfair Contract Terms Act 1977
      103–4, 113–19, 123–4
  voidness   114
Existing duties   65–71
  contractual
    owed to promisor   65–8
    owed to third-party   65–8
  non-contractual   65–8
  public duties   66
Expectation interest   62, 63, 181–3, 212
Extinctive estoppel   73, 79

Factual benefit   59
Factual detriment   59
False statements   128–9

Feelings, injury to 138, 185
Foreseen events 166–7
Forfeiture clauses 190
Fraudulent misrepresentation 131, 132, 133, 137–8
Freedom of contracts 100–1
Frustration 159–79
  contract becomes different 162–4
  death or incapacity 162
  delay or interruption 164–5
  destruction of subject-matter 161–2
  due to negligence 165–6
  effects of 167–72
  events foreseen and provided for 166–7
  illegality 160–1
    see also Illegality
  leases and 166
  questions 173–9
  self-induced 165–6
Fundamental breach 102, 104, 112

Goodwill 218–19

Hadley v *Baxendale* rule 183

Illegal contracts 210–15
  frustration 160–1
  not on *pari delicto* 213–14
  restitutionary claims 212–13
  rights independent of 215
  withdrawal from illegal purpose 214
  see also Illegality
Illegality 210–21
  frustration 160–1
  questions 227–32
  void contracts 216–21
  see also Illegal contracts
Illiterate plaintiff 107
Implied promise
  not to revoke 48
  to pay 64
Implied terms 89–91, 93
Importance attached test 81
Incapacity 162
Incorporation
  by course of dealing 107–8
  by notice 105–7
  by signature 105, 122
  test 118
Indemnity 134
Inducement
  misrepresentation 131–3, 144–5
  to agree to terms 118
Industrial revolution 100
Inequality of bargaining power 218
  duress 221, 222–3, 229–30
  general doctrine 225–7

Inequality of bargaining power — *continued*
  questions 227–32
  unconscionable bargains 221, 225
  undue influence 221, 223–5
  see also Unfairness
Injunction remedy 192–6
Injury to feelings 138, 185
Innocent misrepresentation 82, 133, 136, 158
Innominate terms 84–9
Intentions 80, 81
  statement of 130
Interest
  detrimental 59, 60, 62
  expectation 62, 181–3, 212
  reliance 62, 181–3, 207, 212
  unbargained for 76
Interruption 164–5
Interval test 81
Invitation to tender 49
Invitation to treat 46, 47, 48

Journals 15–17, 28

Lapse of time 135–6
Leases
  frustration and 166
  mistake and 157–9
Lectures 2–7
  note taking 3–6
  preparation work 5
  questions in 6–7
Legal benefit 59
Legal detriment 59
Limitation clauses 109–10, 123
  differential treatment of 112–13
Liquidated damages 189
Loss
  actual 189
  non-pecuniary 185–6
  of profit 184, 185

Mental distress 185–6
Misrepresentation 127–49
  addressed to other party 130
  definition 127–8
  facts 129–30
    statement of intention 130
    statement of opinion 130
  false statement 128–9
  fraudulent 131, 132, 138
  inducing contract 131–3, 144–5
  innocent 82, 133, 136, 158
  negligent 133
  non-disclosure as implied statement 144
  questions 142–9
  reliance on 131, 133
  remedies 81, 133–42

Misrepresentation — *continued*
    damages instead of rescission
        136–7, 145
    other damages 137–42
    rescission 81, 88, 132, 133, 134–7, 145,
        147–8
    wilful, of law 130
Misrepresentation Act 1967 136–7, 145
Mistake 150–9
    common 150–1, 155–9
    leases 157–9
    mutual 150, 154–5
    questions 172–3
    as to identity or attributes 152
    unilateral 150, 151–4
    void and voidable contracts
        151, 152, 156–7, 158
Mitigation 186–7
Money restitution 196–7
Mutual mistake 150, 154–5
Mutuality 194–5

Negligence
    causing death or personal injury
        114
    contractual, and warranty 84
    contributory 187–8
    exclusion of liability for 102, 108–10
    frustration due to 165–6
Negligent misrepresentation 133
    damages 138–42, 145–6
Non-contractual duties 65–8
Non-pecuniary losses 185–6
Notes
    lectures 3–6
    reduction of 29–33
Notice, incorporation by
    blind or illiterate plaintiff 107
    contractual or non-contractual
        documents 106
    existence of terms 106–7
    timing 105–7

Objective test 42–4
Obligations 47
Offers 44–5
    counter-offers 51–2
    see also Acceptance *and* Revocation
Officious bystander test 89, 93
Opinion statement 130

Pari delicto 213–14, 229, 230
Parol evidence rule 82
Part payment of debt 71–4, 76
Party to contract 199–200
Past consideration 61, 63–5
    exceptions 64, 76–7, 78

Penalties 188–9
    for breach 189–90
    forfeiture clauses and 190
Penalty clauses 189
Performance 61
    plaintiff insists on 191–2
    specific 61, 192–6, 203
Personal injury, exemption clauses and
    causing 114
Personal service contracts 208
    remedies 193–4
Pinnel's case, rule in 71–2, 73, 78
Postal rule 45–6, 50, 55
Presentations 18–19
Price, action for 191–2
    accrual of right of price 191
    plaintiff insists on performing 191–2
Privity 75, 82, 199–204
    party to contract 199–200
    questions 204–9
    third-party beneficiaries 201–4, 208
Promises
    implied 48
    secondary 48–9
    see also Consideration
Promissory estoppel 60, 72–4, 76, 78–9
Property restitution 198–9
Public duties 65–8

Quantum meruit 198, 207–8
Questions
    agreements 53–7
    consideration 74–9
    exemption clauses 119–26
    frustration 173–9
    illegality 227–32
    inequality 227–32
    misrepresentation 142–9
    mistake 172–3
    offer and acceptance 53–7
    privity 204–9
    remedies 204–9
    terms of contract 92–9

Reasonableness
    restraint of trade 217–21
    test 114–15, 116–19, 124–5
Recovery *see* Restitution
Relative degree of knowledge test 81
Reliance
    damages 83, 212
    disallowed 103, 125
    interest 181–3, 207, 212
    detrimental 62
    protection of 62
    unbargained for 76
    on misrepresentation 131, 133

Remedies 180–99
    action for price 191–2
    damages *see* Damages
    discretion 195–6
    equitable 192–6
    injunction 192–6
    misrepresentation *see* Misrepresentation;
        remedies
    personal service contracts 193–4
    questions 204–9
    rescission 81, 88, 132, 133, 134–7, 145,
        147–8
    restitution 196–9
    specific performance 192–6, 203
Remoteness 180, 183–5
Representations 81–4, 87, 88, 96–9
Repudiation of contract 92–3, 94
    see also Termination of contract
Rescission 81, 88, 132, 133, 134–7,
        145, 147–8
    affirmation 135, 145
    lapse of time 135–6
    Misrepresentation Act 1977 136–7
    restitution impossible 135
Restitution 196–9
    claims for 212–13
    impossible 135
    money 196–7
    services or property 198–9
Restraint of trade 216–21
    assessment of reasonableness 217–19
    severing clause 219–20
    solus agreements 216, 217, 218, 219
    unreasonable 93, 219–21
Return promise 61
Revision 24–35
    timetable 33–5
Revocation 48, 51–2, 55
    communication of 49–50
    by third party 50
Risk *see* Frustration

Secondary promise 48–9
Self-induced frustration 165–6
Seminars 17–18
Separate collateral contract 82
Separate warranty 83–4
Service contracts, personal 193–4, 208
Services restitution 198–9
Severance of restraint clause 219–20
Signature, incorporation by 105, 122
Silence as acceptance 45, 52–3
Solus agreement 216, 217, 218, 219
Specific performance 61, 192–6, 203
Standard objective tests 96–7
Statutes (study of) 14–15
Stilk v *Myrick* rule 65–6, 68, 69, 70, 76

Study methods 1–19
    essays 18–19
    journals and articles 15–17
    lectures 2–7
    presentations 18–19
    reading cases 9–14
    seminars and tutorials 17–18
    statutes 14–15
    textbooks 7–9
Supervision constant 193–4
Suspensory estoppel 73, 79

Telex acceptance 45
Tender, invitation to tender 49
Termination of contract 84–5, 148
    on basis of effect of breach 86
    as result of fundamental breach
        102
    see also Repudiation of contract
Terms of contract
    classification of 86–9
    conditions 84–9
    implied 89–91, 93
    innominate 84–9
    notice of existence of 106–7
    questions 92–9
    representations and 81–4, 87, 88, 96–9
    warranties 84–9
Textbooks 7–9, 26–7
Third-parties
    beneficiaries 201–4, 208
    communication of revocation 50
    mistakes and 152
    rights 135
Trade secrets 218, 219
Trading with enemy 161
Trusts 200–2
Tutorials 17–18

Unconscionable bargains 225
Undue influence 221, 223–5
Unfair Contract Terms Act 1977, exclusion
        clauses 103–4, 113–19, 123–4
Unfairness 225–7, 231–2
    see also Inequality of bargaining power
Unilateral contracts 46–50
Unilateral mistake cases 150, 151–4
Unreasonable restraint 93, 219–21

Void contracts 216–21
    see also Restraint of trade
Voidness 151, 152, 156–7, 158

Waiver doctrine 74
    see also Promissory estoppel
Warranties 84–9
    collateral 82–4

Warranties — *continued*
   contractual   83–4
   separate   83–4
Wilful misrepresentation of law   130

Williams v *Roffey Bros*   66, 68, 69–70, 71, 72,
   76, 78
Withdrawal *see* Revocation
Wrongful dismissal   185

TITLES IN THE SERIES

SWOT Constitutional and Administrative Law
SWOT Law of Evidence
SWOT Company Law
SWOT Law of Contract
SWOT Family Law
SWOT Land Law
SWOT Criminal Law
SWOT Equity and Trusts
SWOT Commercial and Consumer Law
SWOT A Level Law
SWOT Law of Torts
SWOT Jurisprudence
SWOT Employment Law
SWOT English Legal System
SWOT EC Law
SWOT Conveyancing
SWOT Law of Succession
SWOT International Law